REFORM IN DETROIT

THE URBAN LIFE IN AMERICA SERIES

RICHARD C. WADE, GENERAL EDITOR

STANLEY BUDER
PULLMAN: An Experiment in Industrial Order
and Community Planning, 1880–1930

ALLEN F. DAVIS
SPEARHEADS FOR REFORM: The Social Settlements
and the Progressive Movement, 1890–1914

LYLE W. DORSETT
THE PENDERGAST MACHINE

KENNETH T. JACKSON
THE KU KLUX KLAN IN THE CITY, 1915–1930

MELVIN G. HOLLI
REFORM IN DETROIT: Hazen S. Pingree and
Urban Politics

ZANE L. MILLER
BOSS COX'S CINCINNATI: Urban Politics in the Progressive Era

REFORM IN DETROIT

Hazen S. Pingree and Urban Politics

MELVIN G. HOLLI

NEW YORK
OXFORD UNIVERSITY PRESS
1969

Copyright © 1969 by Oxford University Press, Inc.
Library of Congress Catalogue Card Number: 69–17762
Printed in the United States of America

To Walfred and Sylvia Holli

Foreword

Historians are now generally agreed that Progressivism had its roots in the exploding cities of the late nineteenth century. The rise of the modern metropolis dramatically shifted the focus of American life from farm to city, and the new urban society developed a range of problems that demanded public action. Progressivism was the national climax of an effort that began on the local and state level all across the country. But historians are in less agreement about the movement's exact texture and meaning. Some authors have emphasized the leading role played by the "best" people—businessmen, lawyers, journalists, and intellectuals —in shaping the peculiar progressive approach to politics and public issues. Others have concentrated on the general discontent which provided some of the impetus. Still others find the Progressive movement more a strategy of the business community than a genuine attempt to reallocate power within American society, hence to be more conservative than liberal.

Some of these controversies are simply the inevitable result of the passage of time and the need of each generation to write history with its own view and perspective. Then, too, with the death of the important figures, new manuscript collections become available to scholars, making possible fresh interpretations. Part of the difficulty, however, stems from a long tradition among American historians of writing national history with major figures as the focus. Thus, Theodore Roosevelt and Woodrow Wilson, for example, have many biographies. Yet the scope of national experience is much broader than Washington and much richer than the life of even its seminal leaders. And often a close and detailed examination of a lesser career can reveal more of the texture of a movement than the view from a more commanding height.

This political biography of Hazen S. Pingree provides just such a convenient correction. Though Pingree was never a national figure in the sense of a presidential candidate or a United States senator, he was a four-term mayor of an important city and a two-term governor of a powerful state. Moreover, by the mid-nineties, his crusade for the "three cent" [sic] fare had put him at the center of a lively national controversy. If historians have ignored him, contemporaries did not. And in Michigan, at least, Pingree was a household word.

One reason for his comparative obscurity in Progressive literature was the fact that for the most part he held office before the "official" beginning of Progressivism in 1901. Yet Melvin G. Holli demonstrates convincingly that he was a proponent of most progressive notions a decade before Theodore Roosevelt assumed the presidency. Indeed, there were scarcely any issues that later became nationally prominent which Pingree did not first handle on the city and state level. And the traction question, with its organized private economic power on the one hand and the public interest on the other, reveals all the elements of the classic "trust" issue which so concerned Roosevelt, Wilson, and Debs.

Like most progressives, Pingree came to his political convictions through confrontation rather than ideology. There was little in his first term to distinguish him from other reform mayors. He was the candidate of the Republican party and business interests; his first inaugural dealt almost exclusively with the issue of street paving; and his political ideas were conventionally genteel. Yet even the simple question of adequate paving brought Pingree up against primitive patronage power and the connection between privilege and public contracts. And in this conflict, the new mayor quickly transformed the streets of Detroit from a national scandal into one of the best paved systems in the country.

But what turned Hazen S. Pingree into a social reformer was the transit question. Here private and public interests collided in the most obvious way; here the conventional politics of the nineties ran into the new politics of the progressive era. The mayor fixed the responsibility on the company and then appealed over the head of both parties to an outraged citizenry. He was initially successful in bringing down fares and introducing a precarious competition between two companies. Yet he ultimately became a spokesman not only for the three-cent ride but also for municipal ownership of the transit system.

The same process brought Pingree to a more liberal stance in municipal finance. Detroit's tax system was patently inequitable, favoring wealthier residents and business concerns, or, as the mayor often put it, "the classes are favored over the masses." Worse still, evasion by larger taxpayers was common. The long contest for reform cost the mayor the support of earlier backers and many personal friends. "It takes a lot of pluck to see your old associates pass you by without speaking," he lamented, "and not get disheartened and want to give up the fight." But in the long run he succeeded in establishing a more just distribution of the tax burden and making the single tax principle a possible alternative to traditional sources of city revenue.

At any rate, a genial and successful shoe manufacturer had become something of a radical after a few years as Detroit's mayor. As he did so, Mr. Holli argues, Pingree moved from a "structural reformer" to a "social reformer." And the distinction, the author skillfully asserts, is crucial. For the former dealt largely with the rearrangement of governmental organization and the elimination of graft, corruption, and nepotism in city affairs; the latter sought a fundamental change in economic, social, and political institutions with a larger share of the power going to the dispossessed of the new metropolitan society. Structural reform was superficial; social reform was serious. One depended on the generosity and civic spirit of the successful; the other tapped the deeper discontents of the time. One deflected and defeated fundamental change; the other embraced and encouraged it.

If the period was dominated by "structural" reformers, Mr. Holli demonstrates that there was a larger component of "social reform" among the new mayors than is often assumed. And Pingree was surely one of its most effective practitioners. As he lost his early base of support, he created his own new constituency. A flamboyant and pugnacious scrapper, Pingree dramatized his attacks on his opponents by bold confrontations. He once walked into a public meeting and read an indictment which led to the immediate arrest of some of the presiding officials. When he was unable to defeat the established traction company, he set up a competing corporation and gleefully conducted the first car on opening day. He intruded himself personally (and sometimes physically) into labor disputes, and his language smacked more and more of the emergent radicalism of the day. While many complained, Pingree explained that "eternal fighting seems to be the price of any reform in municipal government."

Melvin G. Holli's perceptive account of reform in Detroit adds another important dimension to our understanding of urban politics in the progressive period. This is the fourth volume in the *Urban Life in America Series* which deals with the politics of the emerging modern city. Lyle Dorsett's *The Pendergast Machine* examines the rise of the Democratic boss; *Boss Cox's Cincinnati* by Zane Miller handles the interplay of reform and machine in a Republican city; and *Spearheads for Reform* by Allen Davis traces the influence of the settlement houses on the Progressive movement. Taken together, they reveal the varieties of public response to the range of problems which accompanied the rapid urbanization of the past century.

RICHARD C. WADE

Chicago, Ill.   GENERAL EDITOR
December 1968   URBAN LIFE IN AMERICA SERIES

Preface

Hazen S. Pingree's Detroit in the years he was its mayor—1890 to 1897—was a socially volatile and ethnically turbulent city undergoing rapid changes with the growth of industry and the influx of new immigrants from Europe. Politics, too, had become deranged in the process: various ethnic and interest groups were pitted against each other and against the older business order in the struggle for control of the city government. Detroit's "good government" forces believed that Satan had turned his heaviest batteries upon the city government. Public peculation, election irregularities, contract fraud, wasteful public works, and moral laxity on the part of municipal officials had shocked the most dignified and respectable elements of Detroit's business and social community. With the help of the Republican federal and outstate machines, they had attempted by state intervention to control a city which newcomers and, later, a maverick mayor were taking away from them. The Michigan legislature had divested Detroit's mayor of control over the police department, exempted certain powerful corporations from city control and taxation, manipulated and altered the city's governmental structure at will, placed a low ceiling on the city's bonded indebtedness, and would deprive many

recent immigrants of political power through alien disfranchisement. Detroit was undergoing the same historical changes which
were being experienced by many, if not most, large cities then.

James Bryce made the first serious effort to seek out the underlying causes of the urban malaise in *The American Commonwealth,*
published in 1888. Bryce's contention that "the government of cities
is the one conspicuous failure of the United States" rested on several
premises. The city's chief faults, according to Bryce, were: (1) incompetent and unfaithful officials who "wasted, embezzled and
misapplied" revenue on needless public works and thereby increased municipal taxes to an unbearable level; (2) the introduction of partisan politics into municipal affairs by spoils-oriented
politicians who catered to "ignorant" newcomers and the "vicious
elements" and thereby discouraged the "thrifty classes from en-
gaging in the 'low business' of politics"; and (3) the intervention
by state legislatures into urban affairs, which undermined the principle of local control. On the third point, Bryce acknowledged that
the subversion of municipal government had brought its own punishment with it, for as a New York study had noted, it was probably
the "good citizens in the supposed interest of reform and good
government" who had first sought legislative intervention to control the city; their "fitful and clumsy" efforts had, however, proved
disastrous.[1] This good-government "ripperism" had backfired, for
urban politicos learned the technique and outmatched the "goo
goos" in using state intervention to enlarge and protect their interests in the city.

Bryce's catalogue of urban ills is not simply the indictment of a
well-bred Englishman but the account of a writer who carefully
reflected the views of the urban patrician class of his time. In addition to the three fundamental causes of municipal misgovernment,
Bryce added a fourth, which he described as the "mechanical
defects in the structure of municipal government."[2] In so doing,
Bryce was fortifying an increasingly popular view which coincided
with the diagnosis of the prevailing business culture and patrician
class. These assumptions about the city undergird what I shall call
the structural reform tradition.

Bryce's assessment is also worth pondering because it has influenced the views that several generations of scholars have held toward reform in the city.[3] This account of reform in Detroit will, I hope, bring into view the dynamic career of an urban leader who saw the causes of municipal demoralization differently and who helped to lay the basis for a social reform tradition in the city, a tradition which neither Bryce nor contemporary American mayors fostered, and which few scholars have recognized even existed at the mayoralty level.

Mayor Hazen Pingree discovered that urban politicking was never merely a struggle between corrupt politicos and virtuous "goo goos," as some civic uplifters had contended. It was instead a serious contest which involved patronage, living costs, dignity, and self-assertiveness for the newcomers, and contracts, lucrative franchises, and preferential treatment for urban businesses and utilities. Through dealing with the crucial problem of urban transit, Pingree began to recognize the unsound business policies of magnates who were manipulating the utilities for speculative profits at the expense of serving the public. Although Pingree's background was that of a self-made manufacturer, he was able to support the needs of the urban laborer. He initiated new relief programs during the depression of 1893 but finally came to realize that the fundamental flaw of most charity work was that it freed entrepreneurs from demands for just wages. Although an Anglo-Saxon Yankee Protestant, Pingree sponsored a vigorous reform program in a city which the United States census declared Catholic. He took Detroit's Republican party with its nativist and rural bias and its business-class orientation and transformed it into a useful instrument for social reform. Later, as Michigan's governor, Pingree continued to press for the same principles that he had followed in his urban career. His efforts at the state house complemented his work in Detroit.

During the course of his mayorship, Pingree, unlike other urban "reform" mayors, realized that the nostrums of "good government" people were inadequate to meet the social needs of the city. Taking this point of departure, Pingree established the first significant social reform administration in any large city of the time. He adopted a reform program which later mayors followed, and which I have called social reform.

Where possible, I have attempted to place this study of reform in Detroit in as broad a context as the material seemed to justify. The similarities in the political and social history of other large cities and that of Detroit are great enough, I think, to make this study one of more than local significance. In the final analysis, the greatest difference between Detroit and other city administrations was the influence of Hazen S. Pingree as mayor.

M.G.H.

Chicago, Ill.
December 1968

Acknowledgments

My heaviest intellectual debt is to Professor Sidney Fine, who read the manuscript at every stage of its development and offered penetrating criticism and helpful guidance. His interest in the manuscript markedly improved the final product. Professor John Higham aided in sharpening a central theme and offered helpful suggestions, as did Robert M. Warner and Joseph E. Kallenbach. My colleagues Gilbert Osofsky, Stanley L. Jones, and C. David Tompkins read and commented meaningfully on various sections of the book. Stephan Thernstrom offered sound advice in the final stages of writing.

The task of research was immeasurably facilitated and made pleasant by the assistance and courtesies extended to me by James E. Babcock and his able staff at Detroit's Burton Historical Collection. Dr. F. Clever Bald of the Michigan Historical Collections and his staff were unfailingly gracious and helpful as were Josephine L. Harper of the State Historical Society of Wisconsin and Geneva Kebler of the Michigan Historical Commission Archives. I would also like to thank the manuscript divisions of the New York Public Library, Columbia University, Yale University, and the Library of Congress.

My research was aided by grants from the University of Michigan, Horace H. Rackham Graduate School, and a summer fellowship from the University of Illinois at Chicago Circle. Finally, Betsy Biggar Holli gave generously both of her time and wisdom in the shaping of this book.

Contents

I. FROM STRUCTURAL TO SOCIAL REFORM

  1. The Road to City Hall   3

  2. The Apprenticeship: Good Government Mayor   22

  3. A Businessman's Mayor Moves Toward Social Reform   33

  4. The Depression and a Commitment   56

  5. The Battle With the Utilities   74

  6. The Mayor Leads a Nationwide Fight for Low Fares   101

  7. The Political Craftsman   125

  8. Social and Structural Reform   157

II. URBAN REFORMER IN THE STATE HOUSE

  9. Urbanite Challenges the State Legislature   185

  Epilogue   219

  Notes   223

  A Note on Sources   259

  Index   263

I

FROM STRUCTURAL
TO SOCIAL REFORM

1

The Road to City Hall

I

Hazen S. Pingree was born on August 30, 1840, near Denmark, Maine. His father was a toil-worn farmer and itinerant cobbler who did his best to provide the necessities of life for his eight children. As a youth Pingree performed the usual chores of a farm boy and traveled with his father as a cobbler's assistant. The Pingree children obtained only sporadic schooling during the winter months. Pingree's early education in economics was probably gleaned from watching his father barter a pair of repaired boots for an unneeded, rusty plowshare, which was in turn exchanged at another farm for a side of beef, a tanned hide, or possibly some cash.

At age fourteen, believing himself confined by the economic limitations of the town of Denmark, Pingree set out for Saco, Maine, where he obtained employment in a cotton factory. Six years later in 1860 he moved to Hopkinton, Massachusetts, and there began his training as a leather cutter in a shoe factory. The Civil War interrupted his apprenticeship in August, 1862, when he became the first of Hopkinton's young men to enlist.[1]

Pingree joined Company F of the First Massachusetts Heavy Artillery. With less than thirty days of military training, his unit received its first taste of war in the Second Battle of Bull Run on August 29 and 30, 1862, an engagement that turned into a bloody

3

rout for the Union forces. Pingree and his defeated comrades retreated to Arlington Heights, where they were garrisoned for two
years.

Pingree's company was reassigned as infantry and was thrown
into heavy combat against the Confederate forces in May, 1864.
Private Pingree participated in the battles at North Anna on May
24 and 25, and on the second day of this engagement he was captured. He spent five months at Andersonville prison, surviving on a
daily ration of a half-pint of corn meal when it was available. Pingree was transferred to the Confederate stockade at Millen, Geor-
gia, from which he engineered a clever but ungallant escape by
answering to the name of a prisoner who was too ill to be exchanged. After a brief furlough he rejoined his regiment and was
involved in combat until the end of the war in 1865.[2]

At Andersonville, Pingree had met several Union prisoners from
Detroit who had impressed him with stories about the economic
opportunities there. Tempted by these prospects, he set out for Detroit shortly after his discharge from the military service.

The Detroit to which Hazen Pingree came in 1865 had changed
considerably during the previous two decades and was shifting
gradually from a city of commerce to one of manufacturing. Once a
fur trading center and a way station for voyagers and shippers, it
had begun to benefit from the exploitation of white pine and virgin
hardwoods of upstate Michigan. Eleven sawmills were operating in
Detroit in 1859. In addition, much of the capital accumulated from
the exploitation of white pine gravitated to Detroit, where it was
used not only for construction of palatial homes but also for investment in local industry. Copper and timber were Detroit's chief
products in 1860, but the rapid economic growth of the next decade
would push the manufacture of iron, steel, and foundry and machine products and the industries of flour milling, meat packing,
and tobacco processing into the lead. Capital invested in manufacturing increased by 256 per cent and the total value of manufactured products by 303 per cent in the 1860's. Detroit's strategic location, always one of the city's chief assets, had been enhanced by
extensive railroad connections.[3]

Postwar Detroit had an aura that attracted not only Hazen Pingree but other fellow soldiers, immigrants, and shrewd Yankees. Many of the future giants of Detroit were numbered among these new "men on the make." Prussian-born August Goebel, a bookbinder who had left Detroit in 1861 to fight for the Union, returned to found a brewery that would eventually become one of the giants in the industry. An Ontario Scotsman named George Hendrie had, by 1864, generated enough capital from the trucking business to take control of the financially wobbly Detroit City Railway, which would bring him a fortune during his lifetime. That same year another Canadian, James McMillan, promoted the organization of the Michigan Car Company, which would become one of the largest car building enterprises in the country. In 1865 a former bookshop errand boy, Dexter M. Ferry, purchased a firm that would bear his name and bring him a fortune in the seed business. Two years later, Dr. Samuel P. Duffield, a chemist, joined Hervey C. Parke and George S. Davis to market the products of a small laboratory that would become the pharmaceutical house Parke-Davis.[4]

Innovation and invention spurred the economic growth of the city. Dynamic and energetic Captain Eber Brock Ward, who was involved in shipbuilding, sawmilling, and canal promotion, installed a Bessemer converter in nearby Wyandotte in 1864 and turned out the first Bessemer steel manufactured in the United States. Hopes soared that Detroit and nearby Wyandotte would become the center of a steel industry based on Lake Superior ores and Pennsylvania coal. Business promoters who shared this optimism founded the Detroit Stove Works in 1864, and many of them lived to see this company spark the organization of other firms which would one day make Detroit the stove-producing center of the country. In 1868 in Detroit William Davis constructed a practical refrigerator car that led to great changes in the meat-packing industry.[5]

Detroit appeared to be a city of exciting promise, a place where hard work, diligence, and individual initiative would be handsomely rewarded and the promise of American life realized. When Pingree left the limited economic prospects of Hopkinton for the expanding opportunities offered by Detroit, he made a sound choice.

In addition to the tangible attractions of Detroit, a panoply of legal weapons for thwarting public control was provided for the Michigan business community by Thomas McIntyre Cooley, Michigan's Chief Justice. Cooley's interpretation of the due process clause as a substantive rather than a procedural guarantee and his justification of monopoly in its most absolute form made him one of the major architects of the businessman's philosophy in the post-Civil War period. His views permeated Michigan jurisprudence.[6] The business community could depend upon a sympathetic hearing from the state and local courts. The business realities of postwar Detroit more than measured up to the tales of economic adventure and entrepreneurial opportunity that Pingree had heard at Andersonville.

When he arrived in Detroit late in 1865, Pingree had ambition, energy, grit, and the shrewdness of a Yankee horse trader, but he lacked the managerial and technical knowledge, the personal connections, and the capital that would ultimately facilitate his rise to prominence as a shoe manufacturer. He secured a job doing the only thing that he knew, leather cutting, in a small boot and shoe factory owned by H. P. Baldwin. After accumulating a modest saving, Pingree and Charles H. Smith pooled $1360 in December, 1866, to purchase the outdated shoe manufacturing equipment of the Baldwin plant. Pingree handled production and sales for the firm, and Smith was responsible for bookkeeping.[7]

By the end of the first year, the partners were able to employ eight people and to gross a modest $20,000. There was steady growth in the following years. Pingree was on the way to updating a primitive operation in the best traditions of nineteenth-century business rationalism. He studied the machinery and manufacturing processes and carefully sought to ascertain customer demands by observing the style and weight of footwear most frequently purchased. In 1868, Pingree sent for his brother Frank C. Pingree to take charge of the sole-leather and designing departments. Frank later assumed supervision of the plant when Pingree began his political career. By 1883 Pingree and Smith was grossing upwards of one-half million dollars annually.[8]

Pingree's first experience with a serious labor problem hurt him economically and caused him to espouse a new solution for industrial problems, marking the beginning of his long romance with the wage-earning class and later the unorganized masses. The shoemakers, members of District Assembly 50, Knights of Labor, struck Pingree and Smith in May, 1885, demanding a union shop, the end of contract labor, and some minor wage adjustments. The company rejected the demands and the union announced a walkout. Production dropped from about 2,000 pairs of shoes per day in early May to 300 pairs per day in June. The strike dragged on until March, 1886, when Pingree finally agreed to arbitration. As later events would demonstrate, the strike made Pingree a champion of arbitration as the method of resolving labor-management disputes.[9]

The company had barely recovered from the protracted 1885 strike when the job of rebuilding once more faced Pingree and Smith: a fire destroyed the entire shoe manufacturing plant in March, 1887. Pingree and his two junior partners, John B. Howarth and Frank Pingree, who had purchased Smith's interest in 1882, rebuilt and expanded the plant so that by 1890 it was classified as one of the largest shoe manufacturing plants in the West. The firm remained a simple partnership and never during Pingree's lifetime accepted the obvious advantages of limited liability that came with incorporation. Its owner and founder considered limited liability an immoral evasion of responsibility.[10]

In 1872, Pingree had married Frances A. Gilbert, a Mount Clemens school teacher. Abstemious in habit and socially withdrawn, she frowned upon the use of alcohol, tobacco, and profanity and looked with a jaundiced eye upon politics. A friend testified that the wealthy manufacturer "lived a quiet and well-ordered life." Pingree was a generous father to two daughters and one son, whose whims and desires he lavishly satisfied. He brought his surviving parent, his father, to live with the family. The Pingrees lived on the upper reaches of Woodward Avenue among the socially prominent element of the city. Their home was outfitted with much of the

garish splendor and overstuffed Victorian opulence then thought
fitting a man of Pingree's station.[11]

Pingree was a booster, a joiner, a member of Detroit's best social
and political clubs, and a respected entrepreneur in the city's business community. He was a Mason, a Maccabee, an active member
of the Detroit G.A.R. Post 384, and regularly attended the Woodward Avenue Baptist Church. His business associations included
memberships on the board of directors of the Preston National
Bank and the Detroit Board of Trade. Pingree was an officer and
member of the Michigan Club, a political organization formed
after the Democratic national victory of 1884 to refurbish Republican political prospects. He was president of the club in 1889 and a
member of its "Big Four," who had customarily played a large part
in determining the strategy of Republican campaigns in Detroit.
Pingree counted as his personal friends such fellow club members
as James F. Joy, James McMillan, Russell A. Alger, James Vernor,
W. H. Elliott, and Dexter M. Ferry, all of them part of the city's
social and economic elite. These personal friends, as representatives
of the Detroit aristocracy, would ask Pingree to accept the Republican nomination for mayor in 1889.[12]

II

In 1889, the time of Hazen Pingree's rise to political power, Detroit
was the most important city in Michigan. It was by far the largest
city in the state, with a population of more than 200,000. The majority of the city's residents were of foreign stock, and had arrived
in Detroit after the Civil War. Although these newcomers were
sensitive to slights to their national heritage and were numerically
dominant in the city, they were not always accorded the political
recognition to which they believed they were entitled. Pingree's
understanding of this fact, and his willingness to act on it, would
drastically alter the political complexion of Detroit in a short span
of five years, and bring to the fore a kind of mayoral campaign
strategy unprecedented in the history of the Republican party. Just
as Pingree had taken over an out-of-date shoe manufactory and
turned it into a million-dollar business, so would his candidacy re-

vive a moribund Republican party by turning the ethnic blocs toward the G.O.P.

The structure of Detroit's government was typical of that of most late-nineteenth-century cities. Rural legislators who doubted the probity of city dwellers had determined its form. The Michigan legislature had prescribed both the substance and procedure of Detroit city government, the mayor-council type that had been codified by the Charter of 1857. The Charter, which could be altered only by legislative action, had been amended in 1881 to provide a bicameral council, with the upper house elected from the city at large and the lower house elected by wards. The upper house, which had been intended to suppress municipal corruption, only added to it, and was abolished by the legislature of 1887, whereupon the city reverted to a unicameral common council elected by wards. The legislature had imposed other handicaps upon Detroit by placing the appointment of the Metropolitan Police Commission in the hands of the governor and by limiting severely the amount of money which the city could borrow.[13]

Detroit's common council in 1889 was composed of thirty-two councilmen representing sixteen wards for two-year terms, with one-half of the incumbents eligible for re-election annually. The mayor was elected at large for a two-year term and possessed a veto power over council resolutions and ordinances, provided that the opposition could not muster a two-thirds vote to override his veto. He was an ex officio member of the Board of Education, whose members were elected by wards; he also appointed the commissioners to the Public Works, Water, Fire, Health, Poor, and Park boards, the city legal counselor, the comptroller, the receiver of taxes, and the tax assessor—all of whom were subject to approval by the council.[14]

The mayor, with council consent, also named the "June appointees," a designation applied to such officeholders appointed in June as hay scale operator, market clerk, city hall janitor, poundmaster, and elevator operator. These political plums were usually the object of a stormy struggle between the mayor and the councilmen of both parties, a conflict that bore little relationship to good municipal government but which reflected directly upon the political future of councilmen who fought to feed their hacks from the city trough. The wretched public service rendered by the June appointees and the fact that most of them were not responsible to the mayor or subject to his dismissal clearly frustrated public attempts to hold city officials politically accountable for misconduct.

Detroit's city elections and ward caucuses were fraught with excitement and political chicanery. The elections for mayor, the city administrative offices, and one-half of the council were held in November of odd-numbered years. The candidates for mayor and for the mayor's administrative staff were nominated at party conventions by delegates who had been elected at ward caucuses. The caucuses were party affairs for which each candidate had his own ballots printed, and he frequently used either muscle or money to sway the ward voters. Some candidates packed the caucuses by importing river front "bruisers" by moving vans, whereas others merely bought the local "floaters," or arranged to rig the count. The city-wide elections proved equally turbulent for, under the Michigan Constitution of 1850, aliens were permitted to vote provided that they had declared their intention to become citizens six months prior to the election.[15]

Many of the aliens and immigrants who had exercised their right to vote were Germans, who, in the decade from 1880 to 1890, began to make their impact felt upon Detroit politics, primarily within the Democratic party. In the late 1870's and early 1880's German-Americans had assiduously worked their way into the common council, but not without clashing with Irish-Americans, who had usually considered the Democratic party as belonging to them. By 1884 at least seven of the twenty-six aldermen were German-Americans; by 1891 a drastic shift in ethnic political power had occurred which broke up the old native and Irish-American monopoly and forced it to share power with a German-American bloc comprising fourteen of the thirty-two councilmen.[16]

Pingree and his Michigan Club associates correctly perceived in 1889 that an ethnic political strategy could be the keystone to transforming normally Democratic Detroit into a Republican city. Detroit was essentially a city of origins-conscious foreigners. The census of 1890 reported that only 42,000 of Detroit's 205,000 people had been born of native parents, some 78,000 came from families in which one or both parents were foreign-born, and some 80,000 were foreign-born. The Germans far outnumbered the Irish and other nationality groups: Detroit in 1889 supported eight German-language newspapers, including three dailies, and Germans, who were antagonistic to the temperance wing within the Michigan Knights of Labor, had played an important role in destroying the Michigan Knights because of their teetotaling tendencies.[17]

German-American ethnic sensitivities were still smarting from the affront that they had received in 1887 when Detroit Democrats nominated a city slate of candidates on which all but two of the positions were filled by persons of Irish descent. One position had been given to a German and one to a Frenchman, but their opponents on the Republican ticket, both Irishmen, had been elected despite a Democratic sweep of the city. Incensed German politicians hurled angry accusations of vote swapping at the Irish Democrats, and as a consequence of the election and the struggle for political position in the 1880's, many German-Americans were vulnerable to Republican overtures. When Pingree and his Michigan Club staff entered the political scene in late 1889, they realized how the ethnic mistakes of the Detroit Democrats could be exploited to Republican advantage.[18]

Just as the politically and economically more advanced German-Americans had felt themselves rebuffed by the Irish Democrats, so had the less fortunate Polish-Americans. Economically unassimilated into the main stream of Detroit's urban life and commonly lacking the mechanical and trade skills that many German immigrants possessed, Detroit's Poles usually found their way into the city's labor force as unskilled workers. They had the lowest average incomes and the lowest living standards of the city's nationality groups and lived either in the industrial districts or on the fringes of the city. Seldom awarded nomination for city-wide or councilmanic office, the Poles had usually been told by the Irish-American chieftains of the Democratic party that their candidates lacked the requisite education and ability to qualify. Their faithful support of the Democrats had never won them a political position of any importance, and so they were vulnerable to G.O.P. overtures.[19]

The Poles were also disaffected because of the increasing Irish domination of the Church. One of the most popular of the few Polish parish priests in Detroit's Roman Catholic diocese, Father Dominic Kolasinski, had been read out of the diocese in 1885 and forcibly evicted by court order from his church the next year. When the Bishop attempted to install a new priest in the church, the faithful Poles had rioted and driven him out. The Bishop, an Irish-American, had further exacerbated ethnic tensions in 1888 by condemning the independent congregation of the wayward Poles as a "church commenced in rebellion and continued in rebellion" and living in the shadow of heresy.[20]

The incipient anti-Catholicism and Protestant middle class flavor of the Republican party, on the other hand, appeared to act as a brake upon the possibility of the G.O.P. winning Polish support. Although the G.O.P. had baited its city slate with an occasional Pole, the Poles in Wayne County and Detroit had not offered the Republicans support.[21]

With their inconsequential role in the political, economic, and religious life of the city and their small number, the Poles appeared hardly worth wooing. The United States census of 1890 reported that only 9,800 Detroiters were born of Polish and Russian mothers as compared to 68,900 Germans, 21,000 Irish, and 17,000 Canadians. The census, however, grossly understated the number of persons of Polish descent in Detroit: Henry M. Utley later estimated that the Poles of Detroit were at least five times as numerous as the census indicated. The disparity arose because most Poles listed their birthplaces or their mothers' birthplaces as Germany or Austria, the nations which had swallowed up Poland. The Detroit *Free Press* estimated in 1890 that the number of those who identified themselves as Poles was at least forty thousand. Harry C. Tillman, a G.O.P. strategist and a major cog in the Michigan Republican machine, concluded on the basis of his enumeration of Polish voters by ward and precinct in a previous city election that the Polish voting population comprised more than 25 per cent of the eligible voters in 1890. Thus Pingree's determination to appeal for the support of Polish voters, despite their long standing antagonism to the G.O.P., was fully understandable.[22]

In the framework of state-wide politics, Detroit's ethnically conscious voters, especially the German and Irish, also exercised some influence by their opposition to prohibition. The liquor issue presented the Republican party with a political dilemma. It had to appeal either to the "dry" sentiments of outstate voters or to the "wet" sentiments of Detroit immigrants. Sensing the growing popularity of prohibitionism outstate, the Republican party adopted a temperance plank in 1888 and renominated as its candidate for governor a "dry," Cyrus G. Luce. Although Luce won the state-wide election, the temperance-tinged G.O.P. gubernatorial candidate was repudiated by an overwhelming and unprecedented electoral margin in urban Wayne County.[23]

Even without the support of Detroit and Wayne County the Republican party could win state-wide elections. From the base of its outstate power, the G.O.P. had carried Michigan for every presidential candidate since 1856, elected every United States senator since 1857, won a majority of the Congressional seats since 1864, provided the state with all but one of its governors since 1854, and controlled both houses of the state legislature since 1855. Conversely, Detroit and surrounding Wayne County had voted against every Republican presidential candidate except two since 1868, generally elected Democratic Congressmen and state legislators, and voted for every Democratic gubernatorial candidate except one since 1854. The G.O.P.'s repeated failures in Detroit were in sharp contrast to the party's remarkable success in state-wide elections.[24]

The stunning success of the Republicans on the state level had strengthened the rural orientation of the party and doomed the G.O.P. to repeated defeat in Detroit. Although Republican sachems Senator James McMillan, Senator Thomas W. Palmer, and former Governor Russell A. Alger were residents of Detroit, they owed their political power to rural Michigan, and they had directed the party toward support of temperance in an effort to maintain that power. The temperance issue, coupled with the G.O.P. legislatures' several unpopular city charter amendments, was hardly calculated to attract Detroit voters. Equally unacceptable was the party leadership in Wayne County, composed of prosperous, socially prominent, native-born persons—manufacturers, investors, and bankers, —whose business interests had created a chasm between themselves and the urban immigrant proletariat. Thus, when Frank J. Hecker, President of the Peninsular Car Company, wanted to run for Congress, Pingree asked him how he expected to win when he paid his men ninety cents a day.[25] The Republican party hardly looked as if it would be an asset to Pingree in his first mayoralty campaign of 1889.

Detroit was then a Democratic city. The Democrats had won nine of the city's fourteen mayoralty elections between 1861 and 1888, had by 1888 controlled eight of the preceding fifteen common councils, and had tied the Republicans for control of two others. In the biennial city-wide elections of 1885 and 1887 the Democrats had taken every city office except that of treasurer, which popular Republican Thomas P. Tuite had secured, apparently on the strength of an Irish-Democratic crossover. The normal Democratic majority was about 2,000, but in the mayoralty election of 1887 Democrat John Pridgeon, Jr. had crushed Republican Charles C. Yemans by a margin of 5,000 votes in a total vote of 22,000. Dr. Yemans, who supported prohibition, had sustained the worst defeat of any G.O.P. candidate in the city's history, a defeat that raised questions about the G.O.P.'s ability to recover its strength in Detroit. Councilmanic victories in the city election of 1888, which extended Democratic control to twenty-two of the council's thirty-two seats, had solidified the party's grip on the city.[26]

The keys to Democratic victory were the construction of a platform that, above all, was antitemperance and the presentation of a slate of candidates for ward and other minor offices that tended to reflect the foreign-born composition of each ward. The success of this system was shown in the city election of 1887, in which Democratic council candidates carried eleven of the twelve wards where

the majority were foreign-born and in which the Democratic candidate for mayor carried every foreign-born ward in the city. Two of
the three Republican victories in the councilmanic election, on the
other hand, were in wards which were described as residential sections with native-born, substantial people and in those where the
foreign-born were outnumbered by those born of native parents.
The same pattern held true in the city elections of 1888, with the
Democrats winning a majority of the council seats with the support
of the foreign-born vote.[27]

Despite its impressive performance in the ethnic wards, Detroit's
Democratic party was afflicted by a division of nationalities. The
Saxon wing of the party was led by John Chris Jacob, a German-
born saloonkeeper who was a cynical and tough-minded ward boss.
Forceful and ponderous Jacob had won the council presidency in
1889 by beating his Irish brethren into line. Despite his heavy accent and use of profanity, he was a parliamentary hedgehog, both
as member and president of the common council. When threatened
with an adverse vote, Jacob would normally drown out the opposition with his booming voice, physically intimidate his opponents, or
invent some parliamentary rule that would send the opposition
scurrying to the rule book, halting council business for a half-hour
while he formed a new coalition to break the opposition. Both in
and out of the council, Jacob cynically exploited his German background by conducting an internecine battle against "dose Irisher
altermanns what is always gombining against der Germans." [28] The
centrifugal forces of ethnicity were constantly tearing at the unity
of the party.

As a crude and effective spoils-oriented politician, Jacob did not
normally permit himself or his fellow city Democrats the luxury of
indulging in issue-oriented campaigns. Seldom could the state and
federal wings of the Michigan Democratic party count upon the
support of Chris Jacob and his cronies; only a question like prohibition could draw them out to work in harmony with the state machine. More often Jacob and his associates engaged in a fratricidal
brawl with the federal wing of the party over who should control
patronage. Postmaster General Don M. Dickinson's installation of

an unpopular "referee system" to dispense federal patronage had deprived Jacob and the Detroit Democrats of a hand in passing out the spoils of office. Nevertheless, as an almost self-contained city party, the Democrats did extremely well: Detroit's election statistics spoke eloquently of Democratic success even though council president Chris Jacob could not.[29]

In the fall of 1889, the party finished a year in office under the blight of charges of corruption. Although Democratic Mayor John Pridgeon, Jr. had kept his office free of scandal, city boss Jacob and three Democratic aldermen came under investigation by a grand jury for bribery. Two municipal contractors charged in October that Jacob had demanded his usual tribute, 10 per cent, from them for a public works job even though the two contractors had submitted the lowest bids. One alderman was indicted for accepting a bribe for a sewer contract, and another for extorting money from a constituent to secure him a city job. It began to appear to Detroit voters as if much of the Democratic machine was involved in "boodling." Each passing day seemed to bring new rumors and revelations of municipal graft. It became increasingly apparent to political observers that the influence of these indictments upon Detroit voters could not be dismissed casually.[30]

Such was the state of affairs in Detroit when several members of the Michigan Club met in October to hand pick the Republican nominee for mayor. Accustomed to directing G.O.P. campaigns in Detroit, the Club's inner circle, including Senator James McMillan, Russell A. Alger, Clarence A. Black, and James F. Joy, convened to canvass the field for candidates. At this meeting, candidate after candidate selected by the Club refused to run. They offered either personal or business reasons for their decisions, but they undoubtedly also thought that an attempt to defeat Pridgeon would prove an exercise in futility. Dexter M. Ferry, the wealthy seedman, had been passed over earlier by the selection committee because he was suspected of advocating temperance. Henry M. Duffield, who was safe on the temperance issue, was the committee's popular choice, but he refused to run. Finally, after an interval of silence, F. A.

"Elder" Blades rose and said: "Mr. President, I can name the next Mayor of Detroit and not go out of this room. . . . His name is H. S. Pingree, and he sits right over there." "No, no, I was never in the City Hall except to pay my taxes," protested Pingree. "I will double my subscription but let me out," he added as he left the meeting.[31] A hastily-formed committee followed Pingree to his shoe factory and again asked him to run, to which Pingree replied: "Mayor? Why, that's political. What in hell do I know about politics. I'm too busy making shoes." [32]

There was much truth in the assertion. Although Pingree had been a life-long Republican and had been president of the Michigan Club since the previous February, he had taken no interest at all in politics and practically none in civic affairs prior to 1889. Pingree, however, was always willing to take a chance.

The well-to-do and conservative members of the Michigan Club applied pressure on Pingree to accept by pledging their support and by circulating a petition which stated that Pingree's business career was a guarantee that economy and a reduction of the "extravagant rate of taxation" would be obtained. The capitalist politicians of Detroit saw Pingree as a mild, tractable businessman whose service as mayor, if he were lucky enough to win, could prove useful. Pingree answered the petition in a letter of acceptance to the Republican City Convention in which he promised strict economy and inflexible honesty, and promised "to lighten the burden of taxation which oppresses our people." Pingree pledged, if elected, to regard himself "not merely as the local figurehead of the republican party, but as the mayor of the whole city, without regard to class faction or party." [33]

The city Republicans, with an eye on avoiding their mistakes of 1887, carefully selected an ethnically balanced slate of candidates. The appearance on the ticket of such names as Howard Weist, John A. Schmidt, Frank A. Rasch, August Marxhausen, and Ernest Burghardt made clear the G.O.P. intention of appealing to the German voters. The Democrats, on the other hand, nominated their customary Irish slate, conceding but one city-wide nomination to a German, Augustus G. Kronberg. The Detroit *Evening News* pointed out that the bid for "racial support sticks out all over the two city tickets." [34] Pingree and the G.O.P. also made a concerted appeal for the Polish vote, hitherto Democratic, by nominating a prominent Pole for justice of the peace and by assiduously courting rebellious priest Father Kolasinski and his band of loyal followers.

More a result of inheritance than the result of calculated political planning was the inclusion of holdover Thomas P. Tuite, a popular Irishman, on the G.O.P. ticket. Although Pingree and his staff made some effort to obtain the Irish vote by charging that Mayor Pridgeon had ignored Catholics and Irishmen in his appointment of a committee to receive the Pan-American Congress, Pingree did not push the appeal to the Irish with any great vigor. Experience had shown the G.O.P. that the Irish would cross from their normal Democratic allegiance to vote for an Irishman on the Republican ticket but that they would not vote for non-Irish Republicans. The Republicans thus could have attracted a large bloc of Irish voters to support their entire ticket only by selecting an entirely Irish slate, a choice which would have been impractical in view of the strength of the German voting bloc in Detroit and the Anglo-Saxon Protestant sources of money for G.O.P. campaigns.[35]

Pingree struck at the heart of the ethnic-political problem in Detroit by beginning his campaign in "Baltimore Red's" saloon, where he demolished the opposition rumor that he was temperance-tainted. He drank "red-eye" whisky with the Irish voters, spoke to German societies, flattered the Poles, called upon his old shoe customers, fraternized on street corners, organized his shoemakers into a political club, and all in all, made a vigorous personal campaign. He avoided issues, condemned the Democrats for corruption, and claimed that he was honest and not a "damn fool" when reporters asked him what qualification he had for office. Lacking favorable coverage from the English-language dailies, Pingree secretly bought the Democratic, German-language *Sonntags Herold* and installed his own editor. The newspaper thereupon reversed its editorial policy overnight and threw its support to Pingree. It was a "red-hot campaign" in which Pingree glossed over his shortcomings as a platform speaker by making one of the strongest personal canvasses on record.[36]

When the vote began coming in on election day, it was apparent that the enthusiasm that Pingree and the "Big Four" had infused into the city G.O.P. had extended to the challengers, whose stiffened vigilance at the polls noticeably curtailed the use of "floaters" and ineligible voters. Even the more careful surveillance, however, did not stop Chris Jacob, who pushed through an unqualified voter over the strenuous objections of a Republican challenger; Jacob silenced the challenger by beating and choking him and pitching him over a rail onto the floor. But not even Jacob's brutal beating could stem the tide that was running against the Democrats.[37]

Pingree won the election by 2,338 votes, polling 13,954 votes to Pridgeon's 11,616. The Republicans also won the council election, carrying nine seats to five seats for the Democrats and two seats for the independents. In the city-wide elections for the six administrative offices, however, only Republicans Tom P. Tuite, who was running for treasurer, and Fitzwilliam H. Chambers, the candidate for associate recorder, were victorious, suggesting that the Pingree-G.O.P. view of Irish voting behavior was correct.[38]

The factors that had a direct influence upon Pingree's election were the corruption issue, the eight-hour day question, and above all, the ethnic appeals of Pingree and the G.O.P. The corruption issue played some role but it was not decisive. The eight-hour day question threw the normally Democratic labor support to Pingree. During the campaign Pridgeon had been harassed and criticized by the Trades and Labor Council for not enforcing an eight-hour day on city jobs. In a ward that had been a stronghold for labor candidates in the 1887 election, the labor vote transferred its entire support to Pingree. Although Pingree did not carry the ward, the G.O.P. increased its vote there from 30 to 47 per cent.[39]

Although the municipal corruption and the eight-hour day issues moved some voters to the G.O.P., the key to Pingree's election was the substantial inroads that he made on the German and Polish vote. Pingree's success in courting the Polish vote is, in part, demonstrable by a study of four key precincts identified as characteristically Polish. The wards in which these precincts were located had all gone Democratic in the city elections of 1887 and 1888, with the exception of one ward in 1888. In the mayoralty elections of 1889, three of the four wards went Republican. In the ward remaining Democratic, only one precinct gave Pingree a majority, and it was characterized as Polish—it was the location of the largest Polish cathedral in Detroit, the Polish Seminary, and a Polish parochial school. In the other three test precincts, Pingree polled a solid majority. In these precincts the average percentage of Pingree's plurality was greater than it was in the city at large.[40]

Locating a characteristically German ward in Detroit is more difficult because of the social and economic mobility of German-Americans and their dispersal into most of the other wards. The fifth ward, which had elected German-American Democrats over German-American Republicans for council since 1887 and which was Boss Jacob's bailiwick, probably qualifies, however. In 1887 and 1888, Jacob and Charles P. Karrer had outpolled their councilmanic opponents by two-to-one margins, and in 1889 Karrer was reelected by a comfortable three-to-two margin. Although Pingree lost the ward, he had increased the G.O.P.'s vote from 31 per cent in 1887 to 45 per cent in 1889 and, one can assume, carried many German-Americans with him.[41]

Another gauge for measuring Pingree's success in garnering German votes is his record in the most foreign-born wards of the city. In six of these wards where German-American political fealty was normally Democratic, Pingree carried three and lost the other three by narrow margins. Pingree's performance strongly suggests that he carried a larger percentage of the German-American vote than had his recent G.O.P. predecessors.[42]

Pingree and the G.O.P. had won a crucial segment of the city's ethnic vote, a result that would have far-reaching consequences for Detroit. Pingree's strength among the Germans had exceeded all expectations. The Detroit *Evening News* pointed out that the Republicans had captured the Polish vote, and attributed this, in part, to a vigorous last minute campaign Father Kolasinski made for Pingree. Pingree, in an effort to hold and enlarge his newly-found base of political power, later appointed numerous Germans and Poles to public office. His recognition of the decisive role that ethnicity could play in urban politics was to revitalize Detroit's Republican party.[43]

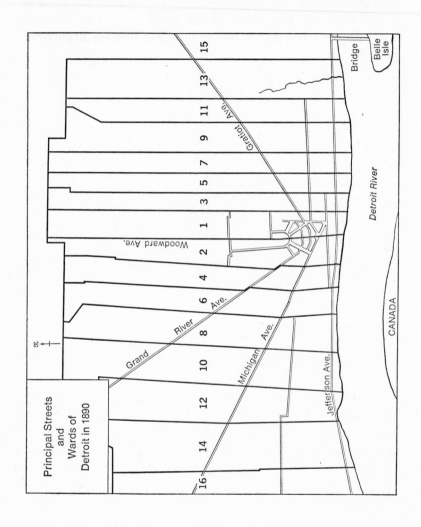

Principal Streets and Wards of Detroit in 1890

2

The Apprenticeship: Good
Government Mayor

During his four terms as mayor, Hazen S. Pingree met many of the problems common to municipalities of his day, and with energy and originality he brought Detroit to prominence among American cities. Yet his first year as mayor in 1890 was a poor, if not deceptive, indication that a social reformer would emerge in 1892 and 1893. Initially committed to a businessman's concept of good municipal government, Pingree first followed a course which other mayors before him had taken and which had done little to change conditions in urban America.

During his first administration, Pingree rooted out dishonesty and inefficiency in a fashion that excited civic uplifters. Pingree struck at what he conceived to be the causes of corruption as ruthlessly and effectively as had any of the "good government" mayors of Eastern cities. Paring away inefficiency, he brought the power of his administration to bear upon crooked contractors, bad workmanship, and the lax policies of municipal departments. Pingree's approach to urban problems also had much in common with the mugwump tradition which sought to upgrade the quality of public service and to lower its cost by the creation of systems which brought in honest and able municipal employees.

Hazen S. Pingree's inaugural message, delivered before the common council on January 14, 1890, dealt with the paving problem. Approaching the problem as a businessman would, Pingree pointed out that Detroit had invested its money badly in 130 miles of wooden block pavements which had been laid on a sand and loam base. He observed that Detroit had spent more than one-half million dollars on Jefferson and Woodward Avenues, two of the city's main thoroughfares, during the previous sixteen years, but that these pavements still remained in poor condition. To lay a pavement of cut stone or asphalt would have required a greater capital outlay, he conceded, but the return would have been worth it. For good pavements would have provided a solid foundation ready for inexpensive resurfacing. The Mayor also asked for better street cleaning and requested that the city "keep apace with private enterprise" by buying "improved machinery." Nothing contributed "so much to the prosperity of a city as well paved streets," concluded Pingree.[1]

Pingree's assessment was correct. The city's streets were, indeed, in such wretched condition that the Detroit *Journal* described them as "150 miles of rotting, rutted, lumpy, dilapidated paving. . . ." The cedar blocks were often set afloat by spring rains or driven deeply into the mud by heavy traffic. During the summer dry season dust storms accompanied every breeze that cooled the city. On streets where the blocks were still on the surface, the resins and pitches that oozed from the cedar frequently caught fire from carelessly discarded cigar butts. Such streets were also difficult to clean, and the sandy loam base prevented drainage and created unsanitary pools of water. Local historian George B. Catlin reported that Detroit was one of the worst paved cities of its size in the country when Pingree assumed office in 1890.[2]

Such inferior pavements in a city of 200,000 people were undoubtedly due in part to public inertia. Also responsible, however, was a group of unprogressive contractors who had failed to equip themselves to handle modern road surfacing and who preferred to hire low-priced unskilled labor to dump blocks and mud on the streets. Although the contractors lacked the skills and equipment to do modern paving, their collusion with the Democratic party was usually adequate to overcome their technological shortcomings. According to the Detroit *Journal*, the contractors' "combine" paid 10 per cent to the Democratic bloc in the city council to keep out low-priced, modern macadam men. Theft and shabby workmanship also played their part. Two foremen for the Talbott Company testified later that they had been paid bonuses by their employer to cut corners and violate city specifications. "I frankly confess I take all the advantage of the city I can on contracts," said a company foreman. Although Pingree's predecessor had broken up the "combine" in 1889 and secured indictments against several leading Democratic councilmen, including Chris Jacob, witnesses had the unnerving habit of disappearing, and prosecution was seldom successful. It was widely believed that the old Irish hangers-on such as councilmen Robert H. Murphy and William O'Regan and Board of Public Works Commissioner James Hanley were deeply implicated with the paving "combine," and their consistent opposition to better pavements in 1890 and 1891 lent credibility to the charge.[3]

Pingree scored his first victory for good streets in May, 1890, when the council adopted some of his paving specifications, including concrete foundations for a few of the heavily-trafficked thoroughfares. In June he pushed an ordinance through the council which authorized concrete foundations and hard-road surfaces for Jefferson and Lafayette Avenues, which serviced two wealthy neighborhoods. During 1892 he secured measures which improved the city's major arteries and obtained brick surfacing for Gratiot Avenue and asphalt for Woodward Avenue. Anxious to complete his program, Pingree, over the protest of churchmen, ordered the contractors to work seven days a week in 1892 because he believed that hard-surfaced streets were an important health measure which would eliminate pools of stagnant water and debris, which spread disease. Distressed by the city's constant surveillance of the private contractors to force them to fulfill obligations, Pingree demanded that security bonds be posted. He also asked Detroit to establish a municipal paving department.[4]

In July, 1893, the Mayor made a major advance when the council accepted the principle that concrete road beds, when economically feasible, would be a routine part of Detroit's future paving policies. In 1893, only Buffalo had more asphalt-pavement mileage than Detroit. Two years later, the Detroit *Journal* declared that Detroit's streets were in better condition than those of any city of comparable size in the country. The Mayor's constant attention to street improvements brought Detroit to the front rank of well-paved cities of the United States.[5]

The same pattern of Democratic collusion with corrupt contractors emerged in the sewer scandal of 1890, and revealed how common graft had become under the old urban order. In March, Pingree ordered an engineering investigation of Detroit's sewage system, which disclosed that many of the recently constructed mains and lines were rotting and crumbling. To win council backing for his improvement program, Pingree led a group of aldermen into the sewers, where they saw concrete as soft as mush, bricks that had fallen out of place, mortar that crumbled with the touch of the hand, water and mud cascading through the walls, and obstructions which backed up the effluence. Although some of the blame lay with faulty craftsmanship, Pingree placed the major responsibility on the city's cement supplier, who had furnished an unsuitable, low-quality product.[6] To end such abuses of the public interest, Pingree established an informal research bureau and converted his office into a concrete testing laboratory filled with jars and bottles of sand and various brands of cement, water, and pressure gauges. Every test of tensile strength of the brand of cement which had been sold to the city showed that it lacked the required hydraulic properties and firmness. Pingree roared his disapproval as the inferior product cracked before the gauges could even register, whereas the Portland and Louisville brands withstood forty pounds of pressure. The supplier of inferior cement threatened to sue Pingree, but his case collapsed when a hardened sample of his cement was presented to an alderman at a public hearing, and he crumbled the sample with his bare hands. A former employee of the supplier testified that floor sweepings which had leaked from other bags had been sold to the Board of Public Works and that the company had a general policy of "short weighting" the city.[7]

Democratic Commissioner James Hanley of the Board of Public Works tried to defend his purchase of inferior workmanship and supplies, but Pingree had already outflanked him with the appointment of two businesslike G.O.P. commissioners who brought an end to Hanley's lax policies. The new Board dropped the cement company from its list of suppliers, established stiffer standards for purchasing, and solicited out-of-town bidders, thus abolishing the inefficient localism which was a part of the Democratic business and political philosophy. To eliminate some of the shabby workmanship that flourished under the patronage system, the Board began purchasing a vitreous, precast pipe to replace sewer masonry for the smaller lateral lines. Even so, in August, 1892, two sewer contractors attempted to bribe the G.O.P. council for several contracts. They were assured by the Pingree administration that competitive bidding and good workmanship were the only requirements for city work. The rational order of the business world had triumphed over the casual corruption of the old Democratic sewer and paving "combines" by 1892.[8]

In another scandal, involving the school board, Pingree moved vigorously to eliminate a long tradition of corruption and collusion. The board, elected on a ward basis, had long been either a nursery for the politically ambitious or a pasture for marginal businessmen who hoped to recoup their private losses at public expense. "Scarcely a session passes that something is not done which has the odor of 'boodle' about it," said the Detroit *Journal*. Pingree was especially irked that the school board awarded lucrative contracts at secret sessions, because of loose budgetary controls, and that the board did not act as a city-wide agent to plan intelligently for Detroit's educational needs. In 1893, hoping to centralize planning and eliminate some of the worst abuses of localism, Pingree secured the enactment of a state law that authorized the Mayor to veto board expenditures. Pingree's goal was not budget cutting but an efficient utilization of the money available for education.[9]

The Mayor's veto power over money measures was, however, inadequate to reform the school board, for the board chose to ignore the state law and reverted to its old patterns of defiance and questionable dealing. Finally, on August 15, 1894, Pingree exposed the corruption and rooted out some of the most dishonest members of the board. "It was like a scene from a melodrama or a page from a sensational novel," reported the Detroit *Evening News*, "for such things happen often on the stage but seldom in real life." At a meeting of the board, Pingree announced: "There are quite a number of the members of this board who are going to jail tonight." He called upon the dishonest schoolmen, as yet unnamed, to resign and to save the city from disgrace. When Pingree was met with stony silence and then opposition, he pealed off the names of the corrupt in slow cadence, repeating the charges clearly and deliberately while issuing warrants. Then he called in police officers from the wings to arrest four board members. When the indicted chairman of the school real-estate committee called Pingree a liar, the Mayor ordered: "Officer, take this man to jail," and a squad of policemen closed in. Pingree then proceeded with his indictment, asserting: "Why, actually members of this board have sold themselves out regularly to this and that and the other contractor. It is frightful. And it made no difference. After they had been bought they frequently sold themselves again, and left the parties they first sold to." [10]

In court it was disclosed that Pingree, determined to leave no loopholes open, had employed several private detectives. They worked in co-operation with a school furniture salesman who had been informed by several board members that a personal payoff would be the price of a contract with the Detroit public schools. The salesman met with the ring in a local hotel room, which Pingree's detectives had rigged in advance for observation. A stenographer recorded the conversation. The salesman led the schoolmen through their usual performance, in which they demanded their bribes and seriously incriminated themselves. [11]

Armed with a dossier of solid evidence, Pingree brought the corrupt board members to trial. Two were sentenced to prison, one jumped his bail bond and fled the state, and the fourth member secured an acquittal. The exposure did indeed shake the town, as Pingree had predicted, and ended one of the long-enduring corrupt practices in Detroit.[12]

During his first term Pingree also attempted to eliminate inefficiency and waste by a number of economy measures. In refusing payment of a personal liability claim against Detroit, Pingree maintained that the city should contest all such cases in court not only to save money but also to force the public attorneys to earn their keep by defending the interests of the city. When the municipal clerks asked for overtime pay to prepare the tax rolls, Pingree vetoed the proposal and asserted that the clerks, who then worked a six-hour day, deserved no additional compensation. The Mayor hoped to plug the continual leaks in the treasury which drained away public resources with needless extras. In turning down a pay raise for the election inspectors, Pingree claimed that their unsatisfactory services did not justify an increase. A pork barrel measure to add to the number of city attendants on Belle Isle Bridge was quashed by Pingree because it provided "for too many high priced employees who would be more ornamental than useful." "Our first duty . . . as representatives of the taxpayers of the city of Detroit is to carefully guard their interests," Pingree said. "How can Detroit taxpayers and business men compete—as they have to—with Chicago taxpayers and business men when compelled to pay from 40 to 100 per cent more for having the same things done?" [13]

The answer of the first Pingree administration reflected the nostrums of an earlier generation of business-minded reformers: eliminate the hacks who were nursed at the "political teat" in the interests of the merit system. The Mayor prodded the garbage inspectors to perform more efficiently, pressed for measures to reduce the pay of sidewalk inspectors, wanted to do away with the gas inspectors who performed few useful functions, strove to eliminate the surfeit of city hall janitors who were political appointees, tried to check the idleness of municipal clerks, and attempted to force public employees to put in a full day's work. Although he opposed the eight-hour day for city laborers (who averaged ten hours) in

1891 because he felt that it would infringe upon their liberty of contract, Pingree supported an eight-hour day for janitors with the hope that they might be induced to work more than their customary four- to six-hour day.[14]

The first Pingree administration had aimed at modifying and improving the mechanisms of municipal government in an effort to make them work as the city charter had intended. Pingree had injected large doses of efficiency into the old system and had tried to scrap many of the agencies whose contribution to good government was questionable. Not only had the Mayor rooted out dishonesty, but he had also worked hard to eliminate the worst excesses of localism and particularism: Pingree had attempted both formally by charter reform and informally by the use of patronage power to centralize administrative and municipal control and to focus power in the office of the mayor. It was clearly an attempt to incorporate the best features of the business world into municipal administration. Responsible, efficient, and clean government had been the goal of countless "reform" mayors; and, in this respect, Pingree's crusade for a better Detroit possessed few features that could not be found within the business-inspired reform movements in other cities.

The prelude to Pingree's concern with the larger social question of transportation came in his struggle to lower ferry rates. Pingree was convinced that the high cost of a ferry ride from Detroit across the Detroit River to Belle Isle Park prevented citizens from enjoying this refreshing respite. When the Mayor threatened to revoke the ferry company's license or to purchase a publicly owned fleet, the company dropped its rates from ten cents to five cents, and a new licensee took over the operation. During the fracas, Pingree examined city-owned water frontage and found that free public access had been blocked by private businesses that had encroached upon municipal property and deprived citizens of their right to the Detroit River at eighteen public landings. Pingree began clearing away the dock areas and winning back for the public free access to water and recreation.[15]

In 1892 Pingree also inaugurated a campaign to eliminate the toll gates which stood astride the city's five main thoroughfares and which levied tribute on two-thirds of the traffic coming into Detroit. The toll roads were in wretched condition because their owners had failed to comply with charter provisions requiring repair and maintenance. Even after the city had repaired and paved the main thoroughfares, some of the plank road companies exercised their ancient charter rights and continued to charge a toll on them for incoming traffic within one-half mile of the city hall. Few escaped the "blackmailing toll-gate," as Pingree called it, for even the Board of Public Works' teamsters had to pay tribute when driving on city streets to the water works. Pingree called the toll roads a "relic of barbarism" and charged that their owners were guilty of legalized robbery. All the Pingree administration's attempts at legislative and legal redress failed, however, for the courts upheld the property rights of the charter holders. Pingree made several attempts to buy out the charters at reasonable prices, but he was rebuffed by the road companies which demanded exorbitant payment. Also opposing the Mayor were a few of the old ward-bound councilmen of narrow vision, but he had little difficulty in lining up votes for the necessary appropriations.[16]

Still it required coercion and harassment of the rawest form to force the owners to sell or even to co-operate. Strathearn Hendrie, one of the principal owners of the Jefferson Avenue gate, obtained a court injunction which temporarily stopped the city from paving Detroit's main northeast highway, Jefferson Avenue. Furious with these "leeches on the municipality," Pingree advised citizens to refuse to pay tolls on the grounds that the plank road charters were forfeit because of gross negligence. "If they won't get out the people should organize and drive them out," said the Mayor. Despairing of legal and reasonable remedies, Pingree struck at Hendrie, the toughest of the toll road curmudgeons, and built what became known as the Pingree bypass around Hendrie's Jefferson Avenue gate. When Hendrie remained obstinate even though vehicles now could pass the gate without paying, Pingree pushed a 60-foot wide macadamized road up to and around the toll house, which was left stranded in the middle of the road. Hendrie then applied for another injunction, but the court ruled that his company owned only the 16-foot strip in the center, and thus his tolls were uncollectable on 44 feet of outside lanes on Jefferson Avenue. The toll companies, having learned the lesson, sold out to Detroit on reasonable terms. By the middle of 1896, every toll company had been ousted from within the city limits. "Now we can drive over our streets feeling that we are free men," declared Pingree.[17]

The struggle for lower ferry rates and a free road system presaged Pingree's concern with the larger question of urban transportation. Pingree was beginning to realize that the social needs of urban Detroiters could not be met by simply tinkering with the machinery of municipal government and wiping out corruption with a Calvinistic zeal.

3

A Businessman's Mayor Moves
Toward Social Reform

A problem of great magnitude that confronted Pingree during his first three terms as mayor was the street railway question. The improvement of transit, the restoration and extension of municipal rights, and the struggle for public control were influential factors in transforming a tax-conscious businessman's candidate into an urban reformer. A strike provided the catalyst by which Pingree moved to the center of the traction issue and gained the leverage to hold public attention on one of the most crucial problems, not only of Detroit, but of the late-nineteenth-century city. Pingree realized that, unlike the private sector of the economy where bad management might adversely affect the fortunes of only a few stockholders and employees, bad management in urban transit intimately affected the lives of thousands who were most often captive consumers of an irreplaceable and vital service over which they exercised no control. During the controversy the Mayor was also discovering that the business concept of urban reform, which had guided his first administration, was inadequate and too limited in scope to meet the larger needs of the urban community. This fundamental shift in emphasis would win for Pingree a new class of supporters as well as convert his old allies into vehement enemies.

The first railway for urban street traffic in the United States was put into operation in New York in 1832. Detroit got her first street railway in 1863, and by 1870 there were horse- and mule-drawn lines in all the nation's largest cities. Privately owned, these railways operated under little or no regulatory legislation, paid but a nominal tax on gross earnings or stock issued, and for slightly more than a modest lobbying fee were usually able to obtain long-term, thirty- to one hundred-year franchises from municipalities or state legislatures. Very little uniformity prevailed in the duration of franchises: Massachusetts granted franchises in perpetuity, subject to revocation by municipalities; Michigan permitted a thirty-year period; and New York, one thousand years. The nation accepted competition as the only regulator of the number of franchises, with the result that during the last half of the nineteenth century Philadelphia had as many as 39 separate street railway companies, while New York had 19, Pittsburgh, 24, St. Louis, 19, and San Francisco, 16.[1]

The installation in 1885 of an overhead electric trolley system in Kansas City signaled the beginning of a technological revolution in the street railway industry. Frank J. Sprague, a naval engineer and inventor, demonstrated the practicability of electricity with his overhead system in Richmond, Virginia, in 1888, and the "electric era" began. Within two years, 51 cities, including Boston, New York, Pittsburgh, Cleveland, Cincinnati, Milwaukee, Minneapolis, St. Paul, Atlanta, St. Louis, and Columbus, had begun to retire horse-drawn cars for electrified rapid transit. By 1891, one-third of the street railway mileage in the United States was operated by electric power or subject to contracts requiring electrification. Detroit, however, was a notable exception to this trend.[2]

During the first decade of the new industry, the advances in street railway technology were not matched by a corresponding increase in business skill on the part of the management of the lines. Unsound financial policies injected a fatal flaw into the industry. Overcapitalization, inadequate depreciation allowances, and the unwillingness of street railway managers to rid the lines of "dead capital" with sinking funds plagued the industry from its inception.

Only in Massachusetts, which restricted and regulated the stock issue of public service corporations, was overcapitalization held in check: by 1897, according to the United States Industrial Commission, Massachusetts street railways were capitalized for $44,683 per mile of track, as compared to $91,500 per mile of track for Michigan, Illinois, Indiana, Ohio, Wisconsin, Minnesota, and Iowa, all of which failed to regulate the issue of street railway stocks and bonds. Edward E. Higgins, a defender of the street railway operators, reluctantly conceded that perhaps one-third of American street railway securities represented "water" in 1897. The relationship between capitalization and actual investment, as cities such as Detroit, Milwaukee, and Columbus were to discover, was of crucial significance because upon this relationship hinged the question of the reasonableness of fares.[3]

"The fixed 5-cent fare," Delos F. Wilcox has noted, "was in the early days the very corner-stone of the towering structure of capital inflation built up by promoters and manipulators of the industry." Low labor costs and the deflationary tendency of the national economy in the early 1890's also appeared to "make the 5-cent fare an inexhaustible goldmine in urban communities." Irresistibly tempted by the "goldmine" psychology, street railway managers continued to carry capital on their books which represented dead and lame horses, light-weight rails and horse-cars, and decaying barns and stables, all of which had been rendered totally valueless by the adoption of electrified rapid transit. Instead of retiring this "waste capital" with adequate depreciation allowances, the operators sapped the vitality of the industry by continuing to pay high dividends, which forced the railways to issue new securities when they had to re-equip their electric lines. This economic spiral continued throughout the 1890's, with most large urban lines being saddled not only with the bonded indebtedness of their new electric systems but also by the burden of their old horse-car systems. After examining the accounts of 799 roads, the Department of Commerce and Labor concluded in 1902: "Doubtless, in many cases, street railways in the past earned profits high enough to enable them to make such depreciation allowances if they had seen fit to do so. Their policy, however, almost without exception, had been to pay out the greater part of net income in dividends. . . ." Even the *Street Railway Journal,* an apologist for the industry, had to admit in 1902 that the industry had gotten itself into a mess by overcapitalization and a refusal to retire dead capital.[4]

The expansion of the electrified street railway system in American cities and the use of free "universal transfers," by which the purchaser of a single fare could travel to almost any point in the city without additional payment, had an important social significance, for they helped to determine the property value, rent structure, and population density of cities. Whether the industrial worker lived in unsanitary, overcrowded, industrial district tenements or in more comfortable circumstances in the suburbs depended to a large extent on the street railway. Whereas a fare fixed according to the distance traveled would have encouraged the lower economic groups to settle in congested areas of the city, the ungraded, low, uniform fare and the universal transfer made it possible for the urban laborer to live in the suburbs. The sociologist Charles H. Cooley asserted that a low fare "brings suburban residence within reach of large classes of the poorest people," and John R. Commons declared that the low fare was the workingman's ticket for escape from the slum. According to the urban reformer Edward W. Bemis, workers at Hull House in Chicago had labored for years with only moderate success in improving the unsanitary and overcrowded conditions of the foreign-born about them when suddenly a new street railway extension induced 5,000 of the slum residents "to move to healthful suburbs." A. H. Sinclair, a student of municipal traction, agreed that expansion acted "as a safety valve to relieve the congested districts. . . ." [5]

Although a recent study of Boston's residential development raises, by implication, some question about the generalizations of the students of urban affairs noted above and shows that street railway expansion in Boston enabled the wealthy class to move to the suburbs and concentrated the working class in the heart of the old city, the pattern for Boston did not hold true for Detroit. There, the upper classes remained concentrated at the geographical center of the city near downtown Detroit as late as 1900 while the foreign-born and industrial workers moved to the outlying districts and suburbs. Although the question of which classes benefited the most throughout the nation might be disputed, the Department of Commerce pointed out that the instrument of amelioration, the street railway, had been "probably the most important single influence in dispersing urban population." [6]

The influence of the street railway in controlling rents and unifying the city was also great. "Broadly speaking," asserted a Department of Commerce study of 1902, "the railways tend to distribute and equalize land values in the residential parts of cities and to prevent excessive rents in certain sections which would follow from overcrowding." Charles H. Cooley noted that "In some cases an actual decrease of rent in thickly settled quarters has been observed to follow the opening of a new suburban railway." The expansion of street railways and the uniform fare also enabled large urban centers to develop in a unified and cohesive fashion, which would have been impossible in the restricted perimeters of the old "walking city." [7]

When Hazen Pingree assumed his duties as mayor in January, 1890, the Detroit street railway was a conspicuous exception to the nationwide trend toward electrification. Detroit's principal line, the City Railway Company, and the main suburban line, the Fort Wayne and Elmwood Railway Company, depended exclusively upon animal power at a time when the last horse cars were disappearing in Cleveland, Toledo, Minneapolis, and St. Paul and were soon to be discontinued in Chicago. In February, 1892, the *Street Railway Journal* pointed out that cities possessing one-tenth of Detroit's population enjoyed more rapid transit, and the *Street Railway Review* asserted that Detroit's horse car system made it "one of the poorest equipped street railway cities in the country. . . ." To overcome this deficiency, Mayor Pingree, in his first message to the common council, called for the adoption of rapid transit and the expansion of the street railway system in Detroit under conditions that would better protect and serve the public interest. [8]

George and Strathearn Hendrie, the principal owners of the Detroit City Railway Company, were determined to continue their horse-drawn lines, and they were unwilling to give the city rapid transit except upon the condition of a franchise renewal. The original franchise, which had been granted in 1862 for thirty years, expired in 1893; but during a period of council complacency in 1879, the Hendries had pushed through a thirty-year extension which advanced the termination date to 1909. The company, however, grew increasingly uneasy about the legality of its 1879 extension, which appeared to conflict with the Michigan constitution's thirty-year limitation on franchises, and the Hendries consequently began to pressure the city for a legal renewal. For the exclusive privilege of operating on Detroit's main thoroughfares for thirty years, a right which was literally worth millions of dollars, the company offered the city only 1½ per cent of their gross earnings in taxes, refused public inspection of the company's books to verify earnings, made no fare concessions, and was unwilling to be subjected to any additional public control. The City Railway met each demand for rapid transit with a counter demand for a renewal, which caused the public to grow increasingly impatient with the retrogressive management of the Hendries.[9]

The delaying tactics of the Hendries were cut short by the street railway strike of 1891, which provided a vehicle for the expression of the city's widespread discontent with its street railway, and pushed Pingree to the center of one of the most important public questions of his career, one that would stir not only Detroit but the nation's major municipalities for the next two decades. The strike began on April 21 after the company had fired twelve union members who were organizing the Street Car Employees' Association, an affiliate of the American Federation of Labor. Also upsetting to the Hendries was the fact that the fledgling union was supporting a ten-hour day bill in the Michigan legislature. The company tried to counter the activity of some of its employees by circulating an anti-ten-hour day petition among its workers and by threatening to cut wages and dismiss union "agitators." [10]

The strike was in essence a three-day riot made up of crowds of workers and citizens, in a vengeful mood, who wreaked havoc on the City Railway. In a heated encounter on Jefferson Avenue, the strike leaders led a rush on an approaching car with shouts of: "Break out the windows. Give them a volley of anything you can lay your hands on. And if you happen to hit the cops and the scabs it'll be all right." Wild with rage, the company treasurer Strathearn Hendrie sprang from the car amid the shattering and splintering glass and shook his fist at the mob, which replied with shouts of: "Kill the Canuck! Kill the Canuck!" [11] On the corner of Woodward and Jefferson Avenues a mob of 5,000 men encouraged the strikers who were derailing a car. The rioting was of a similar character on the Gratiot, Michigan, and other lines. Assisted by workers from the Michigan and Detroit Stove Works, the Motor Works, and by citizen sympathizers, the strikers unhitched horses and drove them off, stoned every car on the streets, tore up tracks, and fought pitched battles against the police with cobblestones and bare knuckles. On Woodward Avenue, where the Pingree and Smith shoemakers' band led a sympathy march down the street, chunks of wood and brickbats pelted every street car that approached. When Strathearn Hendrie, riding on one of the cars, pulled out a revolver to stop a mob which was unhitching horses, a dozen men in the crowd responded by brandishing revolvers. By the third day the barricades of rusty roofing, lamp posts, wooden blocks, and tree stumps and "the wholesale demolition of the company's tracks and other property" had paralyzed much of the city's transit. Finally the Hendries capitulated to Mayor Pingree's request to halt all service.[12]

The streetcar riots were not carried on wholly by a destructive proletariat. As Pingree pointed out, the mob was composed of some of Detroit's most respectable citizens. A future mayor and United States Senator James Couzens was among those who stoned the street cars. The merchant J. L. Hudson placed an iron box in front of his store and sent his clerks out to collect contributions for the strikers and their families. Beals and Selkirk Trunk Company pledged a financial contribution for each day the men were on strike. Mabley and Company and R. H. Travers paid $25 for seats for a union benefit performance, and Mabley arranged for five free omnibuses to ply the city's main thoroughfares. Brewer August

Goebel made a $50 contribution. A Michigan Avenue baker gave baskets of lunches at noon and promised to feed 1,000 men for the duration of the strike. R. H. Fyfe and other prominent merchants expressed open sympathy and condemned the Hendries' antiquated street railway. Ex-Postmaster General Don M. Dickinson and the Reverend Charles R. Henderson, one of the city's popular Protestant clergymen, lent aid and comfort to the strikers by denouncing the company in a rapid transit rally. The following Sunday many of the city's clergy defended the right of the men to organize and pointed out that the conditions that caused strikes required correction.[13]

The large-scale favorable response of Detroiters to the strike was variously interpreted. Some of the union's organizers misconstrued the amount of sympathy and aid from the business classes as a stunning victory for organized labor, whereas it really was, as a representative of the carpenters' union pointed out, the work of "extremely high-tone, law-abiding devoted citizens most of whom had some sort of private spite to work out on the railway company." Clearly, what had happened was that the railway company was "reaping its harvest of indifference to popular sentiment; of its 'public be damned' airs; its purchase of aldermen; its defiance of the public convenience; its lofty demeanor and general supercilious contempt for the community from whom it holds its valuable privileges and franchises. . . ." Hence its treatment of its employees elicited more than ordinary sympathy, noted the Detroit *Free Press*. The strike had given the city an opportunity to express its hostility against the City Railway Company, which had refused rapid transit when it had been demanded with reasonableness, and which had fought every other proposition to furnish modern facilities.[14]

The railway company asked Pingree to call in the state militia to suppress the strike, but he refused on the grounds that municipal protection was adequate. When additional police protection was requested, Pingree replied that the police department was not under control of the mayor but of the Metropolitan Police Commission, appointed by the governor. This brought about some hastily-passed legislation that restored home rule of the police department to Detroit. Although Pingree was in hearty sympathy with the strikers, he advised nonviolence and applied pressure on George Hendrie to submit the dispute to arbitration, which the company did after the three days of rioting. Under Pingree's leadership and with Don M. Dickinson's assistance, the strike was terminated and successfully arbitrated. The agreement that was reached bound management and labor, as Pingree saw it, to the most successful mode of settlement of labor disputes, arbitration.[15]

Although the company had been thoroughly repudiated by the public, it was clear that the Detroit City Railway was still a power in Detroit politics and that the utility would continue to demand a franchise extension as the price of rapid transit. Company secretary Cameron Currie and ex-Alderman DeWitt C. Kellogg, who had "a record as crooked as a dog's hind leg" according to a fellow councilman, applied increasing pressure on the council throughout May and June, 1891; and, in Pingree's words, "When the dust was supposed to be well thrown into the people's eyes . . . a franchise giving the company a further lease of life of thirty years was sprung." As public clamor increased, Pingree assured all callers that he "was with them against the infamous action of the majority of the council that had literally railroaded the job through" and announced that he would veto the extension.[16]

The franchise renewal had been rammed through the council under the leadership of Democrat Chris Jacob over weak opposition led by Republicans James Vernor and Joseph T. Lowry. Stunned by this Democratic betrayal, the president of the Trades and Labor Council, Louis E. Tossy, remonstrated: "It's hard for working people to know who their friends are . . . Now the silk stockings are opposed to the franchise, and most of those who are supposed to be the friends of the laboring people have voted against us. It is infamous and outrageous." [17] Pingree, in a heated confrontation, accused Jacob and the council of accepting bribes and charged: "You and your majority of the aldermen rushed in Wednesday . . . to give the companies these privileges,—rushed as if you would break your necks. . . ." [18]

The city's "best" citizens, led by Don M. Dickinson, Russell A. Alger, Thomas W. Palmer, Henry M. Duffield, Dexter M. Ferry, labor leaders Sam Goldwater and Louis Tossy, the silk stocking aldermen, and merchants of every stripe and station organized a protest meeting to give Pingree's promised veto massive support. At the rally, a committee of fifty men was formed to serve as a watch-dog unit over the council. Dickinson denounced the franchise grab and asked the citizens to support the mayor. Pingree mounted the platform to a round of cheers and shouted that his veto would serve as his speech. The meeting, attended by 4,000 citizens from all walks of life, and characterized as "probably the most magnifi-cently unanimous expression of popular sentiment on a municipal subject that has ever been manifested in Detroit," provided roaring support for Pingree's promised veto.[19]

Pingree's veto message, delivered on July 7, demolished Jacob's railway cabal in the council and gave the street railway company its first taste of defeat in Detroit. He called the private ownership of natural monopolies "a bad financial arrangement" and "the chief source of corruption in city governments" and argued that a fran-chise should be sold for either a cash return to the city or reduced fares for the people. At a time when businessmen were ready to pay millions of dollars for the privilege, he declared that the city could not "afford to buy rapid transit at the immense cost of these franchises," which would "bind this city hand and foot for 30 years." He concluded with the hope that eminent domain might be used to seize the street railway property if the existing unsatisfac-tory state of affairs continued.[20] When the council unanimously up-held Pingree's veto, President Jacob, who was the target of hoots and catcalls of derision from the packed chamber, adjourned the session. Immediately following, the mob rushed over the chamber barricade, overturning furniture and splattering ink, and shouting: "Tar and feather Jacob. Don't let Jacob get away." Jacob, like a "whipped dog," fled to the clerk's office for safety and remained there until tempers had cooled and a bodyguard could escort him home safely.[21]

The whole series of events from the strike to the veto gave evidence of a change that was taking place in Pingree's public personality and his conception of his role as a political leader. No longer reserved in speech, he could "turn loose a fire of profanity" and "career-killing invective" against his enemies that "curled the cedar-block pavements." [22] Pingree had been coaxed out "as a sacrificial offering" who knew nothing about politics. But, "In one year," John Lodge asserted, he "was the most astute politician of the best kind I ever knew." [23] He was not content, as his predecessors had been, to spend but a half hour at noon signing public documents and sending an occasional message to the council. Pingree made the mayorship a full-time job, intervening in the council sessions, guiding legislation, and "jumping into everything." In one alderman's words, "He has the bit between his teeth and is trying to run the town." [24]

Progressive Governor Chase S. Osborn later asserted that when Pingree first assumed office: "No one knew him as a great humanist . . . when Pingree began to find out how things were in a social and political way, he began to raise the dickens." On his business trips, he read Richard T. Ely's books, and absorbed municipal information like "a regular sponge." Pingree was not an intellectual, as the *Evening News* pointed out. "He saw only one fact at a time, but he saw it like a flash of lightning against a midnight sky." A new Pingree had emerged in 1891. He no longer drifted with events but frequently took unpopular actions and left the support of his class far behind him. [25]

During the last year of his first term, Pingree vetoed three other franchise renewals; vetoed a suburban line ordinance which was not in the public interest; denounced the City Railway Company for refusing to pave between their tracks with a durable surface; pushed through a measure requiring the Fort Wayne line to lay concrete foundations; and pressured the council to revoke the City Railway Company's right to maintain three lines on Woodward Avenue. The council upheld all these vetoes. Not until 1891, Pingree recalled, "was the Board of Aldermen really out of the grip of the street-car company." [26]

The fall election of 1891 provided a clear indication of a growing cleavage between Pingree and the economic titans of Detroit whose investments in the street railway industry had suffered at the hands of the Mayor. Officials of the railway complained that Pingree's questioning of their integrity and abuse of their reputations had raised doubts among investors and dried up the markets for their company's bonds. *The New York Times* claimed that "no one's financial interests were more ruthlessly stirred up than those of Senator McMillan." Although Hugh McMillan, the brother of the Senator, had earlier called Pingree "the most unutterable chump that ever occupied the mayor's chair," the attempt of James McMillan's G.O.P. machine to defeat Pingree, first for the nomination and then in the election in 1891, was the first attack upon Pingree by the politician capitalists of Detroit.[27]

In the attempted purge, McMillan's political lieutenants first tried to nominate a popular, German-born candidate, who withdrew his name hours later, complaining that he had been subjected to "the heaviest kind of pressure" to accept. McMillan then apparently threw his support to one of Pingree's principal Democratic opponents for the mayorship, but this too proved a total failure. During the campaign Pingree forced both of them, including the street railway backed William G. Thompson, and ten of the sixteen victorious councilmen to support the three-cent fare and the sale of franchises. Pingree walked away with the election, outpolling the combined vote of his two Democratic opponents. The election demonstrated clearly to Pingree the political potency of the traction issue with the electorate and the interlocking nature of politics and the street railway business in Detroit.[28]

Meanwhile, in July and August, 1891, the Detroit City Railway Company had ostensibly passed into the hands of a slick Eastern promoter, Thomas M. Waller, who attempted to cover any trace of the hated Hendrie ownership by an elaborate face lifting operation that included changing the name of the line to the Citizens' Street Railway Company and packing the directorship and what appeared to be the ownership of the firm with prominent Detroiters. Waller induced Dexter M. Ferry, lumber magnate Simon J.

Murphy, president of the Michigan Central Railroad Henry B. Ledyard, president of the State Savings Bank George H. Russel, and prominent attorneys Charles Stinchfield, Ashley Pond, William A. Moore, and Henry Russell to invest in the company. "Look at the men who have purchased a majority of the stock," Waller told a reporter. "They are men who are honored in Detroit, who have been prosperous and honest in business." Not only did Waller virtually surround Pingree by selecting as stockholders and officials three of his closest friends and neighbors, Ferry, Moore, and Murphy, but he also hired as general manager of the company John B. Mulliken, a Pingree appointed Commissioner of Public Works. In securing Moore and Murphy, Waller had also gained two of the important members of the committee of fifty, the vigilant organization formed to help Pingree combat the "franchise grab." The motive behind Waller's attempt to buy out the opposition and purchase respectability soon became apparent to Pingree, who charged: "The whole scheme is to get the franchises renewed." [29]

Convinced that the Michigan constitution's thirty-year limitation on franchises invalidated the 1879 extension of the Detroit City Railway franchise and assured of the support of some of the best legal counsel in the city, Pingree decided to subject the question of the franchise renewal to a court test. He pushed a resolution through the council to employ Don M. Dickinson and Alfred Russell to represent the city in the legal contest and also secured a companion measure that repealed the 1879 renewal.[30]

Just as litigation was about to commence, Don M. Dickinson withdrew from the city case on March 10, 1892; four days later, Alfred Russell announced: "I can't afford to work for glory, when men like James McMillan and D. M. Ferry offer me a very large amount of money to work for their side of the case. . . ." Sparing Dickinson, who had proved a valuable ally in the 1891 fight, Pingree launched an attack on Russell for betraying a public trust and taunted him with the question: "How much do you want not to sell out?" Pingree continued his verbal assault before the council, condemning the "high-handed and detestable methods" of the company "to enforce their obnoxious and impudent demands" upon the city and called Russell's action "treason or subornation of treason. . . ."[31]

The Russell affair blew the street railway question wide open, revealed a split between the company's stockholders and bondholders, and demolished the Waller myth that the Hendrie interests had been replaced by the "prosperous," "honored," and "honest" of Detroit. The affair demonstrated that the new stockholders did not control the company. Thoroughly shaken by the untoward events, the Citizens' treasurer, George H. Russel, speaking for the stockholders, said: "Do you think the directors are such a parcel of fools as to hire Russell away from the city? Why, if we did so there would be another riot and $100,000 would be raised by subscription in Detroit to employ counsel to fight the company." Senator McMillan issued a similar disclaimer from Washington, and Cameron Currie categorically denied that the bondholders had employed Russell. But Russell insisted that he had been retained by the bondholders, whose interests were paramount to those of the stockholders. Another bondholder attorney called Russell's statement "the most stupid blunder I ever heard of." A prominent merchant, R. H. Fyfe, declared in some alarm: "As I came down in the street car this morning, citizens were mad; they wanted to get out and tear up some street car rails. I tell you, there will be a riot again if the street car company doesn't look out." The whole affair left the Citizens' Street Railway Company weakened and Pingree strengthened in the fight for public control.[32]

Pingree noted that "the street railway company boasts that it has hired or silenced all the ablest attorneys in this city," and he obtained the services of Professor C. A. Kent of the University of Michigan and Benton Hanchett of nearby Saginaw to press the city's case.[33] In a bill of complaint to the Wayne County Circuit Court, the city asked for a judgment on the validity of the 1879 extension and requested that the Citizens' Street Railway Company be ejected and perpetually enjoined from occupying the streets of Detroit after May 9, 1893. The bondholders of the company had the case removed from the Detroit courts to the United States Circuit Court on the grounds of local prejudice. Their attorney argued that Detroit "is so saturated with this law suit that it is impossible to find a citizen who will talk . . . fairly on the subject." Needless to say, Pingree was unhappy about this change of venue and he feared interminable litigation in the federal courts.[34]

In May, 1893, United States Circuit Judge William Howard Taft, writing for the Eastern district of Michigan, sustained the city's contention. In his opinion, he argued that Detroit had no power to grant a vested right in its streets, except as conferred by the constitution and statutes of Michigan, which limited corporate life to thirty years. Taft declared the franchise extension of 1879 null and void and ruled that the company's legal right to the streets of Detroit terminated on May 9, 1893.[35]

The Citizens' Street Railway Company secured a postponement of the judgment of the district court by a complicated series of appeals: the bondholders, supported by George Hendrie and Senator McMillan, appealed to the United States Supreme Court to review the case on a writ of error, and the stockholders sent their case to the United States Circuit Court of Appeals, Sixth Circuit. After the United States Supreme Court dismissed the case, the United States Circuit Court of Appeals handed down a decision in October, 1894, reversing Taft's opinion and sustaining the 1879 franchise extension on the grounds that power conferred by the state to municipalities to grant such privileges had no expressed limitation and that such matters were better left to the "discretion of local government." [36]

In the so-called Workingmen's Fare case, however, the Pingree administration was successful in imposing the city's will and in forcing the Citizens' Railway Company and the suburban Fort Wayne Company to live within the spirit of their contractual obligations to Detroit. Workingmen's fares, a concession made by both companies in 1889 as the price of gaining additional privileges on the city streets, provided for the sale for twenty-five cents of eight tickets which were usable from 5:30 a.m. to 7:00 a.m. and 5:15 p.m. to 6:15 p.m. Since 1890 the railways had practically nullified the use of these tickets by refusing to sell them on the streetcars as other tickets were sold but rather by selling them at distant offices, the barns, or some "out-of-the-way saloon or grocery." The issue was a crucial one. For the average laborer who worked for a dollar a day, the success or failure of Pingree's program could mean the vital difference between 6 and 10 per cent of his meager daily earnings spent on transit. During the protracted depression of 1893, when men worked for as little as eighty cents a day, Jere Hutchins, a traction magnate pointed out that for the hundreds of people who gathered up "broken food and other refuse in the alleys . . . a penny in Detroit looked bigger than a saucepan." Pingree, at various times, had vainly applied pressure on the traction officials to make the tickets available on the cars. Finally, Pingree's secretary Alex McLeod discovered a reserve clause in the Detroit City Railway ordinance which empowered the council to make additional rules and regulations to protect the public interest and safety.[37] Pingree thereupon forced two ordinances through the council, one requiring the sale of workingmen's tickets by conductors and the other levying a $300 fine for violations. On February 15, 1893, when the ordinances went into effect, Pingree boarded a streetcar and asked to buy a strip of workingmen's tickets. The conductor refused. Pingree publicly encouraged workmen to employ the same tactic which caused the Citizens' Company irksome delays. Pingree's strategy was not only to show the bad faith of the traction interests but also to provide a basis for enforcing the law. When sufficient evidence of noncompliance was gathered, the administration took the Citizens' Street Railway Company into the Detroit Recorder's Court. The Court upheld the ordinance and fined the company. The Fort Wayne Company, which had been equally guilty of violating the city ordinance, contested the issue in the Michigan Supreme Court, and, on April 28, 1893, it declared the ordinance legal and binding.[38]

In 1892–93, while decision in the court cases was pending, Pingree embarked upon a program of forcing the lines to undertake physical improvements. Fundamental to rapid transit and the public convenience was the substitution ordered by Pingree of the heavy-weight, girder-grooved rail, which could withstand the added weight of electrified cars and which lay flush to the street surfaces, for the inexpensive, high-profile, and traffic-obstructing flat rail that the traction interests preferred. The administration also sought the replacement of mudsills and dirt roadbeds with concrete foundations, which would support heavier traffic, and the adoption of better paving between the tracks to seal out water seepage that had undermined the city's streets and caused costly repairs. In the struggle to effect these improvements, Pingree took the aldermen on a junket to Buffalo to inspect modern roadbeds, converted his office into a display room for grooved rails, pushed the necessary enabling legislation through the council, and made a personal trip to Johnstown, Pennsylvania, to accelerate shipment of the new rails to Detroit.[39] To the president of the Fort Wayne line, who doubted that the rails would work, Pingree remarked: "You take every street car stockholder, director, officer and superintendent in the city of Detroit down to Buffalo and lodge them at the finest hotel and if they don't find that the grooved rail gives satisfaction, I'll foot the bill." [40] The president declined the offer, and his line complied with the ordinance.

The Citizens' Street Railway Company, however, continued to resist, demanding as the price for such improvements a franchise renewal. This prompted Pingree to accuse the firm of pursuing a "stand and deliver or I'll blow your brains out" policy.[41] Even so, the Pingree administration, by July, 1893, had forced agreements on paving, foundations, and grooved rails from both companies and had substantially advanced the policy of public control over public streets. Frustrated, however, by the amount of energy and money that his administration had to spend to effect basic improvements that were as beneficial to the railways as to the city, Pingree, in December, 1892, asked for municipal ownership of the rails and roadbed.[42] This was a clear break with Pingree's earlier view that private business could be persuaded to operate a natural monopoly in the public interest.

In 1893 and 1894 Pingree vigorously prosecuted his campaign for low fares, sought a favorable franchise for the city, rejected a half dozen renewal schemes, obtained electrified rapid transit on several major streets without sacrificing the city's interests, and won the public over to his ideas of municipal ownership. Reacting heatedly to a Citizens' Company proposal for a renewal with a straight five-cent fare, Pingree called the plan "an insult to the intelligence of the members of the common council" and led the successful opposition to the measure. Adamant on the fare question, Pingree argued that it was only necessary to "wring all the water out of the street railway business and three-cent fares are possible." [43]

The available evidence tends to substantiate Pingree's claim that the Citizens' Street Railway Company system was overcapitalized in 1893. The total value of the horse car system was given as $1,856,627 in 1890, whereas in 1893 the company had at least $3,000,000 in outstanding bonds and $1,000,000 in stock. The only new value added to the system between 1890 and 1893 was the electrification of three streets whose eleven miles, if computed at the highly inflated construction cost of $90,000 per mile, added less than $1,000,000 to the line's worth. In view of the court decision of May, 1893, that decreed the company's franchise expired, all the outstanding capital in excess of the salvage value of the horse lines (then estimated to be worth less than $1,000,000) and the sale price of the electric lines was water. Pingree, as a businessman, understood the problems of the company, but his position was that the company's mismanagement was neither his nor the city's responsibility; his responsibility, as he saw it, was to obtain the lowest possible fares for Detroit.[44] He reasoned that fares should respond to the downward trend of prices just as commodities and wages.

In January, 1894, Pingree specified the ingredients of the model franchise: three-cent fares, a short fifteen-year franchise, and eventual municipal ownership of the rails and lines, with a provision for private operation on a rental basis until municipal operation could be effected. Possibly to discourage the Company's threat to appeal its case to the United States Circuit Court and possibly distracted by a fatal illness in his family, Pingree, uncharacteristically, in March, 1894, scaled down his demands by eliminating the universal transfer from the three-cent ticket. The Pingreeites in the council criticized the proposed ordinance as too weak and amended it to include the universal transfer. For the first time in his career, Pingree had fallen behind council supporters whose unyielding fealty to low fares he had cultivated, but he accepted the ordinance as amended.[45]

Unfortunately, Pingree's backward step in eliminating transfers touched off a rearguard action in defense of the Citizens' Street Railway Company on the part of councilmen whom Pingree had hitherto held in rein. G.O.P. Aldermen James Vernor, Joseph T. Lowry, and Charles Wright capitalized upon the weakness of the Mayor's transfer concession and bolted the administration ranks in the summer and fall of 1894. They then supported a series of franchises that compromised the three-cent fare and forced Pingree to resume his former position as a veto mayor. Vernor, in a fit of spite toward Pingree, sponsored an ordinance which he knew was unacceptable to the Citizens' Company, the council, and the administration. Charles Wright, in an effort to embarrass Pingree, brought in the Mayor's unamended March ordinance, saying "I am going to put Pingree in a box where he won't dare to veto the ordinance which will be adopted." Several efforts were made to delay Pingree's three-cent fare for three years, and one such ordinance was rammed through the council by Vernor. J. L. Hudson and a group of prominent merchants, some of whom had supported Pingree's 1891 veto, asked Pingree to approve the Vernor ordinance.[46] In the battle over these matters, Pingree throttled and vetoed every compromise proposal and bludgeoned his wayward councilmen back into line with tactics that he later explained: "I used to stir up the public by sending out notices, and the people would pack the Council chamber and fairly terrify the Aldermen who wished to go back on their campaign promises [for low fares]. We even told them that we had plenty of rope there and would hang them." [47]

Although Pingree had not secured a three-cent fare, his five-year struggle against the traction interests was remarkable not only because it was without parallel on the national urban scene but also because it had brought some solid progress to Detroit in the form of improved rails, paving, and foundations and had won back for the public its right to buy workingmen's tickets on the cars. Equally important was the fact that Pingree had taught the transit utilities the lesson that the public will and the general welfare could no longer be totally ignored. Pingree had stoutly resisted the blandishments of the traction interests, which, according to his own account, included a $75,000 bribe, and had created an effective counterforce in the council that had stopped every attempted franchise renewal. Rapid transit had been installed on several of the city's streets, as he had predicted, without the "surrender [of] franchises which were worth four or five million dollars in cash." [48] Not content—as Mayor Grover Cleveland of Buffalo had been—merely to defend and restore public rights, Pingree had begun to popularize the significant concept that in view of privileges granted to traction corporations, compensation should be taken in the form of low fares that benefited all the citizens rather than in the form of higher franchise fees that reduced taxation or eliminated the need for tax increases and thus aided the propertied classes. His vigorous promotion of universal transfers also appeared to bear dividends; the *Street Railway Journal* noted in 1894 that this new concept, unthought of five years before, was rapidly gaining adherents. Pingree had firmly implanted the idea of the three-cent fare in the minds of Detroiters, and he had won over the city to municipal ownership. This was demonstrated in an advisory vote in the fall of 1894 in which the electorate cast 80 per cent of its ballots for the municipal ownership of the street railways.[49]

Pingree, however, had paid a personal and social price for advocating and implementing municipal reforms. His attacks upon the "establishment" of the city had been too severe to go unchallenged. Senator James McMillan and the state G.O.P. machine were determined, in Charles Wright's words, to "run him into the ditch." Michael Dee, a journalist, had attempted to form an alliance of what he called the "great powers political and industrial" and journalistic to extirpate Pingreeism. The Preston National Bank had dropped Pingree from its board of directors because, as its President explained, Pingree's public position was "antagonistic to corporate capital" and would, if it had not already done so, place the bank "in an embarrassing position with other financial corporations in the city and state." George A. Gates, president of Iowa College, asserted that the banking community of Detroit had closed its ranks to Pingree and forced his firm to look to Eastern banks for credit. Finally, Pingree had lost his family pew in the Woodward Avenue Baptist Church, ostensibly because someone else had outbid him for this choice seat.[50]

The pressure of Detroit's business elite was also being felt by those who collaborated with the Mayor. A fourth-ward alderman and plumbing contractor resigned from the common council in March and explained: "I believe Mayor Pingree to be right and therefore have supported him, but it is only too plain that if I want to keep up my business I cannot continue in the council and support him. I will not remain and antagonize him, so there is nothing left for me to do but resign. . . . My business depends upon the wealthy class whose interests the mayor is fighting." "I experience the same thing every day," the city controller, Clarence A. Black, asserted. "At my club and at my bank pressure is brought to bear to induce me to leave Pingree, and little insinuations that hurt my business and social standing are thrown out." [51]

Pingree was distressed at the loss of his social register friends and his class status. Some of the most prominent men in the city who had sponsored his nomination and election had turned against him. The railroad promoter James F. Joy, who had convened the meeting that selected Pingree, was busily involved in 1894 with Frank J. Hecker, Peninsular Car Company president, William H. Elliott, a prominent merchant, and S. M. Cutcheon, the president of the Dime Savings Bank, in drafting a city charter that would have curbed Pingree's powers, weakened the mayorship, and decentralized the decision-making processes. The McMillan clan, including William, Hugh, James, and James H., had replaced friendship with hostility toward the Mayor. Three prominent aldermen, who had at first supported the administration had become bitter enemies of Pingree, harassing him whenever possible in the council. Dexter M. Ferry, Simon J. Murphy, and William A. Moore, his former associates, regarded his continued opposition to the Citizens' Street Railway Company as a slur upon their reputations. Henry B. Ledyard and J. L. Hudson, first-term supporters of Pingree, had cooled toward the Mayor. The exclusive Michigan Club had snubbed Pingree and left him out of its deliberations. The Big Four had disintegrated when the last of that group, Controller C. A. Black, had resigned from the Pingree administration.[52] Pingree, at a later date, asserted that the so-called best citizens had offered his programs virtually no support.[53] His loss, from 1891 to 1894, of his upper class supporters had left him socially isolated and shunned by the *nouveaux riches*, who composed the local aristocracy.

Pingree was not impervious to social ostracism and the loss of his personal friends: "It takes a lot of pluck to see your old associates pass you by without speaking and not get disheartened and want to give up the fight," he remarked. Yet he refused to reverse his course. Pingree derived some satisfaction from the knowledge that he was rapidly emerging on the local level as a people's mayor and on the national scene as a reformer's mayor. A Detroit roofing contractor told Pingree: "The Detroit '400' may be trying to down you but there are 40,000 to stick to you." From 1894 Pingree's vigorous fight for urban reform became widely recognized. John R. Commons declared in Detroit in November, 1894, that no matter where he went in his investigation of municipal progress throughout the country, people asked him: "Do you know what is going on in Detroit?" Jane Addams, planning a reform campaign against aldermanic corruption and against traction magnate Charles T. Yerkes in Chicago, asked Henry D. Lloyd: "Do you think that Mayor Pingree would be willing to come and open the campaign with a speech on his street car plans &c. I can think of no one else who would bring out an audience of the 19th Ward and start things up generally." Sheridan Webster, one of the leaders of a utility franchise fight in St. Louis promised: "We are going to do for this town what Mayor Pingree did for Detroit. It means a big fight all along the line, but it means a big saving to the taxpayers and big accommodation to the public." E. W. Bagley of Paducah, Kentucky, said that his city was on the way to municipal ownership and thanked Richard T. Ely for directing his attention to the reforms instituted in Detroit by Pingree. The *New Nation,* a Bellamyite publication, praised Pingree, asserting that "his fight for . . . city ownership of the street railways, has attracted the attention of the country." Henry Demarest Lloyd asked Pingree to "come to Chicago and clean out our Augean Stables. Without some such Hercules as you, the work will never be done." [54]

4

The Depression and a Commitment

Detroit's "400" had other reasons for reading Pingree out of their charmed circle. At the same time he took his vigorous new stance on the traction issue, Pingree had begun to question inequities built into the tax structure. In the case of the railroad, shipping, and car industries Pingree challenged tax-sheltered businesses in which the McMillan clan and the most successful members of Detroit's business community had large holdings. The Mayor's program for equalizing real estate taxes and his application of the personal property tax on a fair basis affected the interests of many in the same group.

The plight of Detroit's unemployed during the depression of 1893 drove Pingree even further from the class that had sponsored his first administration. The depression awakened in Pingree a secular concept of municipal stewardship in which he committed the energies of his administration to a broad scale attack on relieving human misery. He expected the city's industrial and business leaders to do likewise: "I believe that our wealthy citizens, many of whom have accumulated the fortunes which they now enjoy through the sweat and toil of the laboring classes, owe a duty to those who have created their wealth." When they failed to respond,

Pingree castigated the city's largest industrial consortium, the Michigan Car Company, for employing labor "at barely enough to keep body and soul together, without enabling the laborer to save anything against a rainy day," and then for dumping 5,000 "absolutely destitute" men upon the "charity of the community." [1] This abuse of charity and disregard for human suffering brought Pingree even closer to his economic determinist's view of society. The depression clearly settled whatever doubts he may have had about the direction in which his programs were taking him in 1893. Oppression and want excited in Pingree a passion which irrevocably fixed the direction of his future administrations.

I

Pingree had initiated a campaign in 1891 to equalize municipal taxation and to redistribute some of the tax burden to a "privileged class" of corporations which had been exempted from paying local taxes by the state legislature. The railroads, Pingree pointed out, were the main offenders, for they owned some $35,000,000 worth of property in Detroit, more than one-fifth of the property value in the city. The lines, the Mayor noted, did not pay "a single cent" to maintain municipal services such as police and fire protection, street repairs, the laying of new water and sewer lines, health service, public education, which instilled a respect for private property, or the courts, which the railroads used so often to defend their interests. "Whenever an individual pays a dollar of municipal tax, he contributes twenty-five cents to the coffers of these privileged corporations," observed the Mayor. To express the administration's displeasure Pingree directed through the council a resolution, which did not have the force of law, calling for the denial of police, fire, and other municipal services to Detroit's railroad yards, terminals, and depots. He also rounded up petitions, hired lobbyists, and engaged Democratic boss Don M. Dickinson to argue before the legislature for repeal of the tax-evading railroad charters, but the state's lawmakers refused to act. [2]

In 1892 Pingree moved to catch the "millionaire vessel owners, who tried to escape city taxation on their property by hanging up a sign in some barn in Hamtramck" township and by claiming that their principal places of business lay outside of Detroit's city limits. Despite the fact that their ships, docks, warehouses, and business operations lay in Detroit, many of the major shipping lines, such as James McMillan's Detroit Transportation Company, continued to use this tax-dodging technique. Irked by the unjust burden that this practice thrust upon small tax payers, Pingree ordered city assessors to add $1,500,000 in shipping property to the tax rolls and to levy assessments on "their steamboats whenever and wherever found." Justice and equity are on our side, asserted Pingree, and in this case so was the Michigan Supreme Court; it ruled that the creation of bogus offices in remote townships to avoid tax payment was a patent evasion of the law and an unjust attempt by those who employed this practice to shift their tax burden to others. The entry of shipping property on the rolls absorbed much of Detroit's tax increase for 1892.[3]

When Pingree, in 1893, attempted to impose equal taxation upon one of Detroit's largest and most powerful economic enterprises, the Michigan-Peninsular Car Company, he was challenging a combine which was ruled by the city's political, economic, and social elite: James McMillan, Hugh McMillan, W. C. McMillan, John S. Newberry, Christian Buhl, Theodore Buhl, Frank J. Hecker, James McGregor, General Russell A. Alger, and James F. Joy. The Michigan Car Company, the Peninsular Car Company, and their supplier firms, the Russell Wheel and Foundry Company, the Detroit Car Wheel Company, the Baugh Steam Forge, and the Detroit Pipe and Foundry Company, had merged in 1892; the new giant's stock prospectus listed its net value at more than $8,000,000, which sent Pingree digging into the tax records. "This corporation guarantees to pay 8 per cent profit on a capitalization of $8,000,000," Pingree said, but they were assessed for city taxes on a value of only $948,-730. If the stock prospectus were honest, the Mayor argued, the city was being cheated of the tax proceeds from some $5,000,000 to $6,000,000 worth of property (based upon the city's practice of assessing at about 70 per cent) that should have been on the tax rolls. "I only want these people to pay their just proportion of taxes," said the Mayor. What he proposed to do was to "shake up some of these bloodsuckers" to achieve equity, although he knew that there would "be some swearing done by some of the millionaires" before he succeeded.[4]

Pingree underestimated the tumult which would follow. Senator McMillan's commercial allies struck back with a ferocity and intensity which surprised and later concerned the Mayor. "Get out of Detroit as soon as possible," Hugh McMillan warned his fellow capitalists. To underscore his point, McMillan announced that Michigan-Peninsular was considering leaving the city, an action that would have deprived Detroit of its largest single employer. The Detroit *Evening News* picked up the anti-Pingree war chant and warned that such a decision might cost the city from 15,000 to 20,000 people, who could be relocated in a company town such as "McMillan, Ill." "The company would, of course, control the real estate and look after the housing of its employes, a nice chance for big profits on the side," continued the *News*. Thus the dream of paternalism of the McMillans would be fulfilled, and revenge would have been exacted on Pingree. The president of the Detroit Chamber of Commerce was joined by the Mayor's other enemies in the business world in the attack against Pingreeism. The Mayor's challenge to the Michigan-Peninsular Company proved to be more than he could handle, for his administration was also engaged at that time in struggles with the gas, light, and traction interests. The corporation tax question unified the most important sections of Detroit's business community into a solid opposition to the Mayor.[5]

Pingree sought for a way to retreat, and the escape hatch that he found was Henry George's single tax scheme. This tactic helped save face for the administration and, at the same time, had an appeal for many of Detroit's businessmen. At a Chamber of Commerce meeting held in February, 1893, many of the city's most influential businessmen debated the merits of the single tax, which many of them recognized would shift some of the burden of taxation from manufacturers to the owners of real estate. Although Pingree, by his own admission, was never a single taxer, he temporarily substituted the single tax for his Michigan-Peninsular measure to mask the retreat of his administration from a controversy that he could not win. The technique worked, and by January, 1894, anti-Pingree business feeling had abated on this issue. Colonel Frank J. Hecker, president of Michigan-Peninsular, now called the rumor that his company would leave Detroit the "veriest rot." [6]

By contrast, Pingree moved successfully to equalize real estate and personal property taxes in Detroit. When Pingree assumed office in 1890, he found that the assessors were guilty of gross inequities which favored real estate speculators at the expense of small home owners. A typical example of inequality was pointed out by George B. Catlin: "One large farm tract [within the city limits] had been platted so as to make nine lots to an acre. The lots were being sold at $250 each. The land syndicate was assessed at a rate of $60 per lot, but as fast as the lots were sold the assessment was raised to $160 each." [7]

Pingree was also irked by another discriminatory practice which resulted in the assessment of the "most valuable" real estate and buildings in the city at about 40 to 50 per cent of their value whereas the "homes of people of small means" were commonly assessed at 70 per cent or more of their value. "As it stands now," Pingree explained, the "classes are favored at the expense of the masses." Pingree's goal was to assess every man's property at the same ratio to its cash value. As a means of achieving his goal, the Mayor proposed to transform every taxpayer into an "assistant assessor" by publishing in the two leading daily newspapers the entire list of Detroit property, including names and addresses of the owners, thus enabling everyone to compare his rates with rates on comparable property and to redress any inequity. Although this measure failed to pass, by 1895 Pingree was able to point to a marked advance toward tax equality and the elimination of special favoritism toward the real estate interests. [8]

Pingree also launched a campaign in 1893 to secure the taxation of the personal effects of wealthy Detroiters; by 1895 the Mayor was able to press a resolution through the common council directing the tax department to track down and attach assessments to "works of art . . . valuable collections of paintings, statuary, tapestries, pianos, libraries and grand collections of valuable and costly furniture." That luxury items were owned by the Mayor's bitterest enemies undoubtedly accounts for some of the motivation behind Pingree's drive for social justice on this issue. There is no reason, argued Pingree, why such luxuries should not be assessed when the bathtubs of the middling orders and the "humble cottage" of the laborer received no special tax immunity. Pingree directed the tax assessors to begin this important reform by placing the Mayor's personal collection upon the tax rolls of the city on an equal basis with other assessable property. The valuable furnishings and art objects of other wealthy Detroiters were rapidly added to the rolls in 1895, and the old system of tax favoritism which had been linked to a sense of social deference to one's superiors was thus brought to an end.[9]

II

The depression of 1893 had a devastating effect upon Detroit, sending thousands of underpaid workers into the streets and onto the rolls of the poor commission. The crisis created social and ethnic tensions within the community which reached a flash point and exploded in more than one bloody fray. The human misery and suffering touched Pingree more than any other issue of the time and completed his commitment to social reform. His programs and pronouncements assumed an increasingly radical tone, and his attacks upon what he considered irresponsible wealth mounted in intensity. "These vast accumulations of wealth," Pingree told an Ypsilanti audience in 1895, "are more dangerous to the liberties of our republic than if all the Anarchists, Socialists and Nihilists of Europe were let loose on our shores. It will not mend matters, nor can it stifle the conscience of those who, after having become wealthy by robbery and wrongdoing, try to compromise with the Almighty by endowing a university or building a library. These will be but monuments to tell future generations that the income of such a man was $100,000,000 a year and that to reach this figure he had desolated more homes and ruined more men than Goth or Vandal. The poor and honest laborer is more to be envied than such a man." Pingree was appalled by the meager contributions of Detroit's "good millionaires," such as James McMillan, Strathearn Hendrie, and John S. Newberry, to alleviate the suffering of the unemployed whose labor had made them rich. No longer able to recognize his business opponents as honorable men of good will, Pingree began, after 1893, to identify himself and his administration with the aspirations of the foreign-born and the urban working classes.[10]

A change of personnel also took place in the Mayor's office during the depression period which reflected the new orientation of Pingree's reform programs. Alex McLeod, a forthright good government man and speech writer for the Mayor, was replaced by J. W. Walsh, an avowed socialist. Populists like Louis P. Granger and Captain Cornelius Gardner, single tax advocates like Fred E. Farnsworth, and municipal ownership advocates such as Judson Grenell and Francis A. Blades moved into the Mayor's inner circle. Many of Pingree's "respectable" business aides, such as C. W. Moore and Clarence Black, left the administration. At the same time, such political opportunists as DeWitt Moreland and Eli R. Sutton also won the Mayor's trust.

The panic of 1893 and the depression which followed had a devastating effect upon Detroit's financial and business community. Serious money shortages developed during the summer, and in August Pingree informed the common council that $10,000,000 had been withdrawn by depositors from Detroit banks and "locked up" in safety deposit boxes or secreted in "bedticks and old stockings," where the money lay "absolutely idle." Faced with runs by depositors, many of the city's smaller banks collapsed, and even Detroit's national banks underwent a grim experience. One institution went bankrupt, one became part of a merger, and another greatly reduced the volume of its capital stock. The total resources of the national banks dropped from $27,000,000 in 1892 to $21,000,000 in 1893, and commercial deposits dropped from $11,000,000 to $8,000,000 during the same period. In every measurable category, Detroit's national banks met losses, and it was not until 1899 that they recovered their pre-depression level of activity.[11]

The effect of the financial panic upon public and private business was staggering. Short-term loans which normally had cost the city from ½ to 1 per cent per month shot up to 3 per cent per month by the end of 1894, and municipal bonds went unsold for months. Men were being discharged from jobs because of a money shortage, which, according to Pingree, was caused by the "wreckers" and "stock gamblers" of Wall Street. The Mayor asked what could be done to "restore the money to its legitimate channels of circulation?" His answer was to sell the citizens municipal bonds, in small denominations, which would also serve as paper money. Such a plan, argued the Mayor, would not only call out of hiding the money of the middle classes and start public works but it would also place into circulation additional money equal to the face value of the bonds, which could circulate freely. They would, said Pingree, be "better even than the money of the Bank of England, for while they would pass current from one person to another, they would be drawing interest, which cannot be said of any other kind of currency in existence." But Detroiters possessed neither the confidence nor the substance to take up Pingree's "people's bonds." [12]

Private business activity slumped, and the ranks of the unemployed multiplied disturbingly. A report from the Michigan Commissioner of Labor revealed that of the 2,066 factories inspected in the state in the last three months of 1893, only 1,117 were operating at full capacity, and that 43.6 per cent of all operatives had been discharged. Those workers who had been fortunate enough to retain their jobs had suffered a wage reduction of 9.7 per cent. The depression also affected the transportation industry: the Commissioner's survey pointed out that the state's railroads had discharged 12 per cent of their crews by December, 1893, and had reduced wages by 7.9 per cent. Even Michigan's public schools cut back teacher employment by 3.5 per cent despite increasing enrollments during the depression, and Detroit dismissed twenty-five teachers. Detroit's largest industries, including the big stove works and the Pullman Company, shut down operations, and the Michigan-Peninsular Car Company discharged more than 5,000 men. [13]

All contemporary and later estimates placed the number unemployed at about 25,000 men. There were 75,000 males of working age (15 to 70 years old) according to the state census of 1894, so unemployment in Detroit had reached 33 per cent of the male labor force. Worst hit were the foreign-born, who comprised 24,000 of the 28,000 people on Detroit's poor commission rolls. The Polish and German workers drew more than 50 per cent of the "pauper" relief.[14]

The depression provoked severe social and class tensions during 1893 and 1894. During the winter the poor commission was absorbing an additional 250 welfare cases per day. This expanded the case load six-fold to 6,000 families, all of them totally dependent upon alms for survival. The commission rapidly exhausted its funds, and its superintendent warned that if additional money were not made available, rioting might occur. Although some looting was done by the mobs of unemployed men who were milling around the city hall, the police were usually able to suppress it. Cries of "Bread or blood" were heard outside of the doors of the Board of Public Works, and the commissioners worked diligently with "Polish speaking peace makers" to head off disorder. "Long periods of idleness have almost driven [the unemployed] to a point of desperation," asserted the Detroit *Journal*, "and when they hear of a job in any part of the city there are usually 10 times as many Poles on the spot as can be furnished with work." Pathetic sights of the unemployed, especially the foreign-born, could be seen daily as they roamed the streets with their own picks and shovels, desperately hoping to find a job. Many had not been gainfully employed for six months. On Grand Avenue a squad of Poles tried to force a road crew to lay down their shovels and to give others a chance to work. In the bloody clash which followed, the police intervened with their revolvers drawn and clubs swinging to scatter the Poles, who had been attacking with bricks and shovels.[15]

The situation grew progressively uglier. A Polish doctor, W. K. Kwiecinski, who worked diligently without remuneration to secure jobs for his fellow nationals, was threatened, abused, and cursed when he was able to meet but a part of the demand. "There were not enough dirty names in the language to call me," complained the physician, who was forced to call the police to protect himself. Alderman Frank Schmidt signed 1,105 municipal work orders for nonexistent jobs under the coercion of a mob that threatened to smash in the windows of his home if he did not co-operate. A poor commission inspector complained that workless men called at his home until midnight and other groups awakened him at 4:00 a.m. After the inspector finished breakfast one morning and met the usual contingent of 75 supplicants in his yard, he made his way down to city hall. There a mob of 2,000 men rushed him, lifted him into the air, and began to carry him toward the coroner's court. Just as they were about to "plaster him against the wall" three police-men plunged into the crowd with clubs swinging and rescued the terrified inspector.[16]

Religious, ethnic, and social differences were intensified by the crisis. Detroit's anti-Catholic American Protective Association flour-ished in the tense atmosphere and stepped up its attacks against corporate capitalism and Catholicism. The Irish-dominated Roman Catholic church became increasingly critical of the Poles, whom it could not easily assimilate, and the *Michigan Catholic* strongly rec-ommended that its Slavic brethren learn English and integrate themselves into American society. Bishop John S. Foley charged that the Board of Education had dismissed a janitor primarily be-cause he was a Catholic, despite the presence of affidavits which attested to the custodian's laziness and incompetence. Common council president George Beck and Alderman Walter H. Beck op-posed the construction of a new public high school to replace one that had burned because, in their view, it was a waste of scarce money to build an edifice which would educate the children of the rich and not the poor. Smarting under widespread criticism that education was not geared to the workaday world and was "di-vorced from reality," the school board went to great lengths in its reports of 1894–95 and 1895–96 to show that the curriculum was preparing children for the grim and practical realities of society. Even the poor commission came under attack by the Women's Christian Temperance Union, which charged that relief was being dispensed to alcoholics.[17]

The divisive and explosive potential of distress could also be detected at a Polish conclave at Zoltowski's Hall, where violent action was openly deliberated, and a Polish worker attacked Italian-Americans allegedly because "they get work all over the city. They are not citizens, and they come here to get money to send it back to the old country. They do not spend here in the city like we do." "An Italian can live on black bread and onions, whereas a Pole must have good food," asserted Dr. W. K. Kwiecinski. "An Italian can save money at small wages, but a Pole cannot for the simple reason that Italians are mainly unmarried while on the contrary the Pole seldom has less than seven or eight children." In their desperation to obtain jobs, groups of Poles used a "regular football wedge" to crash through the lines of job seekers waiting for work tickets. At a paving site on upper Woodward Avenue, some 200 Poles chased away a large number of Italians with whom they were competing for about 50 jobs.[18]

The bitterest tragedy for the Poles came at the Connor's Creek riot, which occurred at the end of the first winter of the depression. On April 16, 1894, the water board, which was excavating at the creek, substituted the "job-work" or piece work system for the wage system in the mistaken notion that its limited funds could be distributed among more men and that a saving could be achieved for the city. The board had also instituted the system at an Amsterdam Street site, but a mob of 150 jobless men stopped all work with the threat that they would kill the first man who turned a spade full of dirt at eleven cents a square yard. A day later, at Connor's Creek, a group of 500 Poles refused to accept "job-work" and were intent upon stopping others from accepting it as well. "Are we going to stand this?" shouted a Pole. He then led his fellow workers, armed with picks and shovels, over the dirt piles toward the water board supervisors and Sheriff C. P. Collins and his deputies, who were standing nearby in case of trouble. Terrified by the assault, Collins and his six deputies emptied their revolvers into the charging mass but were soon overwhelmed as shovels crashed down upon them and beat them into a "senseless bloody mass." In a frenzied state, the Poles rushed at anyone who was well-dressed, including a hapless spectator, who fled for his life across a field with a group of

Poles in hot pursuit. Within a few minutes the bloody affair was over; Collins lay on the ground with his head "badly caved in," and more than a dozen others lay wounded in puddles of their own blood. At least eighteen men had been felled by gun fire or bludgeons, and three died within the next week.[19]

It was a bitter and chastening experience. Pingree criticized the board for bad judgment in implementing what, in effect, was a wage cut. The board abandoned "job work" and reverted to the wage system. Although evidence was abundant that the "job" system, which had slashed wages as much as 40 per cent, had triggered the riot, Dr. W. K. Kwiecinski and other Polish spokesmen tried to lay the blame on a Bohemian deputy who, they asserted, had touched off the affair by offensively addressing the Poles not in their language but in the Bohemian language. The deputy responded that he had spoken to workers in Polish. He gratuitously added that his own group, the Bohemians, did not "mix up in riots." [20]

The tensions which the depression had created revived old-world hatreds, turned foreigner against foreigner, and even divided men of the same religion. The *Michigan Catholic* asked for severe punishment of the "savage mob" of "howling Poles" and warned them that they could not "dragoon" the American people with violence. Belatedly, the Poles began with increasing numbers to join the Polish Laborers' Alliance, an organization dedicated to using traditional union methods to redress grievances, which had been formed just a few weeks before the riot. Fearful of the divisive influences of nationality upon the labor movement, Sam Goldwater, a union organizer, warned his fellow members of the Detroit Council of Trades to reject the attitude that "they are only Poles and what have we to do with them. Capitalists make no distinction between nationalities, and why should we. It might be a Pole today, but we do not know who it may hit tomorrow." [21]

An anti-immigrant spirit was rampant in Michigan and Detroit in the wake of the panic of 1893. Michigan voters, by an overwhelming majority (117,088 to 31,537), disfranchised aliens in 1894 by a constitutional amendment. The *Michigan Catholic* called for a federal law to stop "alien non-resident labor" in Canada from crossing to Detroit to work. "Chase the Dagos back to Italy," exhorted an American-born brakeman. "To prevent Americans from starving, try restriction on immigration," advised an Irish-born engineer. "It is certainly killing America." [22]

These indeed were the preponderant sentiments of the foreign and native-born workmen polled by the Michigan Bureau of Labor from 1893 to 1896. Of the 5,600 farm laborers canvassed, 3,466 asserted that unrestricted immigration was injurious to their occupations. The foreign-born laborer, noted the Commissioner of Labor, was as "emphatic in condemning immigration as his American brother, and his language is often more forcible." A survey of 9,226 railroad employees revealed that the "most positive" denunciations of unrestricted immigration came from the foreign-born. Of the 3,127 hack and bus drivers questioned 84 per cent also favored restriction. Of the 1,865 street railway employees (45 per cent classed themselves as of a nationality other than American) polled, 96 per cent asked for an end to immigration.[23]

Acting under similar pressures the Detroit common council banned the employment of aliens by a municipal licensee, the Citizens' Street Railway Company, and the city's Park and Boulevard Commission, and prohibited all other city departments and their municipal contractors from hiring "non-resident" aliens. By contrast to his political colleagues and working class supporters, Pingree remained liberal on the issue. By 1895, however, even he felt compelled to retreat somewhat and to request a "rigid enforcement of the laws against pauper immigration." The key to this upsurge of nativism was not a simple xenophobia nor even an involuted form of anti-Catholicism but rather, as the state commissioner of labor pointed out, a bread-and-butter demand by workmen "to reduce the competition for work. . . . It is self-protection that leads them to favor non-immigration." [24]

Few American cities were prepared to deal with the consequences of the depression of 1893, and Detroit was no exception, but Pingree at least took a number of bold and extraordinary steps to combat misery and want. When the poor commission exhausted its funds, the Mayor used methods which did not comply with the strict requirements of law to borrow money for its use and also to transfer other city funds to it. "Necessity knows no law," Pingree argued before the city council, which supported his actions. Whenever the commission exhausted its resources, Pingree replenished them and justified this action on the grounds that thousands of self-supporting people had sold and pawned their household necessities and had "reached their last ditch . . . with starvation staring them in the face after an heroic struggle." Pingree also sent inspectors into the poverty districts to find and help those "poor but sensitive persons" who would rather face personal tragedy than accept charity and its stigma of pauperism.[25]

"While charity is commendable," Pingree argued, "it is far better to furnish work for willing hands." The Mayor called on the city's manufacturers to induce them to accept his proposal of rehiring as many men as possible and, if necessary, to defer payment of part of their wages as a future debt against the company. Pingree used a combination of coercion and persuasion to get the Citizens' Street Railway Company to lay its new girder-grooved rails and concrete foundations at this time. By 1895 employment by the Citizens' Company and the administration sponsored three-cent line was a major factor in reducing the number of unemployed.[26]

"Everything possible will be done by the administrative department to furnish work for the willing and able-bodied," the Mayor promised. Pingree applied pressure on the city departments to expand their public works programs. The water board began extensive pipe-laying at midwinter despite the high cost of digging through frozen ground. The park commission started an elaborate renovation of Belle Isle, including road construction, canal repairing, bridge building, and the erection of a free public bathhouse. The Board of Public Works cut down on the number of public contracts let to private firms and put on two shifts of men daily in an attempt to absorb some of the unemployed. To create even more jobs, Pingree asked the Board to abandon its block-cutting and stone-crushing machinery. Hand-pushed wheelbarrows replaced horse-drawn drays on some of the earth-fill projects, and the Pin-

gree administration initiated the eight-hour day which it had hitherto opposed. The old and less able-bodied workers were given jobs
sweeping the streets and alleys. Public improvements went forward
at such a vigorous pace that the new sewer, paving, and school
construction projects reached Detroit's bonding limit by 1895.[27]

Only the fire commission refused to find "out of door public
work" for unemployed workers, with the result that Pingree harassed the commissioners and investigated them; he called in a public accountant to perform an audit; and he personally tried to seize
the books in a shoving and cursing match in which several burly
firemen physically ejected the Mayor from the station house. Stung
by this rebuff, Pingree carried on a bitter personal vendetta against
the offending commissioners for a full year.[28]

When budgetary cutbacks and wage reductions for the lowest
level of city labor were implemented, Pingree opposed them and
proposed instead that higher paid white-collar workers should bear
the brunt of needed economics. "[R]etrenchment ought in all sense
of right and decency come from those of us who get plenty to live
on." The municipal boards responded by restoring most of the
wage cuts which had effected teamsters and laborers. Pingree also
established a "voluntary" contribution schedule for the city's sala-
ried employees, who were expected to give from $1 to $2 per month
to the poor commission for work relief. Detroit's municipal resources were utilized to a maximum, and although there was not
enough money to provide work for all, Pingree told the common
council that "we must not let any of our people go hungry." [29]

To aid indigent families, Pingree applied pressure on the bak-
eries to lower the price of bread, which sold at five cents per one
pound loaf, and threatened to erect a municipal bakery if two
loaves for five cents were not made available. We must get
"cheaper bread for the poor this winter," exhorted the Mayor. Public pressure was sufficient to convince the bakers that they should
produce an inexpensive loaf, and Pingree secured agreements with
a number of merchants who consented to sell cheaper bread.[30]

During the second summer of the depression Pingree launched
his "potato patch plan," which, as a work relief measure, has been

described as one of the original contributions of the nineties. The Mayor's scheme envisioned the cultivation of vacant lots by the city's unfortunate, who were, in many cases, but a few years removed from a peasant agricultural economy of Europe. Since Detroit's poor commission was near insolvency and the city treasury almost empty, Pingree called upon the churches to contribute funds for the purchase of plows, implements, and seed. "The Mayor proposes to find out if those elegant churches are only for show or for doing some real good," a Pingree aide told a reporter. Most of Detroit's clergymen either ignored or ridiculed the plan. The pastor of the fashionable Jefferson Avenue Presbyterian Church, for example, sarcastically asked his congregation to "give liberally and pray that potatoes might grow as had the . . . [Mayor's] head and then there would not be a single hungry child left in Detroit." The city's churchmen contributed a paltry $13.80. Shortly thereafter Pingree began to advocate the repeal of the tax exemption upon church property.[31]

Most Detroit newspapers also mocked Pingree; the Detroit *Evening News* published a cartoon depicting the Mayor as a despot named "Tuber I" with a carrot as a scepter in one hand and a potato in the other. Absurd charges that potato bugs would invade the city were voiced by the Mayor's conservative opponents, who also argued that unemployed men were too lazy to work and that they would steal one another's crops. Pingree grimly reminded his unco-operative critics that many of them had excused themselves from contributing to the poor fund during the previous winter for precisely the same unproved assumption that jobless men were congenitally lazy and unwilling to work. Most of the unfortunates "would be glad of a chance to raise their own food," Pingree argued. "They are willing to work, and we ought to give them a chance to do it." [32]

The Mayor's appeal fell upon deaf ears: the McMillans, the Ferrys, the Ledyards, and the Newberrys failed to open their pocketbooks. The "pig-headedness" of Detroit's aristocracy was damned to no avail by the Detroit *Tribune*. Pingree sold his $1,300 prize horse for $387 at a public auction in an attempt to shame Detroit's "good millionaires" and to raise money for the potato patch plan. Pingree then solicited the free use of 430 acres of vacant lots for the poor. He laid another levy on the municipal employees and finally raised the funds to buy supplies and to prepare the land for cultivation.[33]

In 1894, 3,000 families applied to the municipal agricultural committee for a chance to till the soil, but because of budgetary limitations only 945 were assigned to one-half acre plots. "Poor people almost fought for a chance to get a piece of ground," reported the Mayor. Captain Cornelius Gardner, who directed the project, reported in the fall of 1894 that indigent Detroiters harvested food which was conservatively estimated to have a retail value of $14,000. Hoping to show the benefits of self-help, Pingree and Gardner asked several prominent merchants to display some of the prize specimens grown, but the merchants refused to do so from fear that they would be "classed as friends and admirers of Mayor Pingree and might be boycotted by their best customers." [34]

The potato patch plan enrolled 1,546 families in 1895 and 1,701 families in 1896, 25.6 and 46.8 per cent respectively of all families on public relief. In 1896 the cash value of the food raised by the vacant lot farmers ($30,998) actually exceeded the sum dispensed by the poor commission ($23,729). In addition to staples such as root crops and potatoes, which provided hundreds of the poor families with a portion of a winter larder, the Pingree plan also varied the starchy diets of the gardeners by providing them with green vegetables throughout the summer. "The unqualified success of the experiment has silenced the croakers," Pingree told the common council in 1895. It had also demonstrated that "at least 96 per cent of the people who are in destitute circumstances, as a result of hard times, are ready, willing and anxious to work," he added. The paramount idea in establishing this plan, the Mayor stated, was to eliminate the stigma of pauperism attached to relief.[35]

Although the Mayor gained wide fame when his potato patch scheme was adopted by such cities as New York, Boston, Chicago, Minneapolis, Seattle, Duluth, and Denver, Pingree had few illusions about the long range value of work relief or almsgiving in any form. He told a Terre Haute benevolent society in 1896: "I think I see where methods of charity lessen wages; where capitalists are secure from the demands of economic justice behind a public tax for the support of the so-called unfortunates; where charity, in short, is the handmaid of economic oppression." Until such a time, however, as society learned to "do justice to all we must depend on the methods nearest at hand," Pingree said.[36]

Pingree had shown a capacity to respond to want and to grow with adversity which had enabled him to complete a fundamental shift in the character and nature of his reform programs. Although this new departure had begun earlier, in the Mayor's approach to the traction question and in his willingness to pursue an equal tax program, it was the economic catastrophe that completed the transition. The Mayor's compassion for those afflicted had sharpened his vision of the city's social responsibility. There was now no question in the minds of either Pingree's friends or his enemies where the emphasis of future Pingree administrations would lie.

5

The Battle With the Utilities

During his years as mayor Hazen Pingree was also engaged in contests with the light, gas, and telephone interests of the city. Although he looked forward to the day when every city would own its utilities, he was primarily a pragmatist. He treated each industry separately and was not governed in his actions by any single ideological approach or by any set of social blueprints. He fought for what he believed was possible and was willing to adjust his reform goals to the practical realities of political power and the peculiar limitations that each industry presented. He sensed that municipal ownership was a fanciful dream on the telephone issue because of the intercity and interstate nature of the service. Conversely he pressed for public ownership on the light issue. On the gas question he sought regulation. He was consistent in championing the cause of people of poor or modest means, and he fought vigorously for what he considered social justice, namely, lower rates for service and increased consumption. The gas and light wars turned out to be two of the "most bitterly contested fights" of the entire administration in 1893, Pingree noted. From the experience Pingree concluded that eternal vigilance may well have been the price of liberty but "eternal fighting seems to be the price of any reform in municipal government." [1] In contending with the privately owned utilities, Pingree was challenging one of the most powerful business institutions in urban America.

I

American city streets had been illuminated by artificial and natural gas lamps since 1821, when Baltimore contracted for public lighting. Gas, however, was not an ideal fuel for street lighting because of its low light intensity, its flickering qualities, and its high cost. From 1880 to 1900 the gas industry met its severest challenge from the electric arc light, which eventually replaced gas for street lighting.

The first central electric station in the nation was established in San Francisco in 1879. In the following year, the Brush Electric Company constructed arc lighting plants in a number of American cities, including New York, Boston, Philadelphia, and Detroit. In all of these cities the firm sought to obtain street lighting contracts for itself. By 1880 the Brush Company controlled 80 per cent of the arc lighting on the nation's streets, and by 1885 the victory of the electric arc over gas for street lighting was virtually complete.

The Brush Company's major rival, the Thomas-Houston Electric Company expanded rapidly, snuffing out competition and absorbing several firms, including the Brush Company itself in 1889. With the aid of its Brush subsidiary, Thomas-Houston had become, by 1890, the dominant firm in the arc lighting industry. Two years later Thomas-Houston merged with the Edison interests, which had developed incandescent lighting, to form the General Electric Company. The new company and a rival, the Westinghouse Electric Company, shared control of 75 per cent of the incandescent and arc light production in the nation by 1896. The incandescent lamp was utilized primarily in indoor lighting whereas the carbon arc light was used to illuminate streets.[2]

Detroit had depended upon gas and naptha lamps to light its streets, but the formation of a local Brush Company in 1880 pitted the arc light representatives against the local gas companies in a stiff contest for a street lighting contract. In 1884 the Brush Com-

pany won a five-year contract with the city. With the assistance of
its parent organization, the Detroit Brush Company fought to ex-
tinguish competition by absorbing its rivals. The firm was not always successful.[3]

In 1889 the Brush Company was underbid and lost its street
lighting contract to the Detroit Electric Light and Power Company
(DELPC), which precipitated a vicious commercial fight between
the two vendors. The Brush Company claimed an exclusive patent
right to the arc lighting process and fought vigorously to oust the
DELPC from the city, first by legal methods and then by a refusal
to sell or lease its towers, poles, lines, and street apparatus to the
new concern. The DELPC thereupon constructed a duplicate system. Claiming that the new system was built too close to its own
system, the Brush Company began to chop down the poles and cut
the wires of its rival. The DELPC brought this destruction to a halt
by securing a court injunction. Each time a new contract was to be
awarded, the rival firms were responsible for a new scandal as they
sought the support of aldermanic candidates and spent money lavishly to purchase influence in the common council. Reacting to this
spectacle of the "caprices and combinations of private corporations," Pingree asked the common council in January, 1890, for a
publicly owned and operated light plant and began to prepare the
city for the municipal ownership campaign that he would prosecute
vigorously in 1893.[4]

The nation's first municipally owned electric plant had been established in Fairfield, Iowa, in 1882. A decade later 16 per cent of
the nation's light plants were publicly owned; but the volume of
power and light produced by these plants was probably less than 5
per cent of the total United States output because most of the
municipally owned stations, with the exception of Chicago and Allegheny, Pennsylvania, were located in cities of less than 10,000
population. This confinement to small towns was the result not of a
"village socialism" but of the difficulty in attracting investor capital
to small communities with limited markets. Many communities
thus did not have a choice between municipal or private electric
power but rather between municipal light or no light at all.[5]

Cities began to consider municipal ownership not only because of the lack of investor capital but often because of the exorbitant rates charged by the privately owned utilities. San Francisco in 1890 paid a private vendor as much as $440 per standard arc (2,000 candle power) per year for all-night service, whereas comparable service was available in Boston for $237 and in St. Louis for $75. To justify the vast differences in rates, the utilities argued that the cost of coal fluctuated from region to region. Professor Frank Parsons pointed out, however, that the variations in both the price of coal and labor could not have increased the price of light more than $10 per standard arc. Parsons further noted that Pittsburgh, which lay in the heart of the coal region, was paying $195 per arc year or 2½ times more than St. Louis and that it would be absurd to argue that coal was more expensive in the former city than in the latter. "The *chaos of prices,*" Parsons contended, "makes it clear that the charge for electric light bears no definite relation to the cost of production." [6]

Poor management was cited by James B. Cahoon, past president and secretary of the National Electric Light Association, which represented the private utilities, as another reason for high electric rates. Cahoon admitted in 1903 that the first promoters had been so dazzled by the lure of massive profits that they had grossly overcapitalized the new firms. Rapid obsolescence of original equipment and a lack of depreciation allowances had weakened an industry which chose to declare large dividends. Unfortunately, public service corporations normally expected the consumer to absorb the burden of such speculative miscalculations. The bugbear of bad management commented upon by Cahoon plagued the Detroit Brush Company, which appeared to be badly overcapitalized by 1891. [7]

The DELPC had secured a three-year contract, commencing in 1890, to light Detroit's streets. During the period of the contract, Pingree began to assemble information to make his case for municipal ownership. He found abundant evidence of the company's poor service, of the high ratio of "outages" because of defective lamps, and of a flagrant abuse of the public interest by private business. "The lights are all paid for as being 2,000 candle power," declared the Detroit *Evening News*, "but they are often so dim that one candle would be a fair rival to the sputtering, fizzling ball of light that hovers between the carbons and only seems to make the carbons more uncertain than if the streets were without any light except the stars and moon." The sight of two sets of lines, poles, and iron pipe towers swaying loftily overhead at heights as high as 160 feet and the fact that one of these sets was totally without function only compounded the absurdity. The Brush Company's harassment of the council with legal threats to hold the city and the contractor liable for patent infringements on the carbon arc added another complicating factor. Finally, the combination of the DELPC and Brush interests through the formation of a holding company in June, 1891, killed competition altogether. Bidding between these two companies had become such a farce that James Vernor had to admit: "In street lighting with arc lamps we can't get competition." [8]

Because of "the manipulation of lighting companies," Pingree later recalled that he was compelled to force through the municipal ownership of a public lighting plant. During his second term, in January, 1892, the Mayor released the results of his personal investigation of the cost of private and public street lighting in 88 United States cities. He concluded that Detroit was paying $33 more for each street lamp per year than was the average in the cities surveyed. The DELPC's high price of $136 per lamp year was thoroughly unjustified, Pingree argued, in view of the company's "notoriously and shamefully poor" service and high "outage" rate. "[N]ow is the time," he declared, "for the city to prepare to do its own lighting." [9]

When he looked into the possibility to purchase an already constructed system in Detroit, Pingree was informed by William H. Fitzgerald, general manager of the DELPC, that "the members of this company are opposed to the municipal ownership of an electric plant" and that his company had no intention of aiding Pingree's effort against free enterprise by selling its system to the city. "I know as an electric man," stated city controller Clarence A. Black, who held $250,000 worth of bonds in Brush Electric, "that all of the electric companies are opposed to selling plants to municipalities and I do not believe that the city could buy either of the local plants." [10]

In 1893, the year the DELPC contract was to expire, Pingree intensified the campaign and publicized his second study of electric lighting in 92 cities in the United States. This study revealed that where lighting was done by the city owned plant, the cost was only about half what it was where the lighting was done by contract. Pingree charged that the large manufacturers of electric lighting equipment had acted in collusion with the major vendors to suppress the sale of appliances to municipal plants. To avoid this problem in Detroit, he visited the officials of Western Electric and Westinghouse, which were both outside the General Electric combine, and received assurances from the two firms that they were willing to sell Detroit the necessary generating and transmission apparatus for a municipal plant. The cost reductions which would result from future "invention and improvement" of machinery would accrue to the public under municipal ownership, asserted Pingree. The "friction between the public and contractor" would also be eliminated under municipal ownership, argued the Mayor, which would take the utility business out of politics.[11]

In answer to the criticism that a municipally owned electric plant might become a patronage plum for the politicians, Pingree declared, "I wonder how many people who mentioned this objection ever stopped to think how much these corporations which are making money out of public service, are, and have always been in politics . . . it would be rather difficult for any branch of municipal service to get into politics to anywhere near the depth reached by one or two corporations which monopolize certain public functions. . . . The pressure of these corporations, having a direct interest in municipal legislation and administration, has been the chief, if not the only source, of corruption in the city governments of America." [12]

Another impediment to municipal ownership that had to be overcome in Detroit was a statute enacted by the previous session of the Michigan legislature prohibiting cities with a population of more than 25,000 from owning electric stations. Gathering support from his fellow mayors in the state, circulating public petitions, and pledging the support of legislators, Pingree took an entourage to Lansing to fight for an enabling act that would permit Detroit to light her own streets. The Pingree forces met the determined opposition of the local electric consortium. "Money was freely offered back and forth to control that vote," the city's assistant attorney later declared. Nevertheless, the DELPC and the General Electric forces, operating without the active assistance of Senator McMillan, who had no economic interest at stake, were unable to halt the passage of the enabling act.[13]

Even though he had won the opening engagement, Pingree still faced the important task of winning the support of the council and the city for his scheme. Recognizing how valuable his street railway junket had been in persuading the city legislature and the voters to accept his traction reforms, Pingree arranged for a similar trip to investigate municipally owned electric plants throughout the country. He took with him twenty-four councilmen, several city officials, and four newspaper reporters, who, Pingree realized, would dispatch daily news columns to Detroiters. The group visited several Eastern cities. By the time they had reached Washington, D.C., Pingree's plan appeared to be succeeding, for the Detroit *Evening News* reported that an informal poll revealed that sixteen of the twenty-four councilmen indicated that they would support municipal ownership. The expedition seemed to have reached its goal on April 3, 1893, when Detroiters in an advisory election cast a vote of 15,282 to 1,745 in favor of a municipal electric plant.[14]

The first display of enthusiasm for municipal ownership that the councilmen had manifested in Washington began to wane after the group returned to Detroit, where utility executives were not accustomed to bending to the sentiments of city officials. William H. Fitzgerald, general manager of DELPC, announced that he did not consider the city's advisory vote for municipal ownership as final and that his firm and General Electric would fight for a lighting contract. "If the city were to do its own lighting at about half what the other companies bid, it would establish a bad precedent or example," Fitzgerald candidly observed, "and other cities that are now lighted by companies owned by the General Electric Company would be apt to follow Detroit's example." [15]

The struggle was transferred to the common council, where Alderman James Vernor secured the passage on April 18 of an ordinance authorizing the city to solicit bids from private utilities for contract lighting. Although Vernor had supported the enabling act that passed the Michigan legislature, he and many of his colleagues evidently were not firmly committed to municipal ownership. The educational value of Pingree's trip appeared to be wearing thin. The following week Pingree vetoed Vernor's ordinance, declaring that "its ultimate object [was] the defeat of the establishment of a public lighting plant by the city." Chafing under the council's dilatory tactics, Pingree warned: "There can be no dodging the issue. The time has come for a show of hands, on this question, and the people intend to find out just where their representatives stand." Pingree's veto was sustained by a 19 to 11 vote.[16]

Nonetheless, Pingree's municipal ownership ordinance was in danger. Recognizing that his public ownership bloc was beginning to come apart under the influence of the electric "combine," on April 25 he silenced his utility opponents and their council allies by exposing a bribe. Pingree walked to the center of the council floor and said: "I have a duty to perform here tonight, most serious and disgraceful. I have to announce that some of these aldermen have been approached by manager Fitzgerald of the Detroit Electric Light & Power Company to pass Alderman Vernor's resolution over my veto. This is a terrible disgrace. It is a disgrace not only to the city but to the whole state of Michigan." Holding up a roll of bills, Pingree shouted: "Here is the money that was paid to one man. This is a terrible thing." Amid the uproar and the applause from citizens assembled in the lobby, Pingree handed the bills to the council president, who, with deliberation, counted $200 as the amount of the alleged bribe. Silence prevailed for a few minutes until finally Alderman Joseph T. Lowry challenged Pingree to identify the source of the bribe. Pingree heatedly explained that the money came from William H. Fitzgerald, with whom Lowry was standing in the chamber. The back of the opposition was clearly broken, and Pingree's veto of Vernor's resolution was hastily reconsidered and sustained again, this time by a 30 to 0 vote. Exploiting the heated events of the moment, the Mayor's forces brought the light plant ordinance to the floor and pressed through a unanimous vote for municipal ownership.[17]

Fitzgerald, who had been involved in a similar lighting contract scandal eight years earlier, was jailed and held for examination in the Police Court until it could be determined if the evidence warranted holding him for trial. It was learned that a few days before the exposure Alderman Charles P. Protiva had informed Pingree's secretary that the electric light company was using large amounts of money to secure the passage of Vernor's resolution over the Mayor's veto. A considerable sum had been offered Protiva and Pingree had advised him to accept the money with witnesses present whose testimony would stand up in court. Protiva, accordingly, met Fitzgerald at the Protiva home, completed the transaction, and turned the money over to Pingree the following day.[18]

Protiva told his story to the Police Justice Court during Fitzgerald's examination. As the hearing proceeded, Fitzgerald's attorney became aware that the prosecution was holding back an unidentified witness or witnesses whom the prosecution hoped to use at the trial. The defense had Fitzgerald corroborate Protiva's story in every detail up to the point where money had allegedly been exchanged, but the defense denied that a payoff had taken place and insisted that Fitzgerald had only pulled out some "documents" for Protiva to examine. Fitzgerald admitted that he had spent money in past elections to elect anti-Pingree councilmen, but he denied that he had tried to bribe the council and Protiva in an effort to stop municipal ownership. The police justice thereupon dismissed the hearing for lack of evidence and refused to hold Fitzgerald for trial.[19]

"It's enough to satisfy any thinking man," Pingree said, "that things are rotten in this town, and that the corporations are bound to rule the town. Rule or ruin." After Fitzgerald was dismissed by the court, it became known that Mrs. Protiva and a servant had witnessed the transaction but that Mrs. Protiva had refused to appear at the hearing. According to George B. Catlin, in the interval between the exposure and the hearing: "Certain interested parties went to the alderman and to the alderman's wife and told them that if her evidence was offered at the coming trial, the attorneys for the defense would make damaging insinuations against her character and so drag her name in the mire that she would never be able to hold up her head again in Detroit." [20] The threat of blackmail was sufficient to silence the chief witness for the prosecution.

Although the Pingree administration had not succeeded in securing the conviction of Fitzgerald, it was able to construct a municipally owned generating plant. Detroit's municipal plant began producing electricity on April 1, 1895, and by October every street lamp in the city was lighted by public power. Pingree also persuaded the common council to push a somewhat reluctant Detroit Public Lighting Commission to extend municipal light to all the public buildings in the city. "This is a step which you will never regret," Pingree told the council on January 14, 1897. "It is to be hoped in the near future you will take another step in this advance direction and take electric lighting out of the luxuries of life, only to be used by the wealthy, and place it within the reach of the humblest citizen." [21] Pingree appointed an able Public Lighting Commission to administer the plant, and a capable electrician, Alex Dow, who built one of the best equipped plants in the country.[22]

Municipal ownership brought with it the economy and improved service that Pingree had predicted. The cost of street lighting in Detroit declined from $132 per lamp per year in 1894 under private contract to $83 per lamp under municipal ownership in 1898 and to $63 in 1902. The lowest price that any private vendor offered the city in 1893, when a decision for private or public power had to be made, was $102 per lamp for a ten-year contract, which was soon demonstrated to be far above the cost of municipal light. The loss of light through defective service also declined sharply under municipal ownership: 86,000 lamp hours were lost under private contract in 1893-94, whereas during a comparable period under municipal ownership in 1895-96, when the number of lamps had increased by 15 per cent, only 4,400 hours were lost. Dow, who as president of Detroit Edison later became a staunch advocate of private power, asserted in 1896 that "It was the right thing to establish a municipal lighting plant in Detroit, because the prices that were being charged here were exorbitant." Professor John R. Commons, who had investigated Pingree's municipal system, concluded in 1897 that "Not only does the city of Detroit get a steadier light but the brilliancy of the same is greater than that obtained from private corporations." [23]

Detroit's plant became one of the major exhibits in the great debate over municipal versus private ownership that raged during the 1890's and into the Progressive period. Scholars, reformers, electrical engineers, and representatives of the private utility interests challenged each other's conclusions in addresses, articles, books, and public debate. Horatio A. Foster and M. J. Francisco, the leading spokesmen for the utilities, marshalled their arguments against Richard T. Ely, John R. Commons, Edward W. Bemis, and Frank Parsons. The controversy was not so much ideological as it was practical, and it invariably drew the contestants into a detailed examination of the cost of operating private and publicly owned plants. The utilities usually chose Chicago as an example of the failure of municipal ownership, whereas the public ownership group generally selected Detroit as illustrative of its success. Bemis, Commons, and Parsons compiled reams of statistics, visited and examined individual plants, and concluded that public power was cheaper. Their contention was supported by the most extensive study of the cost of light production in the nation, which United States Commissioner of Labor Carroll D. Wright released in 1899. *The Fourteenth Annual Report of the United States Commissioner of Labor,* which surveyed 952 electric stations, concluded that in every comparative test which the department could apply, municipal power was cheaper than private power in both incandescent and arc service.[24]

By 1903 the utilities had shifted their line of defense, and James B. Cahoon, past president of the National Electric Light Association, claimed that if the Association's system of accounting and depreciation schedules were accepted, it would prove that private electricity was less expensive than public. To answer the Association's argument, Professor John A. Fairlie used the ultimate test. He hypothetically liquidated the municipal plant of Detroit and rendered it valueless as of 1905. Fairlie was thus able to demonstrate that the total cost for public light in Detroit for the decade ending in 1905 was $87.63 per arc as compared to the lowest private contract price of $102.20. Without even computing the salvage value of the generating plant, which was in excellent condition, Fairlie showed that the city had saved $460,000 during ten years of public power. The Pingree experiment served as a valuable yardstick for the proponents of public ownership. "It is mainly in those cities like Detroit, which have had a hard training for several years in open battle with the franchise holders," John R. Commons asserted, "that we may look for that alert public spirit and jealous determination which will make municipal ownership a lasting success." [25]

The protagonists of municipal ownership and of the utilities also debated the question of whether publicly owned plants had become cesspools of corruption and sinecures for political hacks. In this argument the Chicago station was admittedly difficult for the advocates of public ownership to defend, but in Detroit the results were different. Even after Alex Dow left the system in 1896, the tradition of nonpartisanship was maintained in Detroit. Frederick F. Ingram asserted in 1903 that in the history of the Detroit commission, there had been only three politicians out of thirteen appointments and each had resigned after a short period of service because his political prestige suffered in a job where there was no opportunity to reward loyal followers. Tough-minded administrators such as Ingram continued the Pingree tradition of nonpartisan efficiency which frustrated attempts of the private utilities to attack the Detroit plant.[26]

Pingree's technique of publicizing his investigations of the cost of electric light production appeared to bear results. "The day of secrecy in the matter of accounting by electric light companies has gone by," remarked James B. Cahoon in 1903, "and there is not a single, modern, up-to-date plant in the whole United States which does not stand ready and willing to show to the municipality just what it costs to furnish them with their street lights." [27]

II

Gas had been used as an illuminant in households as early as 1806, and by 1850 coal gas generating plants had been established in most large cities. The high price of gas confined the illuminant to industrial enterprises, city streets, and to the homes of some of the wealthy. Most American householders used candles, whale oil, and kerosene as illuminants until the late nineteenth century.[28]

Although the price of gas in the United States, as one observer noted in 1889, was based not upon its cost but rather upon what the industry could compel the public to pay, the number of cities that sought to lower the cost of gas by constructing municipal plants was very small. Heavy capital outlay and a lack of technical skills appeared to deter the development of city owned plants. In 1891, of the nine municipal gas works, all but the Philadelphia plant were in or near the Appalachian coal fields and located in communities of less than 80,000 population. The average price of municipally produced gas was cheaper than privately generated gas. In a few notable cases, however, the price of private gas was competitive with that of public gas.[29]

In an age of economic optimism and reckless promotion, over-capitalization was a major problem in the gas industry. With the exception of Massachusetts, which controlled the issue of stocks and bonds, there was virtually no regulation of the gas industry in the United States. Capitalization was, of course, a key factor in consumer prices since the overcapitalized firm placed an excessive demand for dividends upon the business, which reasonable charges to the consumer could not satisfy. "It would be very difficult to select any other industry," Professor John H. Gray declared in 1898, "in which during the last decade the capitalization (stocks and bonds) has so largely outrun the increase of business done." In many cities overcapitalization was a major impediment to forcing the gas companies to share the lower production costs of the 1890's with the consumer.[30]

Gas was first used as an illuminant by Detroit in 1851, when production began at the Detroit Gas Light Company. The firm charged $3.50 per 1,000 cubic feet until 1872, when the Mutual Gaslight Company was organized. Faced with a competitor, the Detroit Gas Light Company engaged Mutual Gas in a rate war, in which the price of gas fell to fifty cents per 1,000 feet. Nearly ruined by the battle, both concerns, in violation of a city ordinance, combined to divide the gas market in Detroit and to extinguish competition by allocating the business in the area west of Woodward Avenue to Detroit Gas Light and that in east Detroit to Mutual Gas. By 1890 both firms had linked themselves through an interlocking directorate and had fixed the price at an average of $1.50 per 1,000 feet. The entry in 1887 of a third rival, the Michigan (Natural) Gas Company, complicated the cartel arrangements of the older companies to some degree, but because of the technical problems involved in maintaining the pumping pressure at its gas fields and the uneven quality of its illuminant, Michigan Gas never emerged as a serious competitor to the coal gas companies.[31]

Pingree first concerned himself with the gas problem in 1891, when he became annoyed at the excavation of the pavements and streets by the companies. In 1892 and 1893 the Mayor conducted a probe into the price of gas through an extensive investigation and by consultation with the municipal expert Edward W. Bemis. Pingree concluded that the price being charged for gas in Detroit ($1.75 for illuminating and $1.25 for fuel) not only was too high but was illegal. The combined gas companies are "getting two prices for second-class gas against the plain terms of their franchise," the Mayor declared.[32]

In 1893 already combating the electric light and traction interests, Pingree had, as he saw it, a limited choice of solutions to the gas problem. Never a doctrinaire on public ownership, Pingree eliminated municipal ownership as a realistic solution for the gas problem. About this decision he later said, "We must not . . . wait for public ownership before putting an end to the extortion now practiced by private monopolies. We must, under the present system, compel the corporations exercising public franchises to furnish their services at reasonable rates contemplated in their charters." [33]

Having chosen regulation as the practical means of reducing the price of gas in Detroit, Pingree launched a vigorous campaign in the spring of 1893 to obtain the necessary authorization from the legislature. Together with "his band of crusaders" and armed with petitions and a dossier of evidence that showed the exorbitance of gas prices in Detroit, the Mayor journeyed to the state capital to testify before a legislative committee. "I used my utmost endeavors," Pingree asserted, to obtain "the passage of a law authorizing the Common Council to reasonably regulate the price of gas." The regulatory provision Pingree sought was the prominent feature of a newly proposed charter for Detroit, which would have enlarged the Mayor's power and expanded the city's bonding limitations.[34]

Unfortunately for the cause of gas regulation, however, the bonding section of the proposed charter, which would have increased municipal taxation, united a wide spectrum of business and political interests against the proposed charter. Speaking for the railroad interests, James F. Joy condemned the bonding feature and asserted that "the shiftless thousands who have not a dollar's worth of interest in the city" would support Pingree's projects to build parks and buy street railways and would spend the city into bankruptcy. "The consumer of gas has no more right to regulate the price of gas," Joy added, "than the purchaser of goods from a merchant." Also included among the opponents of the charter were representatives of the gas and real estate interests. Even more important, and ultimately decisive, was the opposition of Senator James McMillan and his G.O.P. machine. The Senator's son William C. McMillan was president of the Detroit Gas Company, which had in 1892 absorbed and consolidated the Mutual Gas Company, the Detroit Gas Light Company, and the Michigan Gas Company into a single business organization. It was reported that Senator McMillan had spent $2,000,000 to secure a monopoly of the city's gas production.[35]

Pingree appeared to have the bad luck of trenching upon Senator McMillan's economic interests almost every time he attempted some municipal reform. McMillan's legislative friends combined with railroad lobbyist Schuyler Olds to compose an unbeatable force at the state house. Their influence delayed the consideration of the charter bill by a committee of the House and determined its final fate. A Detroit reporter overheard chairman D. Judson Hammond solemnly instruct his committee: "We are here for the purpose of protecting the gas companies." It was not surprising, therefore, that the provision authorizing the reasonable regulation of the price of gas "was smothered in the house committee and never saw the light of day" and that the charter itself was not approved. Pingree, angered over the defeat, described "'Sky" Olds as "a d—d ground mole," and denounced Hammond and the legislature. Any hope for gas regulation was dead for the next two years.[36]

Thwarted in his efforts to secure effective regulation of the gas business in Detroit, Pingree turned to competition as the means of solving the problem: he used the threat of inviting a low-cost competitor to the city in the hope that this would drive down the price of gas. In the spring of 1893 Pingree widely publicized the fact that a group of investors was interested in accepting a franchise to sell gas at seventy-five cents per 1,000 feet in Detroit. This proposal, however, turned out to be principally a verbal threat rather than a realistic alternative to the status quo. Pingree explained at the termination of the gas conflict that he had had serious reservations about the wisdom of bringing in an independent competitor which would have had "to tear up our good pavement to lay new pipes" and also construct a new generating facility, which might have caused a delay of several months. Pingree also discovered that no capitalist would invest money in another plant to furnish cheap gas without the guarantee that all existing franchises would be declared invalid. At the time, however, Pingree kept these reservations to himself and continued to use the threat of competition to create the kind of business uncertainty that utility magnates disliked.[37]

Unable to bluff the gas company, Pingree decided to employ his last alternative, which was, as he described it, to wage "a vigorous fight against the company in order to force them to a settlement distinctly advantageous to the city." Pingree doubted the validity of the merger effected in 1892 and suspected that franchise violations had occurred, and in February, 1893, he made an effort to locate the Detroit Gas Light Company franchise, which had been granted in 1851. Unable to find a trace of it in the city records or at the state capitol, the Mayor requested a copy from the company, which brusquely informed him that its files were not available to the city. Pingree then "set a dozen men at work going through two or three carloads of old newspapers stored up in the garret" of the city hall, and he eventually found a news item which demonstrated that the franchise had expired about twenty years previously. Delighted with his discovery and fully aware that he now possessed a weapon to strike the gas company in the securities market, Pingree released his information to the press. The Detroit Gas had just issued $7,500,000 worth of stock, and it was selling at about eighty cents a share. The Mayor noted with pleasure that the price suddenly plunged to fifteen cents.[38]

In an effort to win support for his position, Pingree initiated an educational campaign to demonstrate that gas was overpriced in Detroit. He pointed out that gas was being sold in Cleveland at eighty cents, in Milwaukee at ninety cents, and in Grand Rapids and Cincinnati for $1.00. In a conference with the gas company officials, the Mayor pointedly asked, "Why can't you sell your gas as cheaply as they do in Milwaukee?" Pingree described the gas question as one of the most important raised since he had been mayor. "Gas should be so cheap as to place it within reach of every householder in Detroit," he argued. "If the Detroit gas company can't afford to sell gas for 80 cents," Pingree said, "why don't they get out of the way and let somebody in who can." [39]

The Detroit Gas Company countered Pingree's price demands with the argument that eighty-cent gas was possible in Cleveland only because that city consumed 2½ times more volume annually than Detroit. "Of course they haven't sold as much gas at $1.50 [in Detroit] as is sold in Cleveland for 80 cents and in Buffalo and Chicago for $1. It isn't to be expected . . . ," retorted Pingree. He also answered the volume argument by pointing out that Grand

Rapids, a town not one-third as large as Detroit, had $1.00 gas. Pingree also successfully countered the company's argument that the transportation cost for coal, which was used to generate gas, was more expensive in Detroit than elsewhere. The lake carriers that conveyed coal to Milwaukee, Pingree pointed out, still had several hundred expensive miles to sail when they bypassed the docks on Detroit's river front and before they could discharge their cargoes into Milwaukee's generating furnaces, which produced ninety-cent gas. Lower your prices, demanded the Mayor, and there will be an enormous increase in the consumption of gas in Detroit.[40]

By June, 1893, Pingree's arguments had caught fire. The Detroit *Free Press* commented on the wisdom of the Mayor's exposition. The newspaper explained to its readers the substance of Pingree's high-volume, low-cost equation. The Detroit *Evening News* also stopped its sporadic sniping at the Mayor and admitted the validity of Pingree's arguments. Finally, an overwhelming majority of the city's councilmen were ready to support the Mayor and to pass whatever legislation was deemed necessary.[41]

Pingree next tackled the Mutual Gas franchise and found two important sections that hitherto had been ignored by the company and by city officials. Pingree pointed out that Mutual was specifically forbidden from consolidating with a competing gas company in Detroit, and he began legal proceedings to void the merger of Mutual with the Detroit Gas Company. He also found another subsection of the Mutual franchise which prescribed that the price charged by the company to consumers in Detroit was to be an average of the rates charged in Buffalo, Chicago, Cleveland, Toledo, and Sandusky, Ohio. Pingree obtained the rates of these five cities and showed that Mutual should have been selling gas for $1.06 per thousand instead of $1.50. With this information, he insisted that the gas company accept his payment of his personal gas bill at the $1.06 rate, and demanded a rebate of 44 cents per 1,000 feet for the overcharge of the previous six years. When the firm refused to accept his payment, the Mayor initiated legal action to enforce the franchise and to recover the sum of the overcharges. He also advised Mutual Gas customers to save their old bills because he was convinced that he would win his case and that they would be entitled to similar rebates from the company.[42]

In June, 1893, Pingree took two more actions which threatened to dismember the gas consortium in Detroit. On June 10 the Board of Public Works was informed by the Detroit Gas Company that it planned to excavate trenches in the streets to connect its mains and pipes and thus effect the physical consolidation of its system. Pingree and the Board denied the permits for excavation and sought an injunction from the Wayne Circuit Court to stop the gas company from disturbing the city's pavements. When the restraining order was refused, Pingree ordered public works personnel and police officers to prevent connection of the gas lines. The company challenged this edict by sending out its crews to begin chopping up the asphalt pavements. This brought about a street fight, and the police department arrested the gas men. That evening Pingree explained that although he regretted the use of force, it was the only course of action open to the city. "Possession is a great point," argued the Mayor. "Let them get their gas systems connected and then they could float their $8,000,000 of stock in New York City and become too powerful for the city to control. Detroit would be helpless in the hands of corporations as never before in her history." [43]

Pingree called the common council into special session on June 14 and declared: "Gentlemen—The fight for cheap gas is on." In his message, Pingree argued that the Detroit Gas Company had no legal standing because of the expiration of the former Detroit Gas Light Company's contract with the city, the repeated and open violation of its franchise by the Mutual Gas Company, and because the franchise for the Michigan Gas Company was for natural and not for artificial gas. He pointed out that the city had never granted the new company any rights in the streets. In view of the company's flagrant "defiance of the authority of the Council" and its "subversion of the good order of the community," the Mayor asked for the immediate revocation of all the gas franchises issued by the city. Aldermen James Vernor, Joseph Lowry, Charles Wright, and

Chris Jacob attempted to delay action, but the council complied with the Mayor's request and revoked the three operating franchises. The Detroit Gas Company treasurer called Pingree's action the "raving of a madman who is appealing to mob spirit on the lines of confiscation," and the company's attorney asserted that the council's repeals were wholly illegal. More important, however, was that Pingree had now placed the burden of proof upon the company. Although the franchise repeals may have been of doubtful legality, it would clearly cost the Detroit Gas Company time, energy, and money to prove that point in court.[44]

By August, 1893, the position of the Detroit Gas Company had deteriorated considerably in the eyes of the public, the council, and New York investors. The company had failed to justify its high prices. Under Pingree's attack, the firm had some months previously dropped the price of gas to $1.25, and the value of its securities had fallen on the stock market. Although the concern had monopolized the production of gas in Detroit, it had not been able to connect its mains and pipes to implement physical consolidation. Finally, in September, Pingree won his case against the Mutual Gas Company when the Justice Court declared that Mutual had violated its franchise and ordered the company to reimburse the Mayor for its overcharges on his gas bill for the previous six years.[45]

With the gas combine's resistance severely weakened, Pingree applied increasing pressure on the firm. "We made the fight so hot for the gas company that they finally opened negotiations for settlement," [46] said Pingree. He had by then arranged to meet in New York with Collis P. Huntington, the Southern Pacific magnate who had recently become the principal investor in the Detroit Gas Company. Huntington, however, was not ready to consider a compromise; he believed that he had been swindled by promoters in Detroit who had sold him an investment in a questionable enterprise which lacked a clear title to operate in the city and whose securities had suddenly fallen in price. There was probably a great deal of truth to this, for one of the original promoters of the Michigan Gas Company explained that the Detroit Gas Company's consolidation was "merely a scheme to let the McMillans and others out of a deep hole" and to enable them to sell their inflated securities on the New York market before Pingree would be able to roll back prices.

Pingree met Huntington in two heated sessions and told him: "You're robbing the people of Detroit." He reminded Huntington that if the negotiations failed, Detroit might very well invite an independent to the city to compete with the Detroit gas consortium. Huntington finally agreed to a compromise which Pingree believed was honorable and "as favorable as possibly could be obtained under the circumstances." The agreement provided for eighty-cent fuel gas and $1.00 illuminating gas, with the stipulation that the latter would decrease to eighty cents when a prescribed aggregate volume had been consumed. The settlement also contained a provision for eventual municipal ownership. Pingree pointed out to the council that this would give Detroiters gas as cheap as that in any city of equal size in the United States except Cleveland. The council ratified a franchise based on the agreement on October 31, 1893. Pingree was understandably proud of his eighty-cent gas price for, as the *Detroit Saturday Night* pointed out, it was his "big victory of the year." [47]

Pingree's gas victory served to clear the atmosphere, noted one writer. Instead of the old defiance, "a new policy of fair play was adopted by the gas company." When new methods of manufacture and purification reduced production costs, the company generally shared these savings with the consumer. The Detroit Gas Company made its first voluntary reduction of rates in 1896. Pingree's "gas war" saved the citizens of Detroit several million dollars in gas cost within a few years.[48]

III

The telephone completely escaped not only public ownership but, until 1907, even the most innocuous forms of regulation. The most natural of natural monopolies, as Pingree would discover, proved the least amenable to municipal control or ownership. For seventeen years, no competitor was able to break through the patent claim of the American Bell Telephone Company.

The first commercial telephone exchange was established in New Haven, Connecticut, in 1878, but the telephone remained primarily a novelty and exhibit piece until 1880. For the duration of its patent, from 1876 to 1893, the American Bell Telephone Company retained its absolute monopoly on this new means of communication and easily crushed rival claims. Lacking the capital necessary to construct a nationwide network, the Bell Company licensed local firms to establish systems, rented to them the necessary apparatus, and generally required in payment from these licensees a substantial percentage of their stock. Long distance calls from one local exchange to another were serviced by a subsidiary of the Bell Company, the American Telephone and Telegraph Company, which was the real "whip hand" for control of the local companies.[49]

The expiration of the original Bell patent in 1893 was the signal for the beginning of competition in the industry. The Bell Company, in an effort to prolong its statutory monopoly for an additional seventeen years, had in 1891 applied for and received a patent for an improved telephone. This patent was contested by both the federal government and, later, by the independent companies on the grounds that it had been fraudulently granted. Although litigation continued throughout the decade, more than 1,000 independent companies had been established by 1897.[50]

Two means used with some success in various parts of the nation to break Bell's price structure were "mutualism" and the independent telephone company. The mutual systems were constructed by their consumer owners for convenience rather than for revenue. A farmer who wanted service would usually install his own telephone and run a wire either on or along his fence to his nearest neighbor who was connected to a trunk line that offered communication to a nearby village. Such systems were financed by the assessment of a levy upon each user to defray the cost of operating a switchboard. These "farmer or rural lines" were generally restricted to the corn belt of the Midwest and were seldom found in villages or townships of more than 4,000 inhabitants. In a few isolated cases the mutuals did undercut and drive out the higher priced Bell systems. More often, however, they functioned to fulfill a social need in sparsely

populated areas and for this reason were usually not competitive
with the Bell Company. By 1895, 15 mutual systems had been established. The independent telephone companies, on the other hand,
were organized along traditional lines and sought to compete with
Bell in the large cities. Although the independents were not able to
penetrate the major eastern cities, their incursions in the Midwest
forced Bell to meet the competition by lowering its rates.[51]

The late-nineteenth-century generalization that bigness bred efficiency, economy, and savings which were automatically passed on
to the consumer was not true for the American Bell Telephone
Company. A company born and nurtured under noncompetitive
conditions for seventeen years was not oriented toward lower
prices or mass markets. The average annual rates charged by Bell
for residential and business service were between $75 and $240 in
urban areas which had a population in excess of 100,000. The company, as one contemporary correctly observed, operated on the
principle that "it is better to receive $120 per 'phone per year from
1,000 subscribers than $40 per 'phone per year from 3,000 subscrib-
ers." The nationwide effect of this rate policy was to discourage
telephone use. The Bell system, very much like the gas interests,
was apparently satisfied with low-volume sales and high profits.[52]

Under-consumption was caused in part by the Bell practice of
declaring large dividends for investors and saddling the consumer
with high rates to generate the necessary capital for expansion.
From the point of view of the Bell shareholder, who drew dividends that averaged 18 per cent from 1888 to 1893, there was, of
course, much to be said for this business policy, but from a consumer's viewpoint, it placed a restraint upon consumption. The com-
paratively slow growth of the telephone and its restriction to commercial houses and to a few wealthy residences were the price the
nation paid for Bell's business policies.[53]

It was only after the independents entered the field and challenged it with the business practice of high volume consumption
and low profit margins that Bell decreased its rates—but only when
it was forced to do so by competition. In such cities as Rochester,
Indianapolis, St. Louis, Cleveland, Columbus, and Detroit, where

the independents challenged Bell, service charges were frequently reduced by as much as 50 per cent. The "Independents demonstrated to the Bell interests the capacity of the public to take, use and pay for more telephones," asserted Horace Coon, and they forced Bell to provide cheaper and better service. The independents also performed another valuable service, unwittingly: they so annoyed the Bell company that the firm was willing by 1907 to accept some form of public regulation in order to destroy competition.[54]

The Michigan Bell Telephone Company was licensed by the Bell Company in 1881 to establish a telephone exchange in Detroit. During the same year the company was absorbed by the Michigan Telephone Company, also a Bell licensee. It was reorganized in 1883, the date when telephone communication actually began in Detroit, by James and Hugh McMillan and their business associates. The Michigan Telephone Company, or the Bell Company as it was popularly known, obtained an operating franchise in 1884 which was almost devoid of restrictions. The light burden of taxation on the Bell Company was made even more bearable when the state legislature passed a law exempting the company from personal property taxation in Detroit.[55]

When Pingree began his campaign to secure lower telephone rates, in 1894, the choices open to Detroit and other American cities to force reasonable rates were far more limited than the options which had been available to municipalities in their struggles with the other public utilities. The fact that telephone communication had to transcend city and state boundaries was a deterrent to municipal ownership. Even after 1893 the technical skills and production machinery of the telephone industry remained largely under Bell control, and the few independent competitors who possessed the necessary skills and equipment were more interested in free enterprise than in fostering city ownership. Michigan's unwillingness to enlarge Detroit's bonding authority in 1893, moreover, made it highly unlikely that the city, even had it so desired, could raise the funds necessary to equip a municipal plant. The legislature's refusal to empower Detroit to regulate gas prices had closed the door to any prospect of municipal regulation of telephone rates. Finally, the Michigan Supreme Court's guardianship of the rights of private property and its rigid and narrow interpretation of what was a proper municipal function indicated quite clearly that municipal regulation or ownership of a utility like the telephone would probably be construed as beyond the competence of a local unit of government.

In 1896, during his fourth term as mayor, Pingree began his contest against the telephone company. "The rates charged by the Bell Telephone Company in different parts of the city are not generally known. Only those who have been unfortunate enough to have been robbed by the company are posted as to its system of extortion," Pingree told the common council. "These non-residents, with an impudence unheard of, not only occupy your streets and charge double and treble rates for service," he added, "but pay no taxes on personal property." During the previous year the Mayor had begun to lay the groundwork for his campaign by responding to a charge by the city's physicians and merchants that Bell telephones were priced beyond their reach. The Michigan Telephone Company, under the presidency of James McMillan, charged annual rates that ranged from $72 to $136 for business service, $95 for a doctor's telephone, and between $50 and $125 for residential service. The differential was determined by the distance of the customer's telephone from the central switchboard. "It will be seen," Pingree pointed out, "that the rent for a telephone in some parts of the city is greater than the rent of a cottage, and for those living in the outer wards and in the upper districts of all wards, these rates are absolutely prohibitory." The consequence of high prices was readily evident in Detroit, a city of 250,000 people, which could afford but 4,000 telephones, of which only 1,000 were located in residences. Pingree also argued that toll charges for calls to points outside of Detroit were exorbitant. After he had made a call to Fremont, Michigan, he pointed out that a farmer in that region who wished to check market prices would have to spend "17 bushels of potatoes to talk two minutes over a telephone with a person in Detroit." [56]

Having discarded regulation and municipal ownership as unrealistic alternatives for solving the telephone problem in Detroit and unable to secure lower rates from the local Bell Company, Pingree decided to try competition. Both Grand Rapids and Port Huron, Michigan, which had permitted independent companies to install their exchanges, were enjoying rates that were 50 per cent below those of the Bell systems. Pingree also was encouraged by the independent companies that were making incursions into Bell territory in dozens of other cities with the promise of low prices. "What we want is plenty of competition," asserted Pingree somewhat earlier, for "competition brings low rates." [57]

Pingree pushed a franchise through the council for the Detroit Telephone Construction Company, a concern that was entirely independent of Bell. Many of the Mayor's political cronies, including his legal adviser, Charles Flowers, his former secretary, Alex McLeod, and Sheriff Charles P. Collins were among the directors of the new firm. The franchise provided for $25 residential and $40 business service, 75 free telephones for the city, a personal property tax upon the company's facilities, and an option for municipal ownership which the city could exercise after ten years of private operation. Although it was not feasible in 1896, Pingree thought that within a decade municipal ownership might be "the only method by which the rates can be reduced." [58]

The Detroit Telephone Company finally attracted enough capital to construct its system and to begin operation in 1897. The Detroit Company's low rates and superior equipment and service proved highly attractive, and within a few years it had attracted twice as many subscribers as the Bell Company. The *Electrical Engineer* asserted in 1897 that the Detroit Telephone Company was the largest independent telephone exchange in the world. Appropriately, the Independent Telephone Association held its first annual convention in Detroit in 1897.[59]

The Michigan Telephone Company, with the vast economic resources of American Bell Telephone behind it, could not have been expected to sit by idly and watch the Detroit Company take away its future market. The Michigan Telephone Company cut its rates below those of its competitor and began to improve its customer services. By 1900 the "rate war" had run its course; the independent Detroit Company had capitulated and had been absorbed by the Michigan Telephone Company.[60]

Competition, in the form of the Pingree-supported Detroit Telephone Company, had served a useful purpose, however. It had functioned effectively for a few years as a substitute for regulation and municipal ownership at a time when both of these alternatives had been impossible to attain. By 1900, according to Stephen Mc-Cracken, Detroit had cheaper telephones than any city of its size in the United States. Low rates had also brought a wider use of the telephone: in 1902, Detroit had a ratio of 42 telephones per 1,000 people as compared to Milwaukee's 36, Philadelphia's 34, Chicago's 33, St. Louis' 32, Baltimore's and Washington's 29, and New York's 26. When Michigan Bell later attempted to raise its prices, it was stopped by public protest and a court decision that Bell had to abide by the franchise rates for the original customers of the defunct Detroit Telephone Company. Apparently the rate war had a long-term effect upon Bell's prices, for Edward Burch reported in 1916 that Michigan Telephone Company rates had remained reasonable.[61]

6

The Mayor Leads a Nationwide
Fight for Low Fares

The fall of 1894 witnessed a series of important changes in the street railway situation in Detroit. Then in his third term, Pingree hoped to find a satisfactory solution to the traction problem. Aware of the Michigan constitution's impediments to municipal ownership and sensitive to a depression-worn public "growing weary of delays," Pingree turned to the principle of competition to bring low fares to the city. It was not the ideology of public ownership but the recognition of a public need that guided the Mayor's actions. Pragmatic humanism was the tag line used by friends to describe the administration; his enemies called it political opportunism.

Canvassing the nation during his business trips, Mayor Pingree solicited widely for an investment group to construct a privately owned system which he believed could, if properly financed, prove profitable to the owners because of increased passenger volume. Henry A. Everett, who held streetcar interests in Canada and the United States, joined Albert and Greene Pack, both upstate lumbermen, and accepted Pingree's invitation to construct a 3-cent line to compete with the Citizens' Street Railway Company.

Pingree guided a franchise for the Pack-Everett syndicate

through the council over the objection of Aldermen James Vernor and Charles Wright, two obstructionists whom the administration had marked for defeat. The session took on the flavor of a medieval morality play in which the audience repeatedly hissed and cheered at the respective sides as Vernor, Wright, and Chris Jacob criticized the ordinance and Aldermen George Beck and William B. Thompson pressed the administration's measure to a 29 to 1 victory. Three-cent fares from 5:45 a.m. to 8:00 p.m., six tickets for a quarter for the rest of the night, universal transfers, and a city option to buy the line after thirty years at a price to be determined by arbitration were the provisions of the precedent-making franchise.[1]

The new Detroit Railway Company accelerated its construction schedule to lay the sixty miles of electric track authorized by the franchise. On July 8, 1895, it was able to offer service on some of its lines. Although the Detroit Railway was restricted to the back streets and the less direct routes, this fact did not diminish the magnitude of Pingree's victory. The Mayor donned a motorman's cap to the delight of the cheering crowd, and piloted the first car up the tracks, with the aldermen following symbolically in tow in the second car. Hundreds gathered alongside, many threw bouquets into the Mayor's car, and street crews and paving gangs stopped their work to applaud the Mayor. Men, women, and children rushed out to greet and cheer Pingree, who "received an ovation, the like of which no Roman general, returning from the east with victorious legions, and rich with the spoils of strife, ever received." Pingree reveled in the whole affair and was so busy returning salutes that he almost ran down a herd of cows on Riopelle Street. The occasion showed Pingree at his best, ebullient, confident, waving his hat, gesticulating and shouting to the crowd, and displaying his "pyro-technical" skills. Most important, however, was that Mayor Pingree had broken new ground that made him "a pioneer in the low-fare movement," for his three-cent franchise was the "earliest important low fare ordinance granted by any American city."[2]

The protection and retention of three-cent fares posed a number of problems, the most serious stemmed from Tom Loftin Johnson's presidency of the Citizens' Company in 1895. Tom's brother Albert and the R. T. Wilson interests had purchased the Citizens' Company reportedly for seventy-five cents on the dollar, from the Hendrie-Ferry-McMillan group, who were "not hard-boiled enough . . . to absorb this kind of punishment" that Pingree had delivered. Tom Johnson, who had been raised in poverty, had sold newspapers at the age of eleven to support his improvident family. Shortly thereafter he had invented a fare box that earned him enough cash to invest in the street railway business, and this made him wealthy by the age of twenty-five. Seizing franchises, Johnson had won traction battles in Indianapolis, Cleveland, Brooklyn, and Johnstown, Pennsylvania, and had added two steel mills to his holdings for good measure. His technique was to buy a broken-down street railway, build it up, "pour quantities of water" into its capitalization, and then sell it for more than its true worth. He had capped his career as a self-made man and a self-confessed "monopolist" by serving two undistinguished terms in Congress, the high points of which were delivering a single speech on free trade and teaching "Sockless" Jerry Simpson to ride a bicycle. In his autobiography, Johnson claimed to have been influenced by Henry George in 1883, but none of it was evident during Johnson's years as a traction magnate. In 1894, he was defeated for re-election to Congress and was brought to Detroit to rehabilitate the Citizens' Company fortunes.[3]

Johnson's first task was to root out the three-cent fare. Accepting the Citizens' Company claim that its charter of 1862 gave it the exclusive right to establish railways on every unoccupied street in the city, Johnson initiated a case in the Wayne County Circuit Court. Dissatisfied with the lower court decision that refused to validate the Company's claim and oust the three-cent line, Johnson appealed to the Michigan Supreme Court. "It's for blood," he announced, "and somebody is going to get skinned and skinned thoroughly. . . . This is a fight for gore, and it will be carried right along to the finish." The Pingree administration accepted the challenge and turned back Johnson's assault on July 28, 1896, when the

Michigan Supreme Court upheld the three-cent franchise and ruled out the Citizens' Company claim to an exclusive monopoly of the city's streets.[4]

The second confrontation between Pingree and Johnson came when the Detroit Railway Company sought the joint use of terminal facilities in the downtown area so that it would be able to penetrate the hub and business section of the city. The Citizens' Company, in control of the terminals, resisted. Johnson argued that if the three-cent line obtained the use of the terminals it would freeze out the Citizens' Company, destroy it, or force it to grant three-cent fares. Ironically, as a traction magnate in Cleveland, Johnson had fought for and obtained the free use of downtown lines when it had been in his economic self-interest to do so. The peculiar ambivalence that characterized Johnson's Georgite reform rhetoric showed itself in this controversy when he remarked: "Mr. Pack and I are alike in two things. We are both free-traders and anti-monopolists. Only Mr. Pack wants to put his free-trade theories in operation in this agreement and I don't." [5]

The struggle between the Detroit traction interests was transferred to the state legislature, where the city administration and the Pack-Everett syndicate applied their not inconsequential influence in support of a bill to open Detroit's prime downtown streets. Pingree apparently gambled that the public's low-fare interest could be advanced if it were wedded to a powerful, profit-making enterprise. Pingree and Pack, however, were challenged by Johnson, who called to the rescue Schuyler Olds, a railroad lobbyist, and the McMillan machine. William C. McMillan bombarded the legislature with telegrams that read: "Knowing you are a friend of father, you will vote against the bill." Although Pingree had come to expect just about anything from Senator McMillan, he was surprised by this maneuver because McMillan, as chairman of the Senate committee for the District of Columbia, had permitted the multiple use of lines on Pennsylvania Avenue. Pingree snorted: "Vote for papa! What the people of Detroit want cuts no figure if it happens to conflict in some way with papa's financial interests." [6]

"I don't know what to do," a desperate Michigan legislator muttered. "If I vote against the bill, the friends of the Packs say they will scalp me. If I vote for it I shall be accused of ingratitude to McMillan. I'll get the worst of it either way. It was wrong to bring politics into this matter, and the Republican party will suffer, no matter which way it goes." Representative William E. Rice protested: "I want to ask if Senator McMillan owns this legislature. We paid our debt to him by reelecting him Senator . . . he ought not to try and coerce us into opposing this bill because he may be interested in it." A reporter remarked that "one could almost hear the crack of the party whip" as the bill was defeated. "We could easily have won our fight for terminal facilities on Woodward Avenue," declared Albert Pack, "had not the great influence of Senator McMillan's name and control of public offices, and the active work of his lieutenants been exerted to defeat us." Pingree lashed out at McMillan and concluded that municipal affairs were too intimately linked to state and federal politics.[7]

There is no question that the electrified and modernized Pingree sponsored system had a favorable effect upon Detroit transit. Edward W. Bemis observed that the low-fare franchise had provided several new streets with transit, had demonstrated that three-cent fares were feasible, and had educated the public in the merits of municipal ownership. The Citizens' Company vice-president, Jere C. Hutchins, remarked with obvious displeasure that Pingree's project had raised the devastating question: "If one company could carry passengers for three cents, why not both?" The national significance of Pingree's project was recognized by Wilbur F. Crafts, superintendent of the National Bureau of Reforms, who noted that Detroit's low fare line and its free transfers "beats the world" for cheap transportation. Responding to the challenge, Tom Johnson told R. T. Wilson that he could "not be expected to try to defeat the mayor's three-cent project except by improved facilities on our own lines." Johnson accordingly began retiring horse cars and rebuilding and electrifying the Citizens' system, "complying with the mayor's suggestions as to construction."[8]

Although Johnson had spent a great deal of money and energy in an unsuccessful attempt to smother Pingree's three-cent line in its infancy, his most important task was to bring his manipulative skills to bear upon the Pingree administration to secure a thirty-year franchise renewal for the Citizens' Company. Contingent upon such a renewal was the credit of the firm and the market value of its stocks and bonds, the very life blood of such a highly speculative enterprise as the traction business. Johnson wanted the renewal to contain a five-cent fare, and he tested the feasibility of his proposal by forcing two high fare ordinances through the council that applied to but a small percentage of the total streetcar trackage in Detroit. The ordinances were vetoed by Pingree because they did not include provisions for a three-cent fare, workingmen's tickets, and joint use of downtown terminals. Pingree charged that Johnson's five-cent fare would have enabled the company to float its bonds and "pump water into three million dollars worth of stock until it bulged out to a seven million dollar proportion." [9]

Johnson then decided to try his talents of persuasion to obtain some minor concessions. Although accustomed to the use of power, he was capable of being suave and glib, and this prompted an observer to call him "one of the slickest men that ever came to Detroit." Afraid of what Johnson might secure from the council in his absence, Pingree sought pledges from the aldermen to resist the company's blandishments and then left the city for a G.A.R. convention. With Pingree away from the city, Johnson shrewdly softened the council and said that his company wanted a side street (Baker Street) right-of-way so badly that it might, in return, grant permission to the three-cent line to use a main thoroughfare, Michigan Avenue. Upon his return Pingree discovered that Johnson had been able to push one ordinance through the council over acting Mayor William Richert's veto and had secured a second measure which was still subject to Pingree's purview. Temporarily discouraged by the council's backsliding, Pingree declared: "What is the use of one man trying to do all the fighting," and signed the Baker Street ordinance, which allowed the company to relocate one of its lines. What incensed Pingree was that some of the councilmen had been willing to accept Johnson's verbal promise that he would continue the existing policy of six tickets for twenty-five cents rather than demanding that this provision be written into the ordinance. Pingree warned the council that Johnson's promises of low fares were worthless.[10]

Although he had gained a few minor victories, Johnson still had not obtained the sought-after thirty-year prize. He decided, therefore, to demonstrate to Pingree and the common council what he was capable of doing if a new franchise were not granted. Full of the combativeness that was as much a part of his character as it was of Pingree's, Johnson challenged Pingree with the remark: "I would like to defeat you, mayor; I tell you I'd break my neck to do it." Having previously abolished the exchange of tickets between companies, Johnson announced, on November 19, 1895, that his firm would no longer offer six tickets for twenty-five cents and universal transfers but would charge five cents for a single fare. Although authorized to do so some years previously, the company had not exercised its option. Johnson and Pingree had a heated one-hour conference over fares during which, each gave notice to the other that he was quite a fighter.[11]

Pingree, livid with rage over Tom Johnson's broken promise not to abandon the six for twenty-five cent rate, called for a public boycott of the Citizens' Company. Unaware of what an earlier streetcar riot under Pingree's direction had done to the previous owners and supremely confident of his own ability, Johnson inaugurated his policy on November 21, 1895, eliminating an estimated 20,000 free transfers daily. Johnson's "action raised the biggest kind of howl," observed the line's vice-president, Jere Hutchins. One thousand employees at the Parke-Davis Company, later joined by men at the Novelty Works, initiated a petition condemning Johnson and pledging themselves not to use the Citizens' Company lines. Conductors reported that Polish laborers, school girls, old women, and businessmen complained vociferously all day, shook their fists, refused to pay extra fares to use transfers, and vowed to walk—which many of them did. The Detroit *Evening Press* called Johnson "a cunning, unscrupulous schemer" and charged: "His business methods are treacherous and his political methods are shady. He has deceived the people of Detroit. . . . He has recently attempted to hold up our citizens in broad daylight in order to get revenge on Pingree, the one man who stood like a rock of adamant between Johnson's greed and the People's Rights." The Detroit *Free Press* asserted that if Johnson's gambit was to use the fare increase to wheedle a thirty-year franchise from the city he was doomed to disappointment, for Pingree had fought the old company to a standstill. The city's *Evening News* warned Johnson that Pingree was unbeatable with the city at his back.[12]

Pingree personally led the boycott. He thundered: "This fight ain't going to stop until the old company gets right down on its knees." He harassed the Citizens' line conductors by insisting upon the old rate of six tickets for twenty-five cents and was forcibly ejected from several cars. When not put off, he encouraged others with shouts of, "Demand six tickets or don't pay. That's what we did." He took perverse delight in walking several blocks through the slush and snow to use the three-cent line and declared: "Going to come down that way every morning. Not quite so near, but it's all right. Good service. Got a seat. Warm cars. No smell of gas from the stoves. No old rattletrap cars such as Tom Johnson runs." He used all the prestige and influence of the mayor's office to bring about a reduction of traffic on Johnson's line, publicly ridiculed those few who rode it as "soft-headed dudes," and argued that the company should be driven from the streets as a public nuisance.[13]

Much to Tom Johnson's discomfiture, the boycott, a strategem once used effectively against Pingree, proved a formidable weapon in the Mayor's hands. The volume of traffic dropped precipitously on the Citizens' system. "The company gained no advantage," confessed Jere Hutchins. "On the contrary, so many deserted the lines that revenues fell off materially." The three-cent line, on the other hand, reported that passenger traffic had increased 35 per cent by November 26 and 50 per cent by November 27, when it was carrying an additional 11,800 fares daily. Conceding that Pingree's tutoring of Detroiters in the virtues of the three-cent fare had shattered his program, Johnson capitulated on December 31 and abandoned the fare increases. Pingree hoped that the encounter would teach Johnson that vacant seats were unprofitable and that Detroit, under his leadership, had no intention of being taken in by Johnson's managerial legerdemain. Johnson's reputation as a financial wizard had now plunged to its nadir in Detroit. Not only had he been forced to rescind his fare increase and restore exchangeable tickets, but he had lost what little good will he had gained among Detroiters as the result of his electrification of the Citizens' lines. Senator McMillan, usually a master at understatement, said to his son: "Tom Johnson has made more mistakes than I thought a man of his experience could possibly make and it looks as though Pingree has the best of him." [14]

Johnson attempted to extricate himself from his difficulties with, as he said, a "graceful bow." He proposed an ordinance which, on the surface, appeared to offer an acceptable three-cent package but which, when examined carefully, contained several objectionable features. Among them was a sixty-day trial period during which the Citizens' Company would supposedly experiment with three-cent fares and then decide if it wished to accept the ordinance. In reality the sixty-day trial probably was intended to serve as a cooling-off period during which Johnson, undisturbed by the wrath of the city, could contemplate his next maneuver against Pingree and Detroit.

The ordinance passed the council with the support of Aldermen Charles Wright and Chris Jacob, who publicly identified themselves as single tax advocates when they cast their votes. This must have amused Pingree, because the most vocal proponents of the single tax in Detroit, including Tom Johnson, were the most vehement enemies of municipal reform. Apparently mocking the *ersatz* single taxers and Tom Johnson, Alderman Sam Goldwater remarked that he would like to see the Henry George ideal of no fares effected. Rumors of graft ran rampant. Alderman Frank J. Licht charged that Johnson had offered him a $6,000 bribe to gather support for the ordinance in the council; Johnson admitted only that he had applied pressure upon Licht. Homer Warren had advanced $1,000 to facilitate passage of the measure in the hope of getting Johnson to add a spur line to 140 acres which Warren wished to sell. Pingree, bristling with anger, asked who owned the town, and denounced the "fire-in-the-rear fellows over at the

Chamber of Commerce" who supported the ordinance. "They're dangerous men," the Mayor said, "and the sooner they get out of town the better it'll be for Detroit." In a heavy-handed veto message, Pingree castigated the council for passing an ordinance that gave Johnson a special tax exemption, lacked provisions for a transfer with three-cent fares, a children's fare, and a statement on the hours of labor for employees, and contained no clause for joint use of downtown tracks or for municipal ownership.[15]

Even though the ordinance was defeated, Johnson voluntarily offered a three-cent fare into the summer of 1896, and Pingree began to believe that his efforts were succeeding. In July the suburban Fort Wayne Company dropped its rates to meet the competition. Apparently encouraged by Johnson's concession and secure in the knowledge that the Michigan Supreme Court had quashed Johnson's previous attempt to extirpate the Pack-Everett system, which was required by its franchise to grant three-cent fares, Pingree decided to expand the scope of his reform activity and engaged in a stiff fight for the G.O.P. gubernatorial nomination. Shortly after Pingree had won the nomination, Johnson announced that the Citizens' Company would abandon the three-cent fare and revert to the former rates. Almost simultaneously, the Pack three-cent line began to merge its physical facilities with those of the Citizens' Company. The cat was out of the bag; the Pack-Everett syndicate had been purchased by Tom Johnson.

Pingree realized that Albert Pack's support of his gubernatorial nomination and Johnson's offer of three-cent fares were hardly disinterested attempts to make the Detroit mayor Michigan's governor. Although other factors were involved, the motive for Pack's and Johnson's actions was clearly to get Mayor Pingree out of the way and thereby secure a free hand for traction manipulation in Detroit. Pingree, who recalled Pack's promise not to sell out, called him a Judas and accused him of being "the Tom Johnson of the town now." Pingree sternly reminded Johnson that the merger of parallel or competing transportation systems was prohibited by the Michigan constitution. That antique instrument, replied Johnson, did not prevent a holding company from absorbing rivals and extinguishing competition. Engaged in one of the most heated political campaigns of his career and of the decade, Pingree stormed furiously but helplessly at what he and a majority of Detroiters considered a betrayal. The fabled Pingree luck had run out, and the Mayor seemed to have met his match in the deft promoter. Johnson proceeded to secure a complete monopoly of transit in Detroit for his company by acquiring the Fort Wayne Line in 1897.[16]

Johnson, however, had not obtained what the Citizens' Company still needed to float its securities at par, the thirty-year franchise renewal. His abrasive arguments with Pingree and the city had also measurably decreased the possibility that anyone would be able to obtain such a franchise in the foreseeable future. Johnson's tactics enabled Pingree to drive home the lesson again and again that no traction promoter could be trusted with a thirty-year franchise, that a three-cent fare was the maximum rate the city should accept, and that municipal ownership was the only solution to the traction problem. Neither had Johnson been able to eliminate the three-cent fare, which was locked inextricably into the franchise of the Detroit Railway Company, which he had acquired. Some attempt was made by the Citizens' Company to cripple the three-cent system by curtailing that line's services in an effort to drive passengers to use the more expensive Citizens' cars. Detroit had, however, become hypersensitive by this time to what it considered its hard-earned right to low-cost transportation, and citizen protest and council action defeated all attempts to discredit the low-fare service.[17]

Pingree, a master craftsman of municipal politics, countered Johnson's tactic in the fashion that he knew best. In August, 1896, he announced: "I am going to see that 16 aldermen, favorable to 3-cent fares on all roads, are elected this fall. Three-cent fares will be the campaign cry in the local election." Choosing among the aspirants for nomination, he declared: "I'll fight any man who opposes 3-cent fares." Pingree, true to his word, did secure the defeat of several of those willing to compromise with the company. Next, Pingree announced that he would wage relentless "guerrilla warfare" against the street railways, which would require many additional privileges and favors from the aldermen in the years ahead. What he could not do in the courts, he would do with political power. He also planned to hinder the sale and drive down the price of the company's bonds by advertising widely in city newspapers and informing potential buyers that they assumed an inordinate risk by investing in Johnson's railway consortium, which was in violation of the Michigan constitution and was offensive to the moral sentiments of Detroit. Finally, Pingree initiated a vigorous agitation for a "franchise by [citizen] referendum," which he hoped would prevent unscrupulous railway operators from bribing the city council. Although elected to the governorship of Michigan in November, 1896, Pingree retained his position as Mayor of Detroit until March, 1897. He warned that if Johnson were not resisted: "I'll resign my place as governor of Michigan and go back to Detroit next fall and run for mayor again," and "If none of the men who want to be mayor have the courage to stand out against Tom Johnson and his crowd, I will continue to be mayor until their present franchises run out." [18]

By the end of Pingree's fourth term as Mayor in 1897, his struggle for the improvement of municipal transportation had exerted a profound influence upon urban America. After July 8, 1895, when Pingree drove the nation's first three-cent car up the tracks in Detroit, traction promoters everywhere would never again experience the security that they had enjoyed in the pre-Pingree era. The national contest against long-term franchises and for low fares dated from Pingree's three-cent project in Detroit; city after city had received inspiration not only from Pingree's rhetoric but from the incontrovertible fact that he had implemented low fares. The Cleveland *Plain-Dealer* declared in 1896 that "Until Mayor Pingree won his splendid fight for low streetcar fares in Detroit, very little effort had been made to secure low fares in other cities, but the news of Pingree's victory spread like wildfire and today every wide awake city in the country realizes that it is paying too much for car fare." The Hartford *Weekly Examiner* observed: "The good fight-and victory-of Mayor Pingree . . . for three-cent fares on city railways is having its influence on other cities of the Union," and the Baltimore *News* said: "The agitation for lower street car fares, begun by Mayor Pingree of Detroit, is rapidly spreading throughout the country." Tom Johnson, who held an interest in several street railways in the Midwest and East, agreed with these judgments and admitted to Pingree that his "three-cent plan" had caused trouble over the country. Pingree's argument that the price of fares should respond to national deflation had also caught on. The *Street Railway Review* lamented in 1897 that "The daily press from the Atlantic to the Pacific, in daily, weekly, Sunday and extras, has shouted itself hoarse in the assertion that everything has cheapened in price, but street car fares remain the same." [19]

Pingree, whom the Buffalo *Express* now described as "the most-talked-of Mayor in the United States," vigorously propagandized his low-fare gospel through addresses, letters, speeches, interviews, and his irrepressible off-the-cuff commentary. His proselytizing, unlike that of many public ownership advocates, was not prefaced by any theorizing; his practical mind focused upon the goals of low fares and the elimination of councilmanic corruption, which so frequently accompanied the contracting of urban transportation to private enterprise. Municipal ownership, as Pingree explained, was merely a means to these ends. He told the Providence Businessmen's Association in January, 1896, that "while I am not yet ready to advocate municipal operation of roads—I am strongly in favor of the city owning the tracks of iron, just as it owns the bricks in the pavement. When once you give your streets away, you are no longer master, but servant." A month later he said to the citizens of Milwaukee: "The very stupid persistence of transportation companies in wringing the last cent from the people is forcing the question of municipal and state ownership . . . I do not see why the counties should not own and operate a street rail road as well as a dirt or gravel or macadamized road. What is the difference?" "I believe in cheapening things so that everybody can afford to pay his own taxes," Pingree informed the New York *Sun*. "Every city has come to recognize it now that the weaker class need help and have got to be helped . . . I tell you if I was here I'd pull things wide open on this three-cent business." [20]

Pingree sent William Randolph Hearst, the editor of the New

York *Journal,* a long telegram which Hearst prominently featured
in the newspaper, in which the Detroit mayor explained that New
York's population density and the large number of people who used
public transportation facilities in the city justified demands for a
two-cent and not a three-cent fare. Pingree repeated this argument
to Bostonians and told them that they were "a lot of cowards" if
they did not stand up and fight for low fares and public control. He
presented a paper in absentia to the annual conference of the National Municipal League in 1896 entitled "The Public Control of
Franchises." In an address entitled "Thievery" Pingree shocked
Chicago lawyers and legal students when he condemned the "public plunderers" who played "a high-toned game with marked cards
and loaded dice" to steal franchises and win respectability. "No
reasonable argument," Pingree said, "can be urged against the city
paving a portion of the streets with iron for the use of the street
cars, which are the people's carriages . . . By this system the city
can control the rates." Many of the judges present, including Elbert
H. Gary, president of the Chicago Bar Association, blanched at the
Mayor's unscholarly notions, but William Jennings Bryan and W.
H. "Coin" Harvey, a currency reformer, approved of Pingree's
ideas.[21]

City after city looked to Pingree as a model on the traction question to be followed by local officials. The Pittsburgh *Post* took pride
in the fact that Pittsburgh believed that it had a mayor of Pingree's
mettle to handle the transit problem. The Albany *Press* published a
story of Pingree's public career and requested that the city's mayor
read it to find out how a mayor who really served the people be-
haved. The Philadelphia *Item* held up Pingree as an example to be
emulated, and Professor Frank Parsons, addressing the city's Ethi-
cal Culture Society, explained how Pingree had won the battle for
three-cent fares in Detroit. The New York *World* took cognizance
of Pingree's low-fare project and called upon New York to catch up
with Detroit. The St. Louis *Chronicle* stated that the city's "street
car companies will never reduce fares voluntarily. A Pingree is
needed." The Chicago *Times-Herald* related how Pingree had defeated Tom Johnson in Detroit and suggested that this was the ex-

ample to be followed by Chicago in its struggle against Yerkes. The Chicago *Universalist,* in an article on Pingree, argued that "Chicago needs just such a man, or perhaps a hundred just such men," and the Chicago *Journal* agreed that "Chicago needs a Pingree." The Cincinnati *Post* concluded that it would be better for the nation "if the municipal minds in all the cities were pregnant with Pingreeism." The Boston *Evening Transcript,* the Buffalo *Illustrated Express,* and the Washington *Evening Star* published the same story about Pingree under the headline: "For Lower Fares A Movement on Street Railway Companies Everywhere. Pingree and Detroit Set the Example, New York Threatens to Follow Suit, Philadelphia is Aroused, and There is a Movement for Three-Cent Fares in Chicago." [22]

Pingree's campaigning for low-fare franchises and transit improvement not only elicited widespread comment but also led to action in many municipalities throughout the nation. Professor Frank Parsons accepted the nomination for Mayor of Boston from the Municipal Reform Party and ran on a platform of three-cent fares and municipal ownership. "Boston," he declared, "should not loiter behind the march of progress." Lee Meriwether, an independent Democratic candidate for mayor in St. Louis in 1897, called upon Pingree to help him campaign and said: "We particularly desire you because neither Gov. Stone nor any other man in the United States is so conspicuous in the battle for franchise and taxation reform as you are, and it is upon these two points I am making the race for mayor." John Peter Altgeld, who ran unsuccessfully for mayor of Chicago in 1899, forced the opposition to accept his planks for low fares and municipal ownership. Samuel M. "Golden Rule" Jones, during his campaign for mayor of Toledo in 1897, received Pingree's assistance and adopted the three-cent fare and no extension of franchises as his platform. [23]

In Philadelphia a group of clergymen decided to stage a march to protest an increase in fares and the abolition of free transfers and were encouraged and instructed by a Pingree letter telling them how to beat the traction magnates. Senator Richard F. Pettigrew of South Dakota introduced a bill in the United States Senate in 1896 "to Pingreeize Washington street car lines" with three-cent fares. A New York state senate investigating committee, with a case of "Pingree fever," examined Detroit's low rates in 1896 and "saw no good reason why as cheap a rate of fare should not prevail in the cities of the State of New York." In 1897 the Indiana State Assembly passed a law requiring three-cent fares throughout the state. Finally, in 1915, the National Municipal League belatedly accepted the view that low utility and transit rates were more beneficial to the public than was the income to be derived from the granting of franchises to municipal contractors. Pingree had clearly exerted more influence on the national low-fare movement than any other man of his time. The Boston *Evening Transcript* correctly referred to him as the fountainhead of the movement.[24]

By 1899 three-cent fares were in effect on approximately one-third of the total street railway mileage in Detroit. Pingree, then Governor of Michigan, turned his energies to the urban scene once again in a last effort to extend low fares to every line in the city. He was quite aware of what his administrations had accomplished in Detroit, and it was evident that he wanted to bring his decade of continuous public service to total fruition in his home city. More convinced than ever that there was only one way to settle the problem, Pingree searched for a method to circumvent the Michigan constitution's prohibition of municipal ownership. Although a few cities, for instance, New York, had voted in referenda to support publicly owned transportation, not a single American community, in 1899, possessed a municipally owned or operated transit system. After several conferences with Tom Johnson, Pingree conceived of a quasi-public ownership scheme which would cut through the Gordian knot and bring low fares to every line in Detroit. The details of the plan were enacted into law by the administration supported McLeod Act, which permitted the Detroit common council to appoint a Street Railway Commission which was empowered to negotiate with the Citizens' Company for the purchase of its entire traction system.

The act envisioned that the commissioners, who were quasi-public trustees, would buy the system with a bond issue and would offer a long-term franchise obtained from the city as collateral. The city council, in turn, would be given control over fares, transfers, schedules, track locations, inspection of the books, and the hours of labor. Three-cent fares would be granted immediately, and the city would hold an option to acquire ownership and operation of the system whenever it desired or whenever the state constitution was amended to permit this action. The Pingree plan, in short, would effect almost total municipal control and operation without the immediate burden of purchase. Because the city would not be required to invest any money in the lines or be a party to any financial transaction, Pingree reasoned that the project could meet any constitutional test. Detroit's only risk would be to confer a long-term franchise on Pingree and the commissioners, who would use it as security for their bond issue.[25]

The transaction with the city was not viewed as philanthropic by Tom Johnson and the Citizens' Company, however, because the long-term franchise renewal was likely to raise to par the value of the Citizens' Company bonds, which had been in a depressed state on the market for the preceeding several months. The plan also provided that if Pingree and the commissioners should default in their interest payment on the bonds, the system, enriched by the franchise renewal, would revert to the Citizens' Company.

The Commission, with Pingree as president, began negotiations with the Citizens' Company in the spring of 1899 and found Tom Johnson to be a tough bargainer. As a salesman for the Citizens' Company, Johnson was willing to deduct his commission from the sale price, and he later claimed in his autobiography that he was sincerely interested in assisting Detroit to obtain municipal ownership. The actual negotiations appear to belie that assertion, however. One of Johnson's primary demands was the abolition of the three-cent fare from the security franchise. On this point the commissioners absolutely refused to compromise and went directly to R. T. Wilson, the principal owner of the company, who apparently overruled Johnson.[26]

A second controversy between Johnson and the Commission involved the price to be paid for the railway. Pingree brought in Edward W. Bemis and Professor Mortimer E. Cooley to appraise the value of the system, and they set it at $16,800,000 in 4 per cent bonds or $15,325,000 in cash. The disparity in price between the bond issue and the cash equivalent was based upon the assumption that Street Railway Commission's bonds would sell under par as had those of the Citizens' Company. Johnson opened negotiations by demanding $17,500,000 in 4 per cent bonds and a forty-eight-year security franchise as collateral. After several trying sessions, the Commission whittled the price down to $16,800,000.[27]

The final disagreement in the negotiations between Johnson and the Commission involved the question of who should sell the bonds. Johnson insisted that he personally should handle the bond sale and should turn over to the Commission $15,325,000 in cash to buy the line. Critics quickly pointed out that the difference in price between the bond issue and the cash price, some $1,500,000 would be a windfall to Johnson if the bonds sold at par. It was also convincingly argued that the depressed condition of the Citizens' Company bonds was due to its rapidly expiring franchises and the Company's general posture of opposition to Pingree and the city. A group of New York bond buyers in Detroit testified that the Street Railway Commission's bonds would sell at par with a forty-eight-year security franchise behind them, and local spokesmen argued that since Detroit school bonds had recently sold above par, it was very likely that the quasi-municipal Commission's bonds would sell at least at par. The Pingree Commission pressed its advantage and took from Johnson the right to dispose of the bond issue. With "the fat . . . extracted from the deal" Johnson appeared temporarily to lose interest in the project. He remained, however, as chief negotiator for the Citizens' Company and as an interested party who held securities in the firm.[28]

When the council showed signs of balking in June, 1899, Johnson foolishly suggested that the Citizens' Company should raise its fares to five cents to coerce the city to support the project. The commissioners, who recalled Johnson's ill-fated fare increase of 1895, opposed the idea. Changing his tactics from those of the lion to those of the fox, Johnson then advanced what he believed to be a

more compelling idea, namely, that the rate of fare on every streetcar be reduced to three cents, a proposal that the Commission approved. Pingree then pushed a forty-eight-year security franchise
through the common council over Democratic Mayor William
Maybury's objections.[29]

Although the long-term franchise was in itself difficult for some
Detroiters to accept, and although many of the city's social elite
believed that municipal ownership was the "first tangible move in
the direction of socialism," these factors did not critically affect the
outcome. The principal objection to the plan rose from the fact that
it was widely believed that Tom L. Johnson simply could not be
trusted. As J. L. Hudson pointed out: "The simple fact that [Tom
Johnson] wants to sell should put the city on its guard." City Treasurer William B. Thompson, an erstwhile Pingree stalwart, asked:
"If Tom L. Johnson has not always been an enemy of the people,
then in the name of common sense who has? . . . Since when did
he become a friend of the people?" "The Tom Johnson of five years
ago is the Tom Johnson of today, a smart, shrewd, jollying promoter," charged the president of the common council, William
Beamer. "Have the horns and cloven feet been so suddenly transformed into wings of white?" Alderman Frank J. Licht reminded
Detroiters that Johnson had attempted to bribe him in 1896. The
Detroit *Journal* asked if Johnson had changed. "Is he not the same
as always? There is a mint of money in the thing for Tom Johnson,"
it added, "and Detroit has made him rich enough already." The
Detroit *Evening News* asserted that Johnson's insistence upon handling the sale of bonds would have enabled the Company "to clean
up . . . $2,000,000 by the manipulation of the bonds" and that "all
over 90 cents would have been velvet in Johnson's pocket." The
Free Press characterized Johnson as Mark Twain's "Col. Mulberry
Sellers," who panted with avarice and screamed: "There are millions in it—millions in it." [30]

The distrust and dislike of Tom Johnson were sufficiently intense
to disrupt Pingree's municipal ownership bloc in the common council, and all the indications were that the proposed franchise would
not muster enough support to overcome Maybury's threatened

veto. Although the Michigan Supreme Court had invalidated the act which created the Pingree Commission on July 5, 1899, the fatal blow to the project was the strenuous opposition of Detroiters. This prompted the Citizens' Company, on July 16, to withdraw its offer to sell the railway system.[31]

The failure of the Pingree-Johnson scheme for municipal ownership is full of curious ironies. Detroit, in 1893, had supported Pingree's public light plant project by an impressive 15 to 1 majority, and the public had voted in 1894 for municipal ownership of the street railways by a 4 to 1 majority. Pingree had so effectively educated Detroiters to the belief that low fares could best be obtained by municipal ownership that Edward W. Bemis was moved to assert in 1899 that "no city in America is so thoroughly committed to the theory of public ownership of city monopolies as this." Neither Pingree's sincerity in support of the measure nor the efficacy of municipal ownership had been seriously challenged. That the movement for public ownership failed under all these circumstances after Pingree had finally persuaded the Citizens' Company to co-operate can only be explained by Graeme O'Geran's assertion that "the more interested Tom Johnson became in establishing municipal ownership and three-cent fares, the more opposed were the people." The press clearly believed that Pingree had been "hornswoggled" and cruelly "deceived and misled" by Tom Johnson, and this was also the view of the "Citizens Committee of 62," which painted a nasty picture of Johnson stealing a "fat" commission under the guise of advancing the cause of municipal ownership. It is understandable that Detroiters who knew Johnson as a traction magnate and an enemy of the city would accept such a charge as plausible. Whatever may be the merits of the view that Johnson was genuinely interested in helping Detroit to achieve its long-coveted goal of municipal ownership, it is perfectly clear that the ghosts of Johnson's past as "one of the stiffest of bloated monopolists" had returned to haunt Pingree's municipal ownership scheme to death.[32]

It is unlikely that Johnson, either as a monopolist or later as a reformer, was pleased with the result. All in all Detroit had handed

Johnson a series of defeats. He had failed to obtain a franchise re-newal for his company. He had failed to cripple Pingree's three-cent fare. In 1899, the final indignity had been heaped upon him when the public rejected a municipal ownership plan in which he was involved. It must have struck Johnson as ironical that he could not win either when he was for or when he was against Pingree and the public welfare.

Johnson clearly was not unmarked by the defeats that he had sustained in Detroit, and some of the evidence surrounding his ca-reer suggests that public rejection in Detroit had some influence upon his future decisions. He once complained of the manner in which Pingree had held him up to public ridicule. Later, when he was about to withdraw from the traction business, he declared: "Much as I enjoyed the game, I wasn't willing to take the thumps." Although he was flamboyant, gregarious, and often generous, John-son, as Professor Robert H. Bremner has pointed out, was "greedy too. Greedy for work, greedy for affection and greedy for accom-plishment." "I embarked in this new field [of urban reform] from purely selfish motives," Johnson asserted in his autobiography. "I was seeking happiness and I chose the line of least resistance." In an attempted diagnosis of the factors that had transformed Pingree into a reformer, Johnson wrote that Pingree "crusaded because he loved the fight and the cause" but, above all "he loved to be loved. That is what makes men 'get right' at or beyond middle life." John-son's remarks are a better insight into his own conversion than they are into Pingree's.[33]

The magnitude of Pingree's influence on Johnson can be seen in Johnson's decision to enter politics as a reformer. His brother Al-bert said in 1899 that Johnson was "going to run for office of mayor [of Cleveland], using Pingree's tactics, and all hell can't head him off." This decision may have been in the formative stage as early as November, 1896, when Johnson told a reporter: "Say, you know that paper in Cleveland which the World calls my organ, the *Re-corder?* Well, that paper is demanding a mayor for Cleveland like Pingree." In any event Johnson entered the election for mayor of Cleveland in 1901 and won on a platform calling for three-cent fares and universal transfers. Johnson later acknowledged that he had first been impressed with the idea of the three-cent fare after seeing what Pingree accomplished in Detroit.

Johnson's career as reform mayor of Cleveland from 1901 to 1909 was patterned closely after Pingree's. He used Pingree's techniques, language, and programs, and Pingree's principal issue, the three-cent fare, was also Johnson's political mainstay. Johnson campaigned for municipal ownership of gas, light, and street railways, for low water rates, equal taxation, improved paving and sewers, and the construction of boulevards, parks, public schools, and public bathhouses. This is not to suggest that all of these programs originated with Pingree, but it does suggest that Johnson's model for urban reform was one of the earliest protagonists of these improvements, Hazen Pingree, whom Johnson had had ample opportunity to observe closely for five years. Even Johnson's characterization of his opposition struck a familiar chord: he noted that the fight of "Privilege . . . against Pingree" was "much the same as the fight I was to encounter later as mayor of Cleveland." [34]

The last act of Johnson's career as a reformer in Cleveland in 1908 almost duplicated Pingree's ill-fated attempt to secure municipal ownership in Detroit in 1899. Unable to effect municipal ownership of the Cleveland street railways because this was prohibited by the Ohio constitution, Johnson, like Pingree, turned to a plan in which quasi-municipal trustees would control the traction system in the public interest. Johnson's quasi-municipal ownership plan, however, was defeated by a citizen referendum. The instrument of Johnson's defeat, "franchise by referendum," had been placed on the Ohio statute book with Johnson's assistance and embodied the same principle for which Pingree had striven in 1896 to prevent traction promoters such as Tom Johnson from bribing city councils for franchise renewals. Ironically, the referendum had finally stopped Johnson not as a street railway promoter but as an urban reformer. This reversal finished Johnson's career in Cleveland, and the agony of public repudiation drove him into an "hysterical" condition and made him "physically a sick man." Johnson, during the last weeks of his administration, in August, 1909, tried desperately to grant a franchise to a competing three-cent line, as Pingree had done in Detroit in 1894, but the Cleveland voters defeated this plan. They also defeated Johnson in the November election. This final humiliation drove Johnson into a sanitarium, where he was shielded from all public contact and placed on a "water cure" for six weeks. The traction industry, which had lifted Johnson out of abject poverty, had, as Carl Lorenz pointed out, defeated him and "then swallowed him up like a maelstrom." Johnson's defeat in his bid for re-election is where the parallel with Pingree stops, however, for Pingree, during his public career from 1889 to 1901 was never rejected by the voters of Detroit or Michigan.[35]

Pingree's struggle with Tom Johnson probably had a more profound influence upon the traction question than any other event of the decade. Public awareness and civic action followed in the wake of Pingree's efforts in Detroit. Pingree emerged as the most prominent leader of what was rapidly becoming a nationwide fight for low fares and municipal ownership of the street railways. He left his mark on the urban reforms of the Progressive period. Although not all the programs he advocated in the field of reform were adopted during his lifetime, the impact of his programs for city control of transit and the regulation of public utilities would be felt for decades to come.

Not only did Pingree's encounter with the traction interests provide an important model and some inspiration for Cleveland and other cities as well, but his traction fight forced a redefinition of political issues in Detroit and, in the end, led to the removal of the constitutional impediment to municipal ownership in Michigan. From 1892, when Mayor Pingree introduced the municipal ownership and three-cent fare question, to 1922, scarcely a candidate sought the mayorship or an alderman's seat without advocating these measures. George Catlin asserted that "the street railway question was the main, if not the sole issue in every city election," and William Lovett judged that "no other issue engaged so much public attention as this issue of local transportation." Finally, James Couzens, who consciously groomed himself as a "second Pingree," won the mayorship using his idol's tactics, and in 1922, after a bitter struggle, brought municipal ownership to the whole Detroit street railway system. This resolution of the issue was made possible by a 1908 revision of the Michigan Constitution, which permitted municipal ownership. Among the factors that produced this change in the state's fundamental law, none was more important than Hazen Pingree's long campaign for municipal home rule and its corollary, the right of municipal ownership.[36]

7

The Political Craftsman

During the years between Pingree's first election in 1889 and his fourth in 1895, the Mayor underwent a dramatic transformation which changed him from a poltically untutored shoe manufacturer into a political craftsman. His first year as mayor was a trying one, in which Chris Jacob, a veteran ward boss, blocked many of Pingree's appointments and programs. Learning from his enemies, Pingree developed into an astute politician who beat Jacob on the issues of ethnicity and reform. Pingree increasingly attracted to the Republican party German and Polish voters and workingmen, and they enlarged the size of his electoral pluralities. During Pingree's third term there was evidence that even the Irish, generally faithful Democrats, had begun to defect in noticeable numbers to the Mayor's ranks. Pingree built an effective political machine and purged his own party of its conservative elements. He changed the political complexion of Detroit and practically destroyed the city's Democratic party in the process.

Pingree's first task as chief executive of the city was to appoint representatives to the various boards and commissions which directed the mundane but important work of Detroit, ranging from street paving to fire fighting. These appointments could be made only with the concurrence of the common council, and Detroit's weak mayor system offered no alternative if that body opposed the Mayor's wishes. Ominous from Pingree's point of view was the fact that the G.O.P., despite its upset victory of 1889, controlled but one-half of the thirty-two council seats and had been able to organize the city unicameral legislature under a Republican president only because a few independent Democrats had voted with them in one of the January sessions of the council.

The G.O.P.'s tenuous grip on the council was broken in June, 1890, when Chris Jacob successfully wooed back an independent Democrat and brought two turncoat Republicans into the Democratic bloc. The occasion for this shift in allegiance was the selection of the "June appointees," who ranged from hay-scale operator to market clerk and whose appointment was the least disguised form of political patronage in the city. The G.O.P. councilmen, in their tentative selections for these positions, had committed a serious tactical error by attempting to monopolize all the offices for their own party rather than sharing some of the patronage with a few Democrats upon whose sufferance their power rested. Capitalizing upon this oversight, Jacob, with a three-vote majority, engineered a take-over which caught the G.O.P. by surprise and which resulted in every one of the "19 plums" being "dropped into the democratic basket." In the uproar that followed, the Republicans filled the air with charges against the "traitors," and Chris Jacob and his Democrats responded with a barrage of foot thumping, hand clapping, and shouting. When the tumult subsided, Jacob ran his nominees to the clerk's desk to obtain their official credentials. Jacob had cleverly out-generalled the politically inexperienced G.O.P. council in a fashion that augured ill for Pingree, who still needed council approval for several important appointments.[1]

Jacob, heady with victory, formed an organization called the Jackson Club, apparently to commemorate his victory and also to advance German-American political aspirations within the ranks of the Democrats. The "Jacobites," who appeared at council meetings with sweet peas in their lapels, rejected nomination after nomination offered by Pingree and also overturned one of his vetoes.

With his appointments stymied for several weeks, Pingree changed his tactics and embarked upon an ethnic campaign to break through Jacob's roadblock. Nominating German-American Jacob Guthard to the Board of Public Works and German-born William T. Dust as city assessor, Pingree attempted to put the Democrats "in a hole." Pingree also chose a young Polish-American, Francis J. Ducat, as city accountant. This made it increasingly difficult for Jacob to maintain full control over his veto bloc, which was composed of councilmen who could not afford to disregard their ethnic constituencies. Pingree's "nomination of Mr. Ducat as city accountant has, so to speak, floored us," said a Democratic alderman. "There is no way out of the dilemma but to confirm him. . . . If we do not, we stand a chance of losing the Polish vote, which has become an important factor in politics." Pingree's strategy was based upon his assessment that there were 40,000 Poles in Detroit. Jacob, on the defensive now, challenged the Mayor's assessment and cynically asserted that their number was only 23,000. "You'll find out when the ides of November roll around," Lou Burt, a Republican, told Jacob, "that there are more Poles in Detroit than you wish there were." Burt warned Jacob that the Democratic refusal to confirm Ducat would be broadcast from the housetops to every ward in the city with Polish voters.[2]

By mid-July Pingree's ethnic maneuver had begun to have its calculated and corrosive effect upon the Democrats. The Detroit *Tribune* had warned earlier that the city's Poles fully supported Pingree's nomination of Ducat. To buttress this, during the first week of July, a Polish-Republican club of 258 members was organized in the fourth precinct of the ninth ward, hitherto "one of the strongest Democratic precincts in the city." Detroit's postmaster, Harry C. Tillman, pointed out that the city's Poles could best gauge the political respect accorded their nationality by the shabby treatment the Democrats had given Ducat, and the Polish newspaper *Prawda* praised G.O.P. councilman Lou Burt for his sterling defense of the Poles.[3]

Already cracking under ethnic pressure, Jacob's campaign to reject all Pingree's nominations crumbled on July 30 when three

Democratic councilmen were induced to enter the Mayor's bloc. The new coalition approved a spate of Pingree nominations. Moving into the breach, Pingree resubmitted the name of Francis J. Ducat, and the appointment was confirmed. Although it had taken Pingree three months to obtain council approval for Ducat's nomination, he had learned much about the significance of ethnic politics and the techniques available to a vigorous political leader who was determined to overcome the limitations of the weak mayor system.

A second serious disruption of councilmanic business occurred on October 21 after the G.O.P. had suffered a reduction in strength as the result of the death of one of its aldermen. The question of the appointment of inspectors for the fall election was raised in a stormy session in which Jacob strove to weaken Republican strength by introducing a resolution to unseat a G.O.P. alderman, George Dingwall, on a bogus charge. Unable to control the proceedings, the Republican council president adjourned the session and hastily left the chambers with the G.O.P. members. The Democrats then assumed control of an extralegal rump session, unseated Dingwall, and appointed Democrats to every one of the city's 61 election boards.

The G.O.P. petitioned the Michigan Supreme Court to nullify the actions of the extralegal session. The fall elections were but a week away, and the G.O.P. recognized that it had an issue which could conceivably hurt Jacob and his city Democrats. On October 29 the court ruled that Jacob's rump session was an "inexcusable outrage," declared Dingwall's ejection and the selection of election inspectors to be null and void, and ordered the council to rectify its errors. The next day the council session was the scene of an uproar. Jacob reneged on an agreement made with the G.O.P. and once again pushed a full slate of Democrats into the inspectorships.[4]

In the fall of 1890, Michigan Democrats were part of the Democratic tidal wave that swept the nation. They won an unprecedented victory over the state G.O.P. In addition to securing the Michigan governorship, the Democrats won seven of the eleven United States Congressional seats, gained control of the lower house of the state legislature, and swept every state-wide office. The Democratic gubernatorial candidate drew a solid 57.9 per cent of the vote of Detroit, and he amassed nearly one-half of his state-wide plurality there.[5]

For Detroit's municipal Democrats, the story was different, however; none of the state party's political magic rubbed off onto the city party's councilmanic candidates. Almost inexplicably, Jacob's aldermen, in the very hotbed of Michigan's Democratic Party, failed to win a decisive victory over their G.O.P. opponents. Jacob's crude disregard for councilmanic proprieties, his general obstruction of Pingree's programs, and his undisguised contempt for the Poles, coupled with the Pingree administration's vigorous courting of the ethnic vote, had broken the ranks of Democratic voters. Jacob's party secured but one-half of the 16 contested council seats.[6]

Jacob was not averse to the outright theft of any election which the Democrats could not win legally. In firm control of the city Board of Canvassers, Jacob therefore decided to deny council seats to three victorious Republicans. The Board of Canvassers refused to certify Republicans Henry Schehr, Jacob F. Meier, and John Coll. The Michigan Supreme Court intervened on November 19 to remind the canvassers that their duties were "purely clerical," and directed them to certify the G.O.P. aldermen.[7]

Undeterred by the court decision, Jacob used his Democratic bloc during a council meeting the following week to display his personal power and to signify his contempt for the bench by refusing to recognize Coll's election. He was not a Democrat, said Jacob, and "We don't want him." Jacob persisted on his obstinate course for two weeks, until December 10. Then George F. Reichenbach, a Democrat, defected to the G.O.P., and this gave the Republicans enough votes to recognize John Coll. Jacob thereupon lost all control of himself, brandished his fists at the president, and denounced the court "in language too horribly profane and vile to be printed." Turning on Reichenbach, Jacob, livid with rage, cursed the defector "in the vilest and grossest language imaginable [and] branded him a traitor and a coward." Jacob's language even embarrassed his hardened council colleagues, and they called upon the president to

restrain the Democratic boss. One of Jacob's cronies then burst into
the chamber, stood over Reichenbach, and heaped abuse upon him.
So volatile were conditions that it was feared that bloodshed would
have followed if anyone had struck a blow. The following day
Chris Jacob said: "I meant to smash [Reichenbach], and if he'd
opened his head when I dared him to I'd have knocked him
down." [8]

For most of the month of December, Jacob barred his Democrats
from attending council meetings, and paralyzed the transaction of
city business. The G.O.P. continued to attend the regular sessions
on Tuesday night, and Jacob convoked his extralegal rump sessions
on Thursday night, but neither group accomplished anything.
Meanwhile, the Christmas holidays approached, and the city's laborers, who had gone unpaid for two weeks, grew restive. On December 16 the G.O.P., in an attempt to approve the city payroll,
assembled at the regular session under the watchful eye of 400 unpaid laborers. Since a quorum was lacking by one, the sergeant-at-
arms was sent to fetch a Democrat from a nearby saloon, where the
Jacobites were holding a caucus. Alderman Robert H. Murphy,
speaking for the Democrats, informed the sergeant-at-arms that the
Democrats had no intention of attending the meeting. As public
criticism of the Democrats increased, however, Jacob relented and
permitted the Democrats to attend a session on December 23, and
the payroll was approved.[9] Detroit's city council was in a turbulent
state when the first year of Pingree's administration drew to a close.
It was a distressing introduction to the politics of municipal government for Detroit's neophyte mayor.

In January, 1891, during his second year as mayor, Pingree was
determined to minimize the disorder that plagued Detroit's lawmakers. Another deadlock between the G.O.P. and Democrats, accompanied by councilmanic brawls, threatened to paralyze the
city's government. During the reorganization meeting of the council, Jacob summarily suppressed an Irish revolt in his own ranks
and challenged the G.O.P. contender in a protracted struggle
which involved 119 ballots before the Democratic boss was elected
president. Hoping to avoid the turmoil of the previous year, Pin-

gree effected a *modus vivendi* with Jacob in which the patronage question was settled. Pingree's deal with Jacob meant conceding the more numerous, low-grade June appointments to the Democrats, while retaining for himself the prerogative to pick heads of city departments. Pingree had steered the council away from the tempestuous battle over spoils and gained some time to concentrate on his municipal programs.[10]

The streetcar strike and riot of April, 1891, which culminated in Pingree's veto of a franchise renewal in July, not only transformed the substance of Pingree's programs but brought out his dynamic style and forceful leadership, and these were of crucial importance in exerting control over the aldermen. The Mayor's veto precipitated an overwhelming public repudiation of President Jacob and the street railway sympathizers in the common council. It was a painful and humiliating experience for Jacob, who was driven from the chambers by a "storm of indignant protest." Jacob failed to recover control of the council during the balance of his presidency and Pingree continued to press his advantage and cut into the old veteran's power.[11] By the late summer Pingree had overcome one of his major obstacles; he had learned rapidly from his old enemy, turned the tables on Jacob, and dethroned the foxy tactician of the city council.

By the fall of 1891 Pingree had discarded much of the circumspection and caution that had characterized his first year and a half as mayor. The municipal election in the fall tested the receptivity of the city to Pingree's programs and gauged the effectiveness of the new and vigorous political style which the Mayor had adopted in his battle with the street railway company.

At this time, Detroit Democrats were engaged in an internal struggle for power that split the party into two factions. The William G. Thompson wing of the party contested against the party regulars, led by Daniel J. Campau, Jr., and Don M. Dickinson, to elect delegates to the city convention. During the course of the fight, both sides "bribed, bullied, cheated, [and] broke each other's heads" and brazenly stole primary votes. In one precinct, a group of Thompson supporters forced open the ballot box, and discovered that it had been stuffed with one hundred "early" votes. Tension was so great that in another, two separate caucuses were held to elect delegates. Typifying the struggle was an eighth ward Campau challenger who fought for a ballot box only to be foiled by a Thompson man who seized it and ran into a saloon. It was a battle that pitted "saloon against saloon, bruiser against bruiser," according to the Detroit *Tribune*. In the end, "the Thompson bums beat the morality bums." [12]

The Democratic city convention proved to be as seamy an affair. The Thompson faction broke down the doors of Harmonie Hall, used a ladder to send its advance guard through a second story window, and seized control of the floors and rostrum before the convention had officially begun. The Thompsonites then nominated William G. Thompson as Democratic candidate for mayor. Unable to control the proceedings, the Campau regulars retreated to the basement of the hall and nominated John Miner as their candidate. In the following weeks, the Democratic party tore itself apart as the two wings of the party heaped unrestrained abuse upon each other.[13]

Smelling political victory in the autumn air, members of Senator James McMillan's G.O.P. machine moved rapidly to replace Pingree with a candidate more acceptable to the business and traction interests of the city. Dexter M. Ferry and Russell A. Alger refused to support Pingree's renomination because of the Mayor's antagonism to the street railway companies. Consideration was first given by the G.O.P. sachems to James L. Edson, a conservative and Catholic they believed would remain loyal to the material interests of his class and "would attract the support of his church." The anti-Pingreeites seemed to gamble on the fact that 45,000 of Detroit's 83,000 religious communicants were Roman Catholics and might vote according to their religion. However, Edson, an old friend of Pingree, declined to run. McMillan's lieutenants then called upon a German-born merchant, F. William Lichtenberg, to oppose the Mayor. Pingree thereupon made it clear that he would run as an independent candidate if the McMillan machine succeeded in nominating Lichtenberg. But Pingree's control of the delegates and

Lichtenberg's hasty withdrawal prevented a floor fight, and the Mayor was easily renominated.[14]

Pingree began his campaign with the popular slogan: "Equal rights to all; special privileges to none." "Let us fight for equalized taxation," exhorted the Mayor, who demanded an increased levy on the vast landed estates of the city. He asked support for his programs to force the steam railroads and other tax-dodging corporations to assume their just burden of local taxation. Pingree also demanded that the public utilities and the street railway company make adequate compensation for their privileges by paying higher taxes or lowering their rates.[15] The Mayor's vigorous agitation for rapid transit to replace the slow horse car was also well-known.

Pingree's platform proved attractive to labor. Although disturbed by the Mayor's two vetoes of an eight-hour day measure, the Detroit Council of Trades and Labor Unions was unable to disguise its admiration for Pingree's support of the workers in the streetcar strike and his fight against the street railway. During the last weeks of the canvass, Detroit's most popular labor leaders, Richard F. Trevellick, William J. Law of the Street Railway Employees Association, and many members of the Trades Council campaigned either for Pingree or for his platform. Never in municipal elections had the streetcar employees dared so openly to support an anti-railway candidate for mayor. The "Citizens Committee of 50," which had staunchly backed Pingree during the street railway fracas, formed a bipartisan committee to oppose councilmen who had supported the traction interests, and thereby exerted a heavy influence in Pingree's favor.[16]

Belatedly the Democrats began to recognize that their attempt to use the question of increased municipal taxation had failed. The only way to beat Pingree was to meet him on his own grounds and to find a candidate who was as solid as the Mayor on the traction issue. As the campaign progressed, John Miner assumed a firmer position on the street railway question. The regular Democrats spent most of their fury in assailing Thompson as a "servant of the City Railway Company." [17]

During the closing days of the campaign, Thompson dropped his low tax promises and embraced most of Pingree's ideas on the traction question—a course followed by most of the G.O.P. and a few of the Democratic aldermanic candidates. Nevertheless it was too late to offset the trend that was running in the Mayor's favor on election night. Pingree carried thirteen of the city's sixteen wards, won 51.7 per cent of the total vote, and polled 15,335 votes to Thompson's 9,015 and Miner's 5,263. Political victory apparently hinged upon the traction question. Without this issue, the Detroit *Evening News* said, Pingree would have been "as dead a political duck as could have been found in the city." More substantial evidence of the strength of the street railway question can be gathered from an examination of those wards and precincts that were most closely affected by Pingree's program for rapid transit and low fares. Pingree received a plurality in all Detroit's outer wards, which included the tenth through the sixteenth wards, and the Mayor polled 57.1 per cent of the total vote in the city's sixteen outermost precincts, where residents were dependent upon street railway transit to get to the industrial sections of the river front and the downtown business district. In sharp contrast was the vote of the city's sixteen innermost precincts (which were near the business and manufacturing sections), which gave Pingree a meager 49.2 per cent of their vote.[18]

Neither the eight-hour day nor the increased municipal taxation appeared to have any bearing upon the outcome of the election. In wards nine through sixteen, where the labor vote was concentrated, Pingree suffered no appreciable decline from his previous vote totals; the Mayor won every one of these wards with the exception of the ninth. Pingree actually increased his percentage of the vote in wards ten and fourteen from 53 and 54 per cent in 1889 to 57 per cent and 59 per cent in 1891. This indicated that the Mayor's street railway and urban reform programs had held the labor vote. In the traditionally G.O.P.- and business-oriented first, second, and fourth wards, where resistance to taxation might have been expected to appear, Pingree polled 66 per cent of the total vote and increased his margin of victory over 1889.[19]

The Democrats sustained a devastating defeat in the election.

William G. Thompson, who felt bitter toward the regular Democrats, charged that Dickinson had torn the "heart, viscera, and gizzard" out of the Detroit Democratic party. The returns demonstrated, however, that Pingree had done his share of eviscerating the Democratic party, for he had carried foreign-born wards that were normally Democratic. If the vote of the two Democratic candidates had been combined, it still would not have been enough to overcome Pingree's majority. John Miner, the only Roman Catholic candidate for mayor, polled but 18.3 per cent of the total vote of a city in which more than one-half of the religious communicants were Roman Catholic. Miner's poor performance clearly disproved the assertions of the American Protective Association and those of a recent historian that religion was an important factor in Pingree's reelection in 1891. Even the sixth ward, which lay athwart Detroit's Irish "Corktown," was carried by Pingree.[20]

The G.O.P. won every city-wide office in the election and took eleven of the sixteen contested council seats. Even in the hidebound Democratic fifth ward, a G.O.P. aldermanic contender beat a Democrat whom Chris Jacob had been grooming for the council presidency. The fifth ward boss and the Democratic party had suffered heavily in prestige but even more seriously in political power at the hands of the Mayor.[21]

Pingree's candidacy appealed to the ethnic and economically deprived voters of the city. The Mayor won the Detroit wards with the highest concentration of foreign-born residents, the fourteenth and sixteenth, where 48.8 and 50.2 per cent of the inhabitants respectively were foreign-born and where 88.5 and 89.2 per cent of the residents had either been born abroad or were the children of immigrants. Along Gratiot Avenue in the heart of Detroit's oldest German settlement, Pingree won four precincts and lost two by narrow margins. He also carried the densely populated third ward, which had the highest concentration of people per dwelling and per acre and which experienced the greatest per capita death rate among infants and adults in the city. The sixth ward, which was regarded as one of the poorest in the city, was also registered in Pingree's column.[22]

During the fall election of 1892, Pingree and the G.O.P. enlarged their control of the common council as the Mayor continued to build a political base for his programs by supporting councilmen who were friendly to urban reform. Ignoring the national and state elections, Pingree used his patronage, his appointees, and his political influence to secure the election of G.O.P. aldermen. Eleven of the sixteen contested council seats were won by the Republicans, who reduced the Democrats to an ineffective minority in the council of 1893. Chris Jacob, however, miraculously survived the G.O.P. onslaught. In the presidential, gubernatorial, and congressional campaigns in Michigan, which were directed by Senator James McMillan and the state machine, the Republican candidates failed to win majorities in Detroit and Wayne County. The peculiar political ambivalence of Detroit's voters, who supported the national and state Democratic slate but the G.O.P. municipal ticket, was evidence of the growing political appeal of the revitalized city G.O.P. under Pingree's direction.[23]

The factors that influenced the outcome of the 1892 municipal election in Detroit were Pingree's effective use of his political machine, the Mayor's assiduous courting of the ethnic vote, and the fratricidal battle that had split the Democratic party in 1891 and had left it severely weakened. The readiness of Chris Jacob's Democratic councilmen to spend prodigious amounts of energy in the struggle for political spoils and their inability to initiate and support positive programs for urban improvement were hardly political assets in a city faced with pressing gas, light, and traction problems.

A dispute between the American Protective Association and a number of Roman Catholic lodges had also intruded itself into the 1892 election. The A.P.A. blacklisted Roman Catholic candidates for public office. The Catholic Mutual Benefit Association, the Ancient Order of the Hibernians, the Knights of St. John, and several religious lodges responded with their own blacklists of non-Catholic candidates. In some parishes Polish Catholics were asked by their priests to vote only for Catholics. The G.O.P. candidate for sheriff of Wayne County, Charles P. Collins, a Protestant, complained bitterly to Senator McMillan of a "determined Catholic effort being made to defeat me." [24]

Despite the appeals to prejudice, Detroit's voters appeared to ignore the advice of religious chauvinists and opposed or supported candidates for reasons unrelated to religion. The Church's attack on Collins was neutralized by the city administration's endorsement, and Collins was elected. Although blacklisted by both the A.P.A. and the Catholic lodges, Francis Fildew, a Democratic candidate for the state legislature, proved the political bankruptcy of the religious issue and confounded bigots in both camps by winning office. [25]

The councilmanic election in the eighth ward, won by a Democrat and Roman Catholic, William B. Thompson, was another indication of the political weakness of religious intolerance and the strength of Pingree's organization. Thompson was opposed by the A.P.A., which supported his G.O.P. and Protestant opponent, Charles F. Brown. Because the eighth ward Democrat had proved a valuable ally in the traction fight and a solid supporter of the Mayor's reforms, Pingree brought in his political lieutenants and patronage to fight for Thompson's re-election. In a ward which had but 500 Catholics, Thompson polled 1,613 votes to defeat Brown, who registered 1,334 votes. A study of voting returns demonstrates that in no city contest was the issue of religion strong enough to transcend other factors such as a ward's traditional voting patterns, Pingree's support, or a candidate's general reputation or his stand on social issues. Although the rhetorical fury of the A.P.A. reached its acme in 1892, it was no more influential than the Catholic societies in determining the course of political victory. [26]

By 1893 Pingree had come into his own as an advanced urban progressive. In April the Mayor, as noted, had forced the principal street railway company to sell workingmen's tickets, and he had also won a massive mandate from the public for the establishment of a municipally owned electric light plant. By this time, he was involved in a heated fracas with the gas company in an attempt to force lower rates, a battle which the Mayor won in October. Most of the Mayor's social reform measures had been introduced by

1893, and many of them had been enacted into law. Detroiters in 1893, unlike 1891, had the opportunity to vote not for the promise of urban improvement but upon Pingree's performance as a municipal reformer.

Pingree's attacks upon the public utilities and tax-evading corporations had, by 1893, provoked the intractable opposition of the vested interests of the city. Senator McMillan, whose business enterprises had suffered as the result of the Mayor's reforms and whose personal character had been assaulted almost daily by Pingree, joined with his wealthy and conservative colleagues in mounting a counterattack on the Mayor. The Preston National Bank dismissed Pingree from a directorship, and, as noted, G.O.P. Aldermen James Vernor, Joseph T. Lowry, and Charles Wright, from Detroit's silk stocking first and second wards, began to oppose many of the Mayor's measures.

Pingree, however, had endeared himself to a large number of radical reform organizations and to an ever increasing segment of the city's working class. In January, 1893, the Socialist party of Detroit praised Pingree's actions with regard to the traction interests and natural monopolies. Damning the "blue-blooded monkeys" who lived off the people, Samuel Goldwater called upon the membership to support the Mayor and to follow the actions of the common council. "Let us work that the man Pingree may be successful," he urged. Gustave Herzog repeated Goldwater's message in German, and the Socialist Labor party denounced the capitalists who had "offered Mayor Pingree $100,000 and the Governorship of the state" to kill the Mayor's urban reforms. At Detroit's Plymouth Congregational Church, the Reverend L. Morgan Wood, who was the city's most important social gospel preacher, beseeched the workingmen to stand by Pingree. In their publication, the *Conflict*, the urban Populists asserted that "rank and file will almost to a man vote for him [Pingree] without money and without price. Because he is a friend of the masses and against the classes." [27]

During the municipal campaign of 1893, the Democratic party was united under Don M. Dickinson and Daniel J. Campau, Jr., probably because of the newly acquired patronage power that had come with Grover Cleveland's election the previous year. Determined to avoid the fatal division of 1891 and with their prestige enhanced by the fact that Cleveland had carried Wayne County in 1892, the regulars beat the Thompson faction into line and nominated a respectable businessman and Mason, Marshall H. Godfrey, for mayor. Conservative supporters who had never been able to accept many of Pingree's reforms bemoaned the fact that Godfrey's campaign chairman was a railroad attorney and that his committee was composed of "nice, respectable gentlemen, [who] are absolutely useless" in cultivating the ethnic vote. In their nomination of candidates for city-wide office, however, the Democrats attempted to recoup their recent losses to Pingree and the G.O.P., and put forth a slate which was calculated to appeal to German voters.[28]

Several dissident elements within the Republican party would have been happier if a more "respectable" and less radical mayor than Pingree could have been found. The Detroit *Evening News* specifically objected to Pingree's brusque treatment of the gas, light, and street railway interests, and ridiculed the Mayor and the social gospel ministers who supported him with its own parody of the doxology:

> Praise Haze, from whom all blessings flow:
> Who runs the city here below;
> Praise him ye preachers of all grades
> From Morgan Wood to Elder Blades[29]

Displeased with Pingree's failure to enforce the liquor laws strictly, the prohibition wing, under the leadership of Dr. C. C. Yemans, who had been soundly defeated as a G.O.P. mayoralty candidate in 1887, made an attempt to weaken the Mayor's power in Republican circles. Yemans charged that the cost of Pingree's light and gas junket had been $100,000 and that the money had been spent illegally and in a corrupt manner. Subsequent investigation forced Yemans to reduce his exaggerated figure to $15,000. Pingree then lined up his G.O.P. councilmen, who joined with saloonkeeper Chris Jacob's minority Democrats, and testified that the fact-finding expedition had not only been legal but that the city had received more than its money's worth from the trips. The issue fizzled, whereupon the prohibitionists chose to put their own ticket into the field.[30]

The People's party of Detroit held its city convention on October 7 and adopted a forward-looking, radical platform. The party asked for municipal ownership of the street railways, telephone, gas, and light; the abolition of private contracts for public works; an eight-hour day for city laborers; the approval of bond issues by referendum; strict factory inspection; and the elimination of child labor. Detroit's urban Populists were in the forefront of the municipal ownership movement and were free from the retrogressive tendencies that one historian has attributed to the national movement. The urban Populists chose Pingree to head their ticket, and vowed to back pro-Pingree aldermanic candidates in all the wards. The Mayor received additional support from Detroit's Socialist party, which announced: "The Socialists will not put a city ticket in the field this fall. The most of us will vote for Pingree for a third time as he is in full accord with our views."[31]

Although an internal struggle for power within the Republican party erupted during the city convention, the McMillan forces were not able to stop Pingree. He was easily renominated. Pingree initiated a campaign that developed into one of the most hotly contested elections of his career as Mayor. "I am a plain man, blunt of speech and action as you all know," snapped Pingree, but "this is a struggle of principles and not of men. . . . Much has been done to restore to the people their rightful heritage, but much remains yet to be done." Indicting the public utilities, Pingree demanded "justice for the people from corporations whose wealth has been made possible by the people. Let it be set down as a principle that corporations asking favors of the city shall come as petitioners and not as dictators; that they shall give the people a fair and just return for all concessions given them." The Mayor told the Michigan Stove workers that he was not opposed to capitalists per se. "All I asked of them was not to rob the city. I tried to make them pay their taxes, and I made enemies by doing so." Pingree also campaigned on the issue of cheap street railway fares and denounced the banks, which he charged had acted toward him in a fashion that would have been banned at a gambling table.[32]

In the fever-pitched campaign, the Pingree forces used all the weapons at their disposal to gain re-election for the Mayor. Political appointees were systematically assessed for a war chest and then sent into the precincts to drum up votes. Public works gangs were informed by Commissioner John McVicar that if they wished to keep working eight hours a day at the existing rate of pay, the way to do so was to re-elect Pingree and to contribute "money to fight the battle against boodle." Pingree and Smith shoemakers passed resolutions lavishly praising their chief. Polish, German, Italian, and Negro Pingree clubs were organized, and enthusiasm was aroused by torchlight parades and ward rallies. Labor leaders Richard Trevellick and Joseph A. Labadie joined the Reverend L. Morgan Wood in an energetic round of campaign speeches for the Mayor. Pingree's political aides put together a ditty which was sung to the tune of Yankee Doodle:

> Pingree's fight has always been
> In favor of the masses,
> He's broken up the ring machine
> And boodle schemes he smashes.[33]

Marshall H. Godfrey and the Democrats responded with a hard-hitting campaign of their own. They accused the Mayor of conducting a spendthrift administration and of destroying Detroit's credit in the municipal bond market. William G. Thompson charged that Pingree's antagonism to capitalism had driven business and industry from the city. Equipped with two large flood lights from the electric company and 150 horses from the street railway firm, the Democrats drew attention to the fact that Pingree and Smith had employed convict labor during the 1880's by staging a massive parade that featured a prison van filled with men dressed in prison uniforms. The Democrats liberally sprinkled the city with pamphlets in which they inquired into "The Cost of Grease for Pingree's

Machine" and branded the Mayor as "The Ass in the Lion's Skin." [34]

Hoping to recapture a large proportion of the ethnic vote, the Democrats sent a carload of flour into the northeast side of the city for distribution by Catholic priests to the impoverished Poles. The Republicans responded by passing out work orders for street gangs on a ward basis and by placing a generous parcel of such employment notices in the hands of a Polish priest in the ninth ward. The Polish-language *Prawda*, apparently unimpressed by the free flour, warned that "all rich masons are supporting Mr. Godfrey" and asked every Pole to do his duty and "vote for the man who is with the working men and for the benefit of the city"—Hazen S. Pingree. Joining the German-language *Abend Post*, which had earlier endorsed Pingree, the *Sonntags Herold* called upon German workers and middle class people to re-elect Pingree, who would "fight against rich corporations, [and] corrupt wire-pullers." [35]

When the first reports began coming in on election day from the silk stocking precincts, where the substantial and fashionable voters exercised their franchise early to avoid the evening crush with the proletariat, they were all adverse to Pingree. Undisturbed and confident that the working class vote would offset Godfrey's early gains, Pingree said: "Wait till the gravel train comes in." Later that evening, after the "tin-pail brigade" had been to the polls, a "big chunk of midnight gloom" hit the Godfrey forces as the Mayor's vote grew. When an overwhelming Pingree victory became apparent, "the whole city," according to the Detroit *Evening News*, "went crazy. No other word is so appropriate." Impromptu marches and parades were staged, and spontaneous celebrations developed and continued until the early morning. There had not been a struggle in which the people took so deep an interest and which was of so vital importance to the city in many years. At stake was a choice between the promise of a respectable and businesslike administration under Godfrey and the continuation of Pingree's uncompromising battle for urban reform. Although it was an off-year election, a total of 44,048 Detroiters went to the polls, only a few hundred less than the 44,349 attracted to the presidential contest in 1892. The municipal election of 1893 summoned more voters to the polls than did any municipal election in Detroit's history before 1896.[36]

The G.O.P. not only won the mayoralty election but carried every city-wide office and won 10 of the 16 contested aldermanic seats, giving the administration a 21 to 11 advantage in the common council. Pingree increased his percentage of the total vote cast to 54.4 and carried thirteen of Detroit's sixteen wards, just as he had in 1891, but the pattern of the Pingree vote had been significantly altered. In the silk stocking and traditionally G.O.P. first, second, and fourth wards, where 60 per cent or more of all males of voting age were native-born, Pingree's majorities dropped by 2.5, 5.3, and 1 per cent respectively as compared with 1891. This reflected the stiff opposition to the Mayor's candidacy by conservative G.O.P. elements, including Senator McMillan's youngest son, and the effort by Godfrey and the Democrats to attract these dissidents. In the outer and less prosperous wards, ten through sixteen, where an average of 65.6 per cent of all males of voting age were foreign-born, the Mayor's majorities increased by 4.4, 12.1, 4.0, 18.6, 16.0, 14.1, and 7.8 per cent, respectively. Illustrative of the working class voting pattern was the 65.1 and 56.1 per cent of the vote that Pingree received in the heavily proletarian fourteenth and sixteenth wards. Pingree was not surprised that his support had come from the foreign-born and the workers. "All of the millionaires," he declared the day after election, "were against me; a United States senator and his gang were against me; the collector of the port and his crowd down to spittoon cleaner were against me, . . . but all of the little democrats and all the little republicans were the other way." [37]

Although Godfrey carried the hard-core Democratic fifth, seventh, and ninth wards, the Democratic margin in these wards was reduced as compared with 1891. Pingree increased his vote in these wards by an average of 10 per cent. Analyzing the Democratic failure, William B. Thompson reprimanded the city committee for its faulty election strategy, which was based in part upon an appeal to disgruntled Republicans; and he told the Democrats that it was their inability to campaign on issues which deeply concerned the people that had destroyed the party's grip on the city.[38] Thompson's admonition was not heeded, however, and Detroit's Democracy during the 1890's, with a few notable exceptions such as Thompson and Don M. Dickinson, was never able to abandon its laissez-faire, small government philosophy that made the party an unfit instrument for social reform.

Conscious of the bipartisan and Populist support that he had been accorded, Pingree refused to hold a Republican victory celebration. "Success," he asserted, "was obtained only by voters setting aside political preferences and joining in a grand crusade against the power of monopolistic corporations. A partisan ratification of this victory would be unfair and unjust to our friends of other political beliefs who had stood shoulder to shoulder with us in the fight for the people's rights." Pingree asked that each elected candidate celebrate his victory privately by carrying out the pledges for reform that he had made to the people.[39]

During the municipal campaign of 1894, Pingree fought to eliminate Republican councilmen who had become hostile to his programs and also to increase his control over the G.O.P. political apparatus. He recognized that control of the party caucuses was of primary importance. Committed as he was to social reform, Pingree had few compunctions about punishing those whom he found on the wrong side of the traction, light, and gas issues. Pingree put his political machine to work in Detroit's first ward, and in a "wild and wooly caucus" secured the defeat in the Republican primary of one of his major G.O.P. aldermanic antagonists, Joseph T. Lowry.

Applying the same techniques in the second ward caucuses, Pingree brought in Everard B. Welton to defeat Alderman James Vernor. A bitter and frenetic struggle followed in which both sides enlisted "bums and bloated bondholders, bankers and blackguards, sober and soaked" and marched them through the caucus booths. Vernor's imported Negro voters were challenged by Pingree's sailors and riverfront gangs, who were voted, plied with liquor, given a change of clothing, and voted again. In the end, Alderman Vernor was hit by "Mr. Pingree's City Hall Buzz-Saw" and "was laid out a ragged political corpse," as one journal put it. Welton, although opposed by the ward's 'better people,' was elected to the council.[40]

Pingree's forceful support of the friends of urban reform and the elimination of his party opponents appeared to pay dividends in 1894, for the Republicans swept the municipal election and won 12 of the 16 contested council seats. At least 9 of the G.O.P. victors owed their elections directly to the Mayor's influence. "We elected every alderman we stood up for in spite of the opposition," Pingree boasted. He also took pride in the fact that his program for municipal ownership of the street railway tracks had been endorsed by a vote of 12,619 to 3,044. Significantly, more than one-third of the opposition to citizen ownership came from Detroit's silk stocking first, second, and fourth wards, where political opposition was taking on class overtones.[41]

The Mayor's increased political power and prestige also manifested itself in Michigan's first Congressional district in 1894, where Pingree was able to override the McMillan machine and to name a friend of the city administration, John B. Corliss, as the G.O.P. nominee. Corliss beat the Democratic incumbent by a handsome margin. Pingree also made his political influence felt in Wayne County. This had hitherto been enemy territory under McMillan control, but in 1894 Alex McLeod, Pingree's secretary, was elected county treasurer. The political magic of Pingree's potato patches had proved effective; reporters saw illiterate Poles, the major beneficiaries of the Pingree plan, going to the polls with pictures of Alex McLeod clutched in their hands so that election workers could assist them in casting their ballots for Pingree's secretary.[42]

By 1895 the breach between the Mayor and Detroit's political and social "400" was irreparable. The intense bitterness of the relationship was illustrated by wealthy tobacco scion Oren Scotten, who declared that he would "fight to the middle of hell and back" to defeat Pingree. Colonel Frank Hecker had proposed ejecting Pingree from the exclusive Michigan Club, but Senator James McMillan vetoed the suggestion because he realized that such an action would only provide the Mayor with additional political ammunition with which to fight the federal machine.[43]

Pingree had developed effective techniques to use against his enemies. For example, he directed Detroit's prosecuting attorney to conduct a thorough investigation of a liquor dealer who had vehemently opposed his re-election; the investigation revealed that the dealer was unlicensed and guilty of tax evasion. This was sufficient to silence this antagonist and put him out of business. In a more celebrated affair, Pingree, acting upon information from a friend, made a foray into Detroit's "tenderloin" district and caught a prominent Michigan Club member and merchant in a house of prostitution. The merchant, who had previously been a major buyer of Pingree and Smith shoes, had cancelled his contracts with the company and had become a vitriolic critic of Pingree. While the merchant was inside with the inmates, Pingree ordered the bawdy house quarantined for smallpox and posted guards at both entrances. The following morning Pingree casually strolled by the house, running his walking stick down the picket fence. A familiar voice called out from a shuttered second-story window. "Well, I'll be damned!" declared Pingree. "What on earth are you doing up there." An agreement was arranged whereby the shoe contracts were restored and the merchant agreed to retire from political activity. Pingree obligingly lifted the quarantine and permitted his opponent to return home to his wife and family.[44]

Because of his refusal to root out certain vices, such as after-hour liquor sales, Pingree lost the support of the civic uplifters and the "goo goos." Detroit's Civic Federation was unhappy with the Mayor's unwillingness to commit his administration to an anti-saloon campaign. The Mayor later explained that although the Civic Federations were well meaning, they were ineffectual and had wrongly diagnosed what needed reforming. The city's Christian Endeavor Society was also disturbed that some of Pingree's political appointees had been seen in saloons consorting with a less reputable element of the community. Dismissing such criticism as relatively unimportant to the cause of reform, Pingree argued that the important job was not to scrutinize the personal morals of a few insignificant appointees but to fight the "battle against privately organized greed and tyranny." He derided the society for its attempt to avoid the "rough road of life, where fierce and often deadly antagonisms are encountered" and for its failure to take up the grim and hard work of social and political reform.[45]

During the fall of 1895 a victim of an earlier Pingree purge, James Vernor, led a hard-fought effort to check the Mayor's domination of Republican politics in Detroit. Joined by twenty-one disgruntled businessmen and several state legislators who were friends of Senator McMillan, Vernor formed an anti-Pingree committee which sought to challenge the Mayor's control of the city convention and to nominate a majority of anti-Pingree candidates for the common council. Vernor's maneuver failed, however, for Pingree won 104 of the 111 delegates to the city convention, secured the selection of fifteen G.O.P. aldermanic candidates whom he had endorsed, and easily won renomination.

Continuing his efforts to defeat unreconstructed conservatives, Pingree struck again at the second ward, where he had previously deposed Vernor. The target this time was the last surviving silk stocking alderman, Charles Wright, a ring leader of the conservative cabal against Pingree and a close friend and confidant of Senator McMillan. The Pingreeites selected as their candidate William P. Sumner, an unknown haberdasher and political nonentity. "I can hardly believe I am nominated," said Sumner. "I took no active interest on my own behalf at the caucuses. The use of my name for alderman was unsolicited on my part, a committee simply called on me and obtained my consent to have my name used." Sumner was elected. The humiliating defeat which Pingree had inflicted upon Wright and the Vernor committee caused the Detroit *Evening News* to complain bitterly about the "political asexuality" of the G.O.P.'s "kid-gloved citizens" who were unable to control the Tartar in their midst.[46]

Six years of Pingree and of Republican victories had sapped much of the vitality of Detroit's Democracy and had begun to attract to the G.O.P. in some numbers an element that had previously been conspicuous for its absence: the Democrat's monopoly on the Irish vote had begun to crack. Evidence of this appeared in Detroit's twelfth ward, where the rough-and-tumble struggle for ethnic supremacy normally involved German against Pole. An Irish contingent, however, appeared at a Pingree Club meeting in 1895, at which councilman Bernard Gerecke sought renomination. "It seems to me dot I see some rader Irish faces here this evening," announced ward boss Ferdinand Flicker in a heavy German accent, "and I vant to say right here dot if the Irishmens vant an alderman in this ward next time, dey can have him if dey will stand by Mr. Gerecke, und the Dutchmens vill stand by dem." After lapsing into German to eulogize the candidate, Flicker concluded his talk with a summary of Gerecke's philosophy, which he described as, "Bread, meat und coal, vat in h—l else do ve vant?" R. H. Murphy followed with a few remarks about the German standard bearer and asserted that although Gerecke was not a Lincoln, a Clay, or a Webster, he "compared favorably in statesmanship with Grant, neither of the two knowing anything about it." [47] After this remark the meeting broke up, with the Irish contingent apparently united behind Gerecke.

When the Democratic city convention opened in late October, the party was still looking for a candidate to pit against the Mayor. "Pingree could be elected on any ticket," said the city chairman, Hugh Guy. "Most of the democrats want him, that's all there is to it. He's the best mayor Detroit ever had." The former chairman of Michigan's Democrats, Daniel J. Campau, Jr., was equally pessimistic and declared that it was clear that the masses wanted Pingree. "The Democratic party seems to be afraid to do anything," said beer baron August Goebel from the floor; "We are wasting our time talking of a candidate to oppose him. Let us vote for Pingree." Delegate after delegate, when offered a place on the ticket, threw up his hands in dismay, shouting: "Not me!" Paul Gies, when offered the nomination, said that he would blow his "brains out" before accepting.[48]

Embittered by Don M. Dickinson's control of federal patronage, which he had refused to share with the city Democrats, a vengeful Chris Jacob led a movement to humiliate Dickinson by nominating him for mayor at the city convention. Voicing a widespread discontent, eighth ward councilman William B. Thompson charged that Dickinson had "loused up the machine. . . . and hence the demand that he be put up as a sacrifice was not unnatural." Responding measure for measure, Dickinson struck back at his enemies. With the backing of his legion of federal officeholders, he seized control of the convention and foisted a hopeless and hapless philosophical anarchist, Samuel Goldwater, upon the convention as its nominee for mayor. Dickinson then left the state for the duration of the campaign. Detroit's Democratic party, as James Kelly, a politician, pointed out, was "a wreck, a physical, mental and moral wreck." [49]

The nominee, Samuel Goldwater, had been born in Poland of Jewish parents, and was known to Detroiters as a radical labor leader, a socialist, an anarchist, and, as a councilman from the twelfth ward, a staunch supporter of many of Pingree's municipal reforms. Used as a pawn in the struggle for power between Dickinson and the city Democrats, Goldwater was literally ignored in the campaign by the party which had nominated him. Dickinson's spoilsmen in the post office, the customs house, and the revenue service refused to offer Goldwater the support normally accorded a candidate for mayor. Two Democrats on the city-wide administrative ticket refused to run with Goldwater and withdrew from the election. The campaign committee vanished like chaff before the wind, and the loyal mouthpiece of the party, the Detroit *Free Press*, and its iron-bottomed, conservative editor, William Quinby, lapsed into silence. Even Tom L. Johnson, who had been a reliable source of money for anti-Pingree candidates, closed his coffers to Goldwater.

Goldwater was an extremely bad campaigner, and his speeches, which included a heavy dose of anti-government anarchy mixed with a great deal of pseudoscientific Marxist and Darwinist jargon, left his working class audiences numb and perplexed. He spoke of having discovered the "social sensorium," which neither the reporters nor the audiences understood. So ineffectual was Goldwater's canvass that neither his own party nor the opposition took him seriously. The sole contribution of Goldwater's candidacy to the election was that it forced the campaign leftward and gave Detroit's capitalists the Hobson's choice between Pingree, "the deadly enemy of trusts and corporations, or Ald. Goldwater, the deadly enemy of the corporations and trusts." [50]

Despite the weakness of the opposition, the campaign of 1895 released all the volatile and dynamic energy of the Mayor. "He's a tireless worker and a splendid vote getter," said city assessor William T. Dust. "Pingree can eat more, drink more, and smoke more for political purposes only than any other man on earth. He will work every night until 4 o'clock in the morning, and be down at 8 o'clock as fresh as a rosebud. There aren't any of the boys that can keep the pace the old man sets." Ignoring his opponent, Pingree preached his gospel of social reform and demanded abolition of the toll road system in the city, the extension of free water to all householders, the imposition of additional controls and lower rates on the traction system, and the advancement of his program of equal taxation. The Mayor pointed with pride to his accomplishments, which included a new, municipally owned light plant, a three-cent street railway, lower gas rates, a new tax policy which had apprehended tax-dodging real estate and shipping companies, sewer and paving improvements, and a systematic attack on the depression, which included the cultivation of vacant lots and public works. At the end of the campaign Pingree issued a blistering attack upon Detroit's Chamber of Commerce for obstructing rather than advancing the important work of urban reform. He pointedly asked the members of the Chamber where they had been when he had waged his war against the light, gas, traction, and real estate interests. [51]

The results on election day provided Pingree with the most spectacular victory of his municipal career. Leading the G.O.P. ticket, he carried every ward in the city and beat Goldwater by a 2 to 1 margin. With an impressive 67 per cent of Detroit's voters supporting him, Pingree broke the Democratic party's grip on the fifth, seventh, and ninth wards, which he won by majorities of 56 per cent and better. Administration-endorsed aldermen won 12 of the 16 council seats at stake in the election, and relegated the Democrats to a hopeless minority of 8 for the 1896 council session. [52]

The election of 1895 was a critical one for Detroit's Democratic party. During a period of increasing immigration, rapid municipal growth, and industrial crisis, depression, and unemployment, the party had lost its hold on the urban voter. In a city where more than one-half of the males of voting age were foreign-born and where more than one-half of the church members were Roman Catholic, the Democratic party had ceased to represent a majority of the voters.

This loss of support for the Democratic party is surprising in view of the social and political conditions which prevailed in Detroit and which should have contributed to the enhancement of the power of the party of Jefferson and Jackson. Low wages, hazardous factory conditions, and unemployment were the lot of the city's average industrial worker. Detroit was also bedeviled by one of the strongest American Protective Association chapters in the nation, and although the organization failed to impose its nativist sentiments upon the G.O.P., its attempts to do so were broadcast at every election by the Democrats. The "best people," conspicuous in the Christian Endeavor Society and the Civic Federation, were generally Republicans who spent most of their energies attempting to save the workingman from the evils of drink at a time when nearly one-half of the foreign-born were of German background and Sunday beer was a way of life. In 1894, the state G.O.P. had successfully sponsored a constitutional amendment which disfranchised alien voters, and in 1895 it had passed a registration bill whose intent was to reduce the number of foreign-born voters in Detroit.[53] The political climate in Detroit, in short, seemed highly favorable for the growth of the Democratic party, the traditional political party of the immigrants and the masses.

Instead, the Democratic party during the "Pingree era" went from a position of power to one of weakness from which it never recovered during the period of partisan elections in Detroit. When faced with the prospect of uniting behind Samuel Goldwater, who stood for reform, the city organization disintegrated. Spoilsmen like Jacob and debonair horse fanciers and sportsmen like Daniel J. Campau, Jr., offered the voters the same old nostrums—lower taxes and retrenchment; both these leaders and their aldermanic colleagues had refused to support Pingree in his struggle to secure social justice for the urban masses. Unable to accept the narrow outlook of their conservative Democratic colleagues were two notable exceptions, eighth ward Democrat William B. Thompson and state boss Don M. Dickinson. Dickinson, although he controlled federal patronage, was, however, virtually without honor or influence among Detroit Democrats, and Thompson, who was potentially an able and vigorous reformer, was unable to rise to a position of leadership until late in the Progressive period. The state Democratic organization, which had come under Campau's control, was as sterile and unprogressive as the city party. This was underscored in 1896 when the Democrats had to go outside their own ranks to get a free silver Republican, Charles R. Sligh, to represent them in the gubernatorial election. The Democratic party of Detroit and Michigan was, during a time of urban crisis, intellectually and politically bankrupt, and it remained so almost until the advent of the New Deal.

The state Republican party was even less sympathetic to the needs of the city and the masses. Although the Michigan G.O.P. refused to pass social reform measures, it readily bestowed special favors upon large interests within the business community when asked to do so. To placate the transportation, communication, and mining interests, the G.O.P. had granted them special tax immunities. In order to curb labor should it become restive, G.O.P. Governor John T. Rich asked Senator James McMillan in 1894 to assist in equipping the Michigan National Guard with a few federal field pieces "for the moral effect of having these guns might save many lives and much property" in the event of a strike. The Republican support at the state level for prohibition and the disfranchisement of aliens was clearly not designed to attract the votes of immigrants and workingmen.[54]

It was Pingreeism and not Republicanism that had installed the G.O.P. in power in Detroit. When G.O.P. state and national candidates lost elections, Pingree and his municipal party won them. The Democrats swept Michigan and Wayne County in 1890, but the city Republican party won one-half of the council seats, and the Mayor went on to win re-election in 1891. The Democratic presidential and gubernatorial candidates carried Detroit and Wayne County in 1892, but Pingree added additional council seats to the G.O.P. column and registered his third victory as Mayor the next year. Throughout his career Pingree heaped abuse and recrimination upon conservative Republicans in general and upon Senator McMillan in particular. In 1894 and 1895, when the political tide was once again running with the G.O.P. in both Michigan and Wayne County, Pingree purged the council of three of its most prominent and respectable Republicans. The Mayor had broken the traditional bonds of fealty which strengthen parties and had reversed the tendency of Detroit's voters to prefer Democrats. By 1895 Pingree had almost obliterated the Democracy as a municipal party.

In a desperate attempt to make pre-Pingree political techniques work, the Democrats had thrown two former mayors, a respectable Mason, a Roman Catholic, and finally a socialist labor leader into the ring against Pingree, and all had been defeated. The party had repeated the time-honored tactic of touching upon what it believed to be every sensitive issue that motivated Detroit voters at the polls. Democratic strategy had proved faulty, however, for the party had underestimated the power of social reform.

The key to Pingree's victories after 1890 was his single-minded fight for social reform. Although clean government, honest contracts, public efficiency, and a businesslike administration never completely ceased to interest the Mayor, he increasingly came to focus his attention on issues of social reform. Theories or abstractions meant little to Pingree. He started with the observation something was fundamentally wrong with a society in which economic and political power gravitated into the hands of only a few. Although his notion was hardly original or unique in the 1890's, it is significant that he was the first large-city mayor to make a serious and sustained attempt to change that state of affairs. Clean government, low taxes, and a city-wide aldermanic system, Pingree recognized, would not redistribute economic and political power, but regulation, public ownership, trustbusting, and the transfer of the workingmen's tax burdens to previously tax-exempt corporations would. Pingree doubted that the large corporations were sharing the benefits of large-scale organization with the consumers.

Reporters observed that issues like the traction question attracted voters to Pingree, and a McMillan spoilsman pointed out that for every upper class voter the Mayor lost, he gained a "score" among the masses. The only elections which lend themselves to testing these generalizations are those of 1891 and 1893. In the former the returns showed a much higher incidence of support for the Mayor in the outer wards and precincts, which were intimately affected by the transit problem, than in the city at large. The election of 1893 clearly demonstrated a shift of upper class and native-born voters away from Pingree, but this was more than compensated for by the electoral gain achieved by the Mayor among working class and for-eign-born voters. A study of the voting patterns in these elections supports the contention that it was the social reform programs espoused by the Mayor that drew votes to his support.

Although Pingree was loath to admit it, his effectiveness as an urban reformer was undoubtedly due in part to his creation of a well-disciplined political machine. Pingree used his machine to con-trol the variety of choices that the voter had at the polls. Pingree's purges eliminated from the Republican ticket the most outspoken defenders of the utilities and business interests and anti-reform candidates and replaced them with men inclined toward the Mayor's views.

The Mayor's machine was also important in getting the faithful to the polls on election day and in insuring a uniformity of view among city employees. "I don't care a d—n about a man's politics or religion, but there's one thing I do care about, and that's his attitude toward Mayor Pingree," said Detroit Water Commissioner DeWitt Moreland. "If any man in the employ of the water board goes around abusing Mayor Pingree, or running him down, he's going to get fired—that's positive. I won't have a single Pingree-hater on the board." No "bomb throwers" would be permitted in any of the city departments, Pingree warned, in an unusual slip of candor. The Mayor noted that if any man worked for a private firm and injured the business, he would be discharged. "Now, it's the same with the city government," added Pingree. "If a man does not want to sympathize with the principles of the administration let him get a new job." [55]

When the city's most powerful business and political interests united solidly in 1893 to defeat the Mayor, Pingree's political aides applied the powers of machine suasion more ruthlessly than they ever had before or were ever to do again. In September a new battery of health inspectors began their house-to-house canvass, and the Detroit *Free Press,* an avowed enemy of the administration, described the political manner in which the inspections were conducted:

> Health inspector: "Will you support Pingree for Mayor?"
> Householder: "Yes sir."
> Health inspector: "The sanitary condition of your residence is admirable, sir."

> *Next Door*

> Health inspector: "Do you think pretty well of Mr. Pingree for another term?"
> Householder: "Not well enough to vote for him."
> Health inspector: "This house is in awful shape. The sanitary conditions are enough to give the whole neighborhood Asiatic cholera. You must have a plumber here without delay." [56]

Although excesses of this kind were bound to occur in an administration that commanded more than 1,000 partisan employees, even Pingree's enemies conceded that there was not a single instance of thievery or corruption of the Tammany or Pendergast variety during the "Pingree era" in Detroit.

Although Pingree had no compunctions about accepting the loose ground rules of urban machine politics, he absolutely refused to tolerate dishonesty or theft. Pingree told the city convention in 1895 that he did not want "men attentive at the spigot and lax at the bung hole" but men who would advance the cause of social reform without besmirching it. Morgan Wood, a social-gospel minister, in defending the Pingree administration, explained the necessity of the Mayor's having a political organization: "The affairs of the city of Detroit can not be run without a machine; but it should be a righteous machine, well oiled to move in the interests of greatness and goodness and with the people's good always uppermost." [57] It was, indeed, the use of machine politics to further social-reform objectives that enabled Pingree to give Detroit seven years of urban reform that were unmatched in pre-Progressive America.

8

Social and Structural Reform

I

Before 1890, there was not a single municipal model after which Pingree could have fashioned his social reform programs for Detroit. Most of the nation's big city reform mayors had been cast from the same mold and had focused the force of their administrations upon cutting taxes, driving out corruption, and bringing honesty into municipal government. Pingree, too, had used the "drive the rascals out" approach but found it wanting at the end of his first administration and turned to fashioning his own brand of reform. "Collision" with the unpleasant facts of city life had stirred the Mayor toward a quest for equality and social justice and transformed Pingree into an urban pioneer in the social reform movement.[1]

During his four terms as mayor Pingree had moved progressively toward a social justice position which had culminated in the Mayor's fight for lower gas, light, telephone, and traction rates. Pingree had reconstructed the sewer system, brought Detroit to the first rank as a well-paved city, inaugurated a conduit system for unsightly and dangerous overhead wires, constructed schools, parks, and a free public bath, exposed corruption in the school board and bribery by a private light company, broken the paving "combine," implemented his equal-tax policies in the city, forced down the cost of ferry, gas, telephone, and streetcar rates, sponsored the entry into the city of a competitive street railway company and a telephone company, established a municipal light plant, forced the adoption of electrified rapid transit, ousted the toll roads, and initiated a work-relief program that had as its goals both aid to the unfortunate and a change in the climate of public opinion toward "paupers." The authority of the mayor in Detroit had, moreover, been tremendously enhanced and enlarged under Pingree's leadership.

In addition to these tangible achievements, Pingree had become a vocal proponent of the abolition of child labor, the popular election of United States senators, the direct primary, the graduated income tax, and municipal ownership; he remained throughout his life both a foe of monopoly and an advocate of state regulation of big business. Moral questions, which civic uplift groups considered paramount, Pingree ignored. The Mayor had no desire to enforce the Sunday saloon-closing law, and prostitution was tolerated by his administration as a "necessary evil." When the school board adopted Bible readings for the curriculum, Pingree vetoed the measure. "I do not believe in stirring up any religious strife among the people," the Mayor asserted. "The Jews, the Catholics, the several thousand atheists among the Germans as well as many Christians of various denominations who are opposed to the introduction of this book are entitled to the same consideration as all the other taxpayers." It would be far better to teach natural history than religion in the public schools, Pingree observed. In his personal religion, Pingree became a practical social gospeler. After having watched a Salvation Army soup kitchen distribute its limited resources to those in distress, he declared: "This is my kind of religion —divide and help your neighbor." [2]

Pingree's achievements as Detroit's social reform mayor were impressive and unmatched by those of any reform mayor of the nineties. "Men who are willing to fight corporate wealth at the present time are rare," B. O. Flower, an editor, told the Mayor in 1896. "I thank you for the work you have done for the people." In the wake of the presidential election that year, Professor Richard T. Ely advised Henry Demarest Lloyd to come into close personal relations with Pingree while he continued his social reform work to help him avoid any serious mistakes which might count him out as a Presidential nominee in 1900. Lloyd told Samuel "Golden Rule" Jones on the eve of his mayoralty career in Toledo that "Pingree [was] the best Mayor America ever has produced." [3]

Several factors appear to have been influential in shaping Pingree's career. Pingree's tough-minded sense of righteousness, his unflinching view of an honorable businessman's responsibility, the public approval he reaped from the traction controversy, his social ostracism, and his warm compassion for the masses all appear to have had some bearing upon his conception of the role of a responsible urban executive. Several of these elements had been foreshadowed in his life as an entrepreneur. As a shoe manufacturer, he had placed a high premium upon good quality and business integrity. As a successful businessman, he had imposed his will, his discipline, and a rational order on an obsolete shoe-making operation and built it into a million-dollar business. Pingree carried the systematic planning and surveying of customer wants and needs that he had conducted as a sales employee with him into his mayoralty administrations. He analyzed the quality of concrete, made engineering surveys of the sewers and streets, examined franchises, and gathered statistical information from other cities about the price and quality of gas, light, and telephones; and he used all this to support his reform proposals. Rationalizing the business process was clearly a technique that had served him well both as an entrepreneur and as an urban reformer. Yet techniques do not make reformers. New York mayors Abram Hewitt, a successful iron master, and William Havemeyer, a sugar manufacturer, were probably superior to Pingree in rationalizing the business process, but neither became a social reformer.

Pingree was an omnivorous reader of both popular and serious periodicals and quality monthlies. He read the essays and articles of Richard T. Ely, Benjamin O. Flower, Albert Shaw, and Washington Gladden; visited and corresponded with John R. Commons,

William T. Stead, and Henry Demarest Lloyd; associated with Edward W. Bemis; and knew of the work of Professor Frank Parsons and Governor John Peter Altgeld. He eclectically took bits of the ideas, notions, and social attitudes of these men. However, none of these men held a major municipal office and thus they were not able to provide Pingree with a practical blueprint for urban reform. Pingree gained the support of urban populists and labor radicals whom he took into his inner circle. It is doubtful if this radical reform tradition ultimately explains Pingree, for part of this intellectual legacy was just as available to New York's Seth Low, San Francisco's James D. Phelan, and dozens of other mayors, but they failed to heed it or to initiate programs of social reform in their cities.

The sociological concept of a "status revolution" appears even less satisfactory in explaining the Mayor. Pingree's background was not that of a middle class professional or a genteel small businessman who reacted with fear to the rise of a newly rich, uncultured, industrial class and thus stumbled into reform. Pingree was part of that postwar generation which rose from humble origins to wealth and a comfortable station in life.[4] The same was true of later reformers who followed the social reform tradition that Pingree helped to establish: "Golden Rule" Jones, a Welsh-born oil field roustabout and Tom L. Johnson, a newsboy who came from a poor Southern family, had come up through inventions and sharp deals, and then embarked upon urban reform careers. If anything, midwestern urban reform seemed more related to the dynamics of that class of newly arrived, scantily educated, urban capitalists than to the status anxieties of upper class patricians or middle class professionals.

Fundamentally Pingree was an economic empiricist who drew his conceptions and built his programs from his own experiences. Despite the fact that he was a capitalist, he accepted the labor theory of value during his mayoral years, and he argued that labor deserved greater consideration because it was the creator of all value. The idea was hardly novel during the 1890's, nor was it to be found exclusively in the province of social theorists: it was as much a part of the popular philosophy of the urban working classes as it was the agrarian philosophy of the populists.

Although Pingree's untutored brand of political economy sounded Marxist to some, Pingree's ideas were a product of his own observations of industrial life and the class structure of Detroit. He had seen Detroit transformed from a wayfarer's station into an industrial center in the brief span of twenty-five years. He had observed how new industrial wealth had taken over control of the city and state G.O.P., and how it controlled access to the highest offices the party had to offer. The old political regime which supported powerful bosses like Zachariah Chandler, a dry goods merchant, had been superseded by the new order of G.O.P. sachems such as James McMillan who stood at the very pinnacle of industrial, commercial, and business affluence and power in Michigan. In Detroit Pingree had personally observed traction, light and gas interests exercise their economic sway over councilmen and city officials in the process of buying valuable franchises and monopolies. Pingree himself had been offered a bribe of $50,000 to permit certain franchises to pass and another of $75,000 to take the pressure off the Citizens' Street Railway Company. What Pingree had personally experienced in Detroit confirmed his views about the national scene.[5]

Economic determinism was a strong article of faith for Pingree, who believed that every man had his price. When challenged on his social theory and asked why, if that were the case, had he not sold out, Pingree's reply was that no one had yet met his price. Pingree firmly believed that the social and political structure of society reflected the wishes, desires, and aspirations of those who controlled and owned the means of production.[6]

II

Pingree's brand of social reform—whose objective was to lower utility rates for the consumer and which attempted to place a larger share of the municipal tax burden on large corporations—was not the prevailing mood of urban reform in late-nineteenth and early-twentieth-century America. Far more prevalent in the programs of large-city mayors who earned the epithet "reformer" was the effort to change the structure of municipal government, to eliminate petty crime and vice, and to introduce the business system of the contemporary corporation into municipal government. Charter tinkering, elaborate audit procedures, and the drive to impose businesslike efficiency upon city government were the stock-in-trade of this type of urban executive. Mayors of this kind of reform persuasion could be found in New York, Brooklyn, Buffalo, San Francisco, and countless other cities.

Although most of these structural reformers did not articulate their positions as eloquently as Seth Low or attempt to install business methods as ruthlessly as John Purroy Mitchel, they all shared a certain style, a number of common assumptions about the cause of municipal misgovernment, and, in some instances, a conviction about which class was best fitted to rule the city. Few of them were as blatantly outspoken in their view of democracy as Samuel S. McClure, the publisher of the leading muckrake journal. He instructed Lincoln Steffens to prove that popular rule was a failure and that cities should be run by a dictatorship of wise and strong men, such as Samuel S. McClure or Judge Elbert Gary. Similarly New York's former reform mayor, Abram Hewitt asserted in 1901 that "ignorance should be excluded from control, [and] the city business should be carried on by trained experts selected upon some other principle than popular suffrage." [7]

None of the structural reformers had the unqualified faith in the ability of the masses to rule themselves intelligently that social reformers Hazen S. Pingree, Samuel "Golden Rule" Jones, or Tom L. Johnson did. "I have come to lean upon the common people as the real foundation upon which good government must rest," Pingree told the Nineteenth Century Club in 1897. In a statement that represented more than a rhetorical flourish, "Golden Rule" Jones chastised Reverend Josiah Strong for his distrust of the masses and told him that the "voice of the people is the voice of God." Tom Johnson, asserted Brand Whitlock, knew that "the cure for the ills of democracy was not less democracy, as so many people were always preaching, but more democracy." When Johnson was defeated by the Cleveland electorate at the very pinnacle of one of the most productive urban reform careers in the nation, he told Whitlock, "The people are probably right." [8]

The structural reform movement was in sharp contrast to the democratic mood of such a statement. It represented instead the first wave of prescriptive municipal government which placed its faith in rule by educated, upper class Americans and, later, by municipal experts rather than the lower classes. The installation in office of men of character, substance, and integrity was an attempt to impose middle class and patrician ideals upon the urban masses. The movement reached its height in the second and third decades of the twentieth century with the city-manager and city-commissioner forms of government, which called for the hiring of nonpartisan experts to decide questions hitherto viewed as resolvable only by the political process. Like the structural reform movement of the late-nineteenth-century, the city-manager movement reflected an implicit distrust of popular democracy.[9]

New York's Mayor William F. Havemeyer was a prototype of the twentieth-century structural reformers. Having inherited a substantial fortune, he retired from the sugar refining business at the age of forty and devoted most of his career to public service. Elected mayor in 1872 during the public exposure of the Tweed Ring, Havemeyer was a reformer who championed "clean government," "economy," and the business class point of view. Obsessed with tax cuts and retrenchment, he and his fiscal watchdog, city Treasurer Andrew H. Green, cut wages on public works and demanded elaborate procedures to account for all petty expenditures of public funds. Green's painstaking scrutiny of every claim snarled the payroll so badly that the city's laborers rioted when their pay checks got lost in an administrative tangle.[10]

To practice economy, Havemeyer sacrificed important public services and, in the process, "crippled downtown development." During a three-month period in 1874 the Mayor vetoed more than 250 bills related to street grading, paving, and widening, board of education contracts, and appropriations intended for public charities. In justifying his liquidation of work relief, Havemeyer told the Harvard Association that contributions of private individuals and Christian and charitable associations were generous enough to meet the needs of the poor. According to Seymour Mandelbaum, the lower classes and the promoters of new areas of the city suffered most from Havemeyer's policies.[11]

During his second year in office, the aging Mayor fought with the city council and accomplished nothing of lasting importance. Havemeyer and the New York Council of Political Reform were so obsessed with "honest, efficient and economical government" that they indicted every public improvement as a "job" and labeled every politician who supported such measures as an "exponent of the class against which society is organized to protect itself." The Mayor's death in 1874 mercifully ended the agony of a reform administration which was strangling the city with red tape generated by its own economy programs. Ironically, Havemeyer helped to perpetuate the widespread belief that reformers were meddling, ineffectual reactionaries, or, as George Washington Plunkitt charged, "morning glories" who wilted in the heat of urban politics.[12]

Buffalo's "fighting mayor," Grover Cleveland, 1882, was another one of the progenitors of the structural reform tradition. Preoccupied as much as Havemeyer with cutting taxes and municipal expenditures, Cleveland had no positive programs to offer, with one notable exception: he fought and won authorization for a massive interceptor sewer system to diminish the dumping of refuse into the Erie Canal. He made his mark in Buffalo by the veto of a corrupt street cleaning contract, the "most spectacular single event" of his administration in Allan Nevins's view. In addition, Cleveland fought to stop the constant proliferation of city jobs, exercised a Havemeyer type of vigilance over all claims made against the city treasury, and directed city employees to stop closing their offices at 4:00 p.m. and to perform a full day's work. His inflexible drive for economy and efficiency and his contempt for the dishonesty of city machines won him a reputation as a rugged veto and reform mayor.[13]

Seth Low, a wealthy merchant, philanthropist, and university president, was mayor of Brooklyn (1882–85) and later of New York (1902–03). Perhaps more than any other American mayor, he possessed the qualities of a high-minded, nonpartisan structural reformer who attempted to infuse a large dose of businesslike efficiency into municipal government. He was widely recognized by his generation as one of the most prominent practicing reformers on the urban scene, but he also built a considerable reputation as a scholar of municipal affairs. In countless addresses, Low argued that the answer to urban problems was charter reform to bring nonpartisanship and a centralized administration into city government. Reform of this sort would arouse a new civic consciousness and create a cohesive corporate government that could be run along business lines, free from outside influences.[14]

Under the aegis of a silk-stocking Citizens' Committee, Low, with his refined eloquence and business support, had waged an effective campaign against political spoilsmanship and partisanship and won Brooklyn's mayoralty election in 1881. Low disregarded political affiliation and based his appointments on ability and merit. Although his two terms proved to be unspectacular, Low had advanced what he considered the cardinal principles of municipal reform: he had reduced the city's debt, tightened up the tax system, and conducted a vigorous campaign at Albany to stop special state legislation from interfering in Brooklyn's affairs. Such social questions as tenement house reform and aid to the aged, the poor, or workingmen were for Seth Low but special benefits which could not be considered until local partisanship had been wiped out and municipal government had been reorganized along the lines of authority and responsibility. Low's name had become synonymous with efficiency, responsibility, and clean government.[15]

After a particularly flagrant period of municipal corruption under Tammany Hall, a reform-minded Citizens' Union, which counted J. Pierpont Morgan and Elihu Root among its founders, asked Seth Low to enter the lists as an independent candidate for mayor of New York against the Tammany favorite in 1901. Low ran on a platform of home rule and nonpartisanship, avoided the social-welfare planks endorsed by the Citizens' Union, and discussed honesty, economy, and responsibility in his speeches. Low was known to the voters because he had assisted in drafting the first charter for Greater New York, which consolidated hundreds of small towns and three large cities into one unit. Low's victory in 1901 was probably less an endorsement of his brand of reform than a public reaction against the excesses of Tammany.[16]

As New York's mayor, Low brought in experts to operate the various departments, pared away Tammany's payroll padding, and set himself up as the businessman in office. He cut salaries, increased the length of the working day for municipal employees, and reduced the city's annual budget by $1,500,000. In the public transit and utility field, Low saw to it that franchises were carefully drafted to safeguard the city's interests and to provide for additional revenue. He failed to press for lower rates, to agitate for a public rate-making body, or to instruct his district attorney to investigate the corrupt alliances between private business and politicians. He balked at appointing one of the best-qualified housing reformers, Lawrence Veiller, to head the tenement house commission, apparently because Low did not wish to disturb the conservative real estate interests. Low was willing, however, to use the full force of law against Sunday drinking, petty gambling, and prostitution, which were commonly found in the immigrant and lower class sections of the city. The Bureau of Licenses also cracked down on the city's 6,000 pushcart peddlers who were operating without licenses, and the Department of Law prosecuted residents whose tax payments were delinquent. With similar zeal, the Department of Water raised nearly $1,000,000 in income from overdue water bills.[17]

Low's tinkering with the machinery of government, his charter revision and rewriting, his regularization of tax collections, his enforcement of the city statutes, his appointment of men of merit, and his reduction of city expenditures were laudable actions by almost anybody's test of good government. Unfortunately, these measures bore most severely upon the lower classes. Low's structural reforms were also very impolitic, as his defeat in the election of 1903 demonstrated. Low never seemed to realize that his municipal reform had nothing to offer the voters but sterile, mechanical changes and that fundamental social and economic conditions which pressed upon the vast urban masses of immigrants and poor could not be changed by rewriting charters or enforcing laws.[18]

San Francisco's reform mayor James D. Phelan, a wealthy banker and anti-Bryan Democrat who held office from 1897 to 1902, was also a structural reformer like his model, Seth Low, whom Phelan frequently quoted. Phelan's program for reform included the introduction of efficiency and economy to ensure "scientific, systematic and responsible government," which was also the goal of the San Francisco Merchants' Association. Franchise regulation, lower traction rates, municipal ownership, and equal taxation were not part of Phelan's design for a better San Francisco. The distinguishing mark of the Phelan administration was its sponsorship of a strong mayor, and a short ballot charter that provided rigid fiscal controls over expenditures, city-wide elections for the council, and a merit system. Known as a "watchdog of the treasury," Mayor Phelan supported a low tax rate that forced the city to withhold schoolteachers' salaries, suspend many of the essential functions of the city health department, subject patients at the city hospital to inadequate care, and turn off the street lights at midnight. Phelan crippled his administration when he permitted the president of the police commissioners (who was also president of the Chamber of Commerce) to protect strikebreakers and club pickets during a teamsters' and a dock-workers' strike against the open shop. Although the 18 unions lost their strike, they retaliated by forming their own political party and defeating the reformers in 1901. In the famous graft prosecutions after 1901, Phelan continued to act like a "member of his class" or, as Fremont Older put it, "a rich man toward a great business in which he is interested."[19] Like Low, Phelan failed to attack what social reformers recognized as the basic problems confronting the city.

Equally ineffectual in his attempt to make New York the best governed city in the nation was Mayor John Purroy Mitchel, who served from 1914 to 1917. He was an "oddly puritanical Catholic" who represented the foibles and virtues of patrician class reform.

Mitchel's election in 1913 was the result of voter reaction to a decade of brazen looting by Tammany Hall. Like his reform predecessors, Mitchel was responsible for little of lasting importance and
did not generate enthusiasm among the large mass of voters with
his structural reforms.[20]

Mitchel's failure was due to his misconception that city government could be conducted by the "ledger book ethics of the corporation accountant." So dedicated was Mitchel to budgetary cutbacks
that he adopted the Gary Plan of education, which enabled New
York City to cram more children into the existing schools. He decreased appropriations for the city's night schools, thus seriously
hampering the entire program; for the summer program, Mitchel
asked the teachers to volunteer their services without remuneration.
Mitchel also appointed cost-cutting charity agents who began
either to return feeble-minded children to their parents or to
threaten to charge the often hard-pressed parents if their children
were kept in public supported institutions. In addition, he instituted an investigation of the city's religious child care organizations, hoping thus to cut the city subsidy; but this action brought
the wrath of the Catholic church down upon him.[21] Mitchel, although well-intentioned, had a kind of King Midas touch in reverse: everything he touched seemed to turn to ashes.

Robert Moses dismissed the Mitchel administration's efficiency
drives as "saving rubber bands" and "using both ends of the
pencil," but its flaws were much greater. The Mitchel administration and the structural reform movement were not only captives of
a modern business mentality but sought to impress middle and
upper class social values upon the urban community and to redistribute political power to the patrician class.[22]

Built upon a narrow middle and patrician class base and a
business concept of social responsibility, the structural reform
movement, with its zeal for efficiency and economy, usually lacked
staying power. As George Washington Plunkitt pointed out, such
crusaders were usually repudiated by lower class voters after a
brief tenure in office. Unlike the social reformers, who were also
interested in economy, the structural reformers had a blind spot

when it came to weighing the human cost of their programs. They failed to recognize that a dose of something as astringent as wage-cutting and payroll audits had to be counterbalanced with social welfare programs if the public were to be served effectively. Too often they blamed the immigrant for the city's shortcomings or directed much of the force of their administrations to exterminating lower-class vices, which they saw as the underlying causes of municipal problems.[23]

Unlike the structural reformers, social reform mayors such as Hazen S. Pingree (1890–97), "Golden Rule" Jones (1897–1903), Tom Johnson (1901–09), Mark Fagan (1901–07), Brand Whitlock (1906–13), and Newton D. Baker (1912–16) began with a different set of assumptions about the basic causes of misgovernment in the cities. They shared the view, which Lincoln Steffens later publicized, that big business and its quest for preferential treatment and special privileges had corrupted municipal government. The public service corporations, the utilities, the real estate interests, and the large industrial concerns all had vested interests in urban America. They sought special tax advantages, franchises which eliminated competition, and other municipal concessions. They bought aldermen, councilmen, and mayors to protect these interests and, in the process, demoralized urban politics and city government. Mayor Tom Johnson's aide Frederic C. Howe was shocked when he was berated by his upper class friends for opposing a franchise steal; they explained that the public utilities have "millions of dollars invested" and had to "protect their investments." "But I do say emphatically," declared Mayor Pingree in 1895, ". . . better take [the utilities] out of private hands than allow them to stand as the greatest corruptors of public morals that ever blackened the pages of history." [24]

The programs of the social reform mayors aimed at lower gas, light, telephone, and street railway rates for the community and higher taxes for railroads and business corporations. When they were unable to obtain the regulation of public utilities, these mayors fought for municipal ownership, the only technique to redistribute economic power available to them as urban executives.

Establishment of free public baths, expansion of parks, schools, and public relief were similarly attempts to distribute the amenities of middle class life to the masses. The social reformers recognized that the fight against crime in its commonly understood sense (i.e. rooting out gambling, drinking, and prostitution) was an attempt to treat the symptoms rather than the disease itself and that such campaigns would burn out the energies of a reform administration and leave the fundamental problems of the urban masses untouched. Pingree, like Jones and Johnson, believed that such binges of "Comstockery" were irrelevant to municipal reform. "The good people are always insisting upon 'moral' issues," asserted Toledo Mayor Brand Whitlock, "urging us to turn aside from our large immediate purpose, and concentrate our official attention on the 'bad' people—and wreck our movement." [25]

The saloons where drinking, gambling, and other vices flourished, Pingree, Jones, and Johnson agreed, were but poor men's clubs and offered the workers but a few of the comforts that most rich men enjoyed. "The most dangerous enemies to good government are not the saloons, the dives, the dens of iniquity and the criminals," Pingree told the Springfield, Massachusetts, Board of Trade. "Most of our troubles can be traced to the temptations which are offered to city officials when franchises are sought by wealthy corporations, or contracts are to be let for public works." For refusing to divert public attention from the "larger and more complex immoralities" of the "privileged" interests, as Brand Whitlock put it, to the more familiar vices, the social reformers earned the bitter censure of the ministerial and "uplift" groups.[26]

The whole tone of the social reform movement was humanistic and empirical. It did not attempt to prescribe standards of personal morality nor did it attempt to draft social blueprints or city charters which had as their goals the imposition of middle class morality and patrician values upon the masses. Instead, it sought to find the basic causes of municipal misgovernment. Pingree, the first of the broad gauged social reformers, discovered the sources of municipal corruption in his day-to-day battle with the light, gas, telephone, and traction interests, the latter represented at the time by Tom

Johnson. Johnson, like Mayor Newton D. Baker, knew from his own experience as a utility magnate why municipal government had been demoralized. Mayor Mark Fagan discovered that Jersey City could neither regulate nor tax the utilities and the railroads because both parties were dominated by these interests.[27]

In attempting to reform the city, Pingree, Jones, Johnson, and Whitlock lost upper class and business support and were forced to rely upon the lower classes for political power. The structural reformers, on the other hand, were frequently members of and sponsored by the very social and economic classes which most vehemently opposed social reform. "If we had to depend upon these classes for reforms," Pingree told the *Outlook* in 1897, "they could never have been brought about." "It is not so much the undercrust as the upper crust," asserted Professor Edward Bemis, who served as a Pingree aide, "that threatens the interests of the people." [28]

The inability of the structural reformers to pursue positive programs to alter the existing social and economic order was probably a reflection of their own business and class backgrounds. Their high regard for the sacrosanct nature of private property, even if obtained illegally, limited them to treating but one aspect of the municipal malaise, and then only when corruption by urban machines reached an intolerable point. This half-way attempt at urban reform prompted Brand Whitlock to observe in 1914: "The word 'reformer' like the word 'politician' has degenerated, and, in the mind of the common man, come to connote something very disagreeable. In four terms as mayor I came to know both species pretty well, and, in the latter connotations of the term, I prefer politician. He, at least, is human." [29]

III

The structural reform tradition drew much of its strength from a diverse group of theorists composed of good government people, spokesmen for the business community, civic uplifters, representatives of taxpayers' associations, editors, and college professors. The most prominent and influential spokesmen of this persuasion were the Englishman James Bryce, college professors Frank J. Goodnow and William B. Munro, and the editor and scholar Albert Shaw. These theorists diagnosed problems of the city differently from the social reformers. Of fundamental importance to the models they formulated to bring about better city government was their view of the basic causes of the urban malaise. New York's problems, according to Professor Frank Goodnow, had begun in 1857, when the "middle classes, which had thus far controlled the municipal government, were displaced by an ignorant proletariat, mostly foreign born." Three decades later, James Bryce, who dealt with the problems of the city in one of the most influential books of his age, observed that the same "droves of squalid men, who looked as if they had just emerged from an emigrant ship" were herded by urban bosses before magistrates to be enrolled as voters. Such men, said Bryce, were "not fit for suffrage" and "incompetent to give an intelligent vote." Furthermore, their odious habits and demeanor had driven "cultivated" and "sensitive" men out of political life and discouraged the business classes from assuming their share of civic responsibility. One of the most able students of comparative municipal government, Albert Shaw, agreed with Bryce and Goodnow and concluded that the foreign-born had provided the opportunities for the "corruptionist and the demagogue," [30] who had demoralized city government and lowered the tone of civic responsibility. The immigrant was central to the analyses of the theorists: although a few of them admitted other contributing factors, it is doubtful that any of them believed that the quality of civic responsibility, the level of public morality, and the honesty of urban administrations could have sunk as low had not the immigrant been present in overwhelming numbers in American cities.

Unlike the immigration restrictionists, the theorists did not distinguish between the new and old immigrants but lumped them together with the urban lower classes and attacked the political agencies that had facilitated the rise to power of these new groups. Even the newcomers from Northern Europe "know nothing of the institutions of the country, of its statesmen, of its political issues," Bryce argued. "Neither from Germany nor from Ireland do they bring much knowledge of the methods of free government." Lower class representatives from the wards were not welcome in municipal circles, for presumably the district system produced "inferior men" of "narrowed horizons," or as Alfred Conkling put it, permitted the balance of power to be held by the "worst class of men." "Wards largely controlled by thieves and robbers," Cornell's Andrew D. White warned, ". . . can control the city." Harvard's Professor Munro argued that the ward system elected councils that only wasted time and money in "fruitless debate" and sent to councils men "whose standing in the community is negligible." The ward system of representation was denounced by Professors Goodnow and Munro and Delos F. Wilcox for producing the worst representatives in the city. The National Municipal League's model charter called upon municipalities to abolish local representation. In Goodnow's view there were no local interests worthy of political representation anyway.[31]

In building their case against the ability of a mass urban electorate to rule itself, the theorists also drew upon psychology and history. The "craving for excitement" and the "nervous tension" of the city had a degenerative effect, Delos F. Wilcox argued, for "urban life tends to endanger the popular fitness for political power and responsibility." City populations were "radical rather than conservative," and "impulsive rather than reflective," asserted Goodnow, and far less inclined than rural populations to have "regard for the rights of private property." This was caused in part by the fact, Goodnow continued, that urban residents, unlike rural, had "no historical associations" with the cities in which they lived and thus had a poorly developed "neighborhood feeling." The elective system that depended upon familiar relationships and a cohesive community for its success was thus a failure in the city. Goodnow was also disturbed by his study of the larger contours of Western municipal history which convinced him that when city populations had been permitted to develop free of outside control, they evinced an "almost irresistible tendency to establish oligarchical or despotic government." American cities that were under Boss rule, in his opinion, showed similar tendencies.[32]

The first solutions proposed by many spokesmen of reform were hardly original. Outright disfranchisement had been suggested frequently since the end of the Civil War. Some cities had enacted stiffer registration requirements to pare down the vote of the unwashed, and some states had followed the pattern of Michigan, which revoked the alien franchise in 1894. Just as effective, although less direct, was the 1876 recommendation of the New York commissioners for the creation of an upper house with control over money bills in New York City, which was to be elected by propertied voters.[33]

The theorists, however, appear to have been inspired by a contemporary historical event. Drawing upon the Southern experience of disfranchising the Negro, Albert Shaw and Frank Goodnow suggested that such a measure might be applied to Northern cities. The "grandfather clause" apparently convinced Goodnow that the nation was not irrevocably committed to universal suffrage: once the people became convinced that "universal suffrage inevitably must result in inefficient and corrupt government, it will be abandoned," he predicted. The safeguards of suffrage, Fourteenth and Fifteenth Amendments, did not pose insurmountable obstacles, argued Goodnow. He dismissed the Fourteenth Amendment as merely an appeal to Congress, and he pointed out that the Fifteenth left room for educational and property qualifications.[34]

Accepting the Southern solution as reasonable, Shaw argued that the franchise in the North should be "absolutely" restricted to those who could read English, and "in the case of the foreign-born, to those showing positive fitness for participation in our political and governmental life." Furthermore Shaw argued that European immigrants should be directed southward where they would provide competition for Negroes which would result in a beneficial "survival of the fittest." In order to upgrade the quality of the urban electorate, Professor Munro recommended that the literacy test for the franchise should be extended throughout the nation. Universal suffrage was a "sacrifice of common sense to abstract principles," Bryce asserted. "Nobody pretends that such persons [immigrant voters] are fit for civic duty, or will be dangerous if kept for a time in pupilage, but neither party will incur the odium of proposing to exclude them." [35]

Although demands to purge the unfit elements from urban voting lists were often voiced during the 1890's, it became apparent that such a solution was too drastic. Few civic federations and even fewer politicians picked up the suggestion. Despite the prestige and influence of the theorists, it was evident that disfranchisement was unacceptable to the American public as a way to solve its urban problems. Clearly, less abrasive and more refined techniques would have to be found.

The theorists often spoke of installing into office the "better" classes, the "best" citizens and civic patriots. Excluded were labor, ethnic, or lower class representatives. As Goodnow put it, their choice was "men engaged in active business" or professionals, presumably associated with the business community. The theorists did not distinguish between big and small businessmen, or between entrepreneurs and financiers. What they wanted, as Conkling expressed it, was "any business or professional man . . . who has been successful in private life" and who was reasonably honest. As Richard T. Ely observed, the battle cries of the good government crowd in the 1890's had been: "Municipal government is business not politics." "Wanted, A municipal administration on purely business principles." If one accepted the premise it followed logically, as Ely noted, that businessmen were the "natural and inevitable directors of local affairs." [36]

The theorists argued that the business of city government was business and not politics. The "purely administrative functions—that is to say business functions—outweighed the political functions nine to one," declared Walter Arndt. They extensively used the modern business corporation as a model in their discussions of city government; some called the citizens "stockholders," and others referred to the council as the "board of directors" and the mayor as the "chairman of the board." They spoke of the pressing need for efficiency, the complexity of urban problems, and favored the use of experts to replace elected amateurs. Goodnow argued that a clear distinction must be drawn between legislative and administrative duties and that municipal departments must be staffed by experts. Munro warned that public opinion was the "worst" enemy of the expert and therefore should be rendered less influential in municipal decision-making. In short, the theorists were arguing that the role of public opinion and political expression should be substantially reduced in governing the modern city.[37]

In urging the reconstruction of city government, the theorists called for far-reaching changes in city charters. They advocated a strong mayor system, which accorded with what most of them knew about New York City politics: at least once during each decade since the end of the Civil War, "reformers" had been able to win the mayoralty, although they repeatedly failed to control the city council. The theorists also recommended that the mayor be given complete authority to appoint members to the various municipal boards. Board members, they argued, should serve without pay since this would remove the mercenary motive that prompted professional politicians to serve and, incidentally, would eliminate most of those without substantial wealth as well. If those who got their "living out of their salaries" could be excluded from municipal office, Goodnow argued, the way would be open for the "business and professional classes" to assume control of the city.[38] At the lower levels of municipal administration, Shaw, Goodnow, and Munro recommended a thoroughgoing application of the civil-service system, which also tended to eliminate ethnic and lower class representatives. A professional civil service at the lower grades, the theorists argued, would create a good technical and supportive staff and, as Goodnow put it, "make it possible for the business and professional classes of the community to assume the care of public business without making too great personal sacrifices."[39]

The recommendations of the theorists aimed at weakening popular control over the legislative arm of government, the city council. Goodnow was convinced that the council system, since it provided so many "incompetent if not corrupt men," should not be a powerful force in municipal government. Goodnow was more favorably

impressed by municipal arrangements in Berlin, Germany, where a
propertied electorate comprising less than 10 per cent of the voters
elected two-thirds of the city council. "This gives to the wealthier
class the directing voice in municipal affairs," commented Professor
Leo S. Rowe with approval. Andrew D. White argued that men of
property should be represented by a board of control, "without
whose permission no franchise should be granted and no expendi-
ture should be made." The English system which in effect disfranchised most lower class slum residents also met with Goodnow's
favor. Councils elected by a nonpropertied franchise disturbed
Goodnow, for such bodies often prodded cities into "undertakings
which are in excess of the city's economic resources." Evidently
pessimistic about changing the basis of municipal suffrage to one of
property, Goodnow reversed the formula and suggested that to extend the tax-paying obligation to more citizens might produce better councils. That failing, he supported state intervention to limit
taxing and spending of municipal governments. "The trouble with
leaving our cities to govern themselves, at least along purely democratic lines," argued C. E. Pickard, is "that they are utterly un-
worthy of trust." [40]

The theorists also argued for fewer elective offices and smaller
city councils. "Men of little experience and less capacity have found
it easy to get themselves elected to membership in large city councils," asserted Munro. Smaller councils would presumably concentrate responsibility and produce better men. The at-large election
was a favorite device of the theorists and one of the most important
structural changes they proposed. City-wide elections to the council, in their opinion, could be won only by men of commanding
presence and city-wide prominence. Obviously the lower class politician or the ethnic representative who served his ward well would
come out second best if pitted against a prominent businessman or
professional. Not until late in the Progressive period, after the at-
large system began to elect the "better classes" into office, did the
theorists return to decentralizing authority and to expanding the
powers of councilmen who then would be known as city commissioners. The ideas of the theorists make it difficult to quibble with

Frederic C. Howe's observation: "Distrust of democracy has inspired much of the literature on the city." [41]

Agencies to regulate utility rates, to investigate tax inequities, or to foster and advance social reform were not on the drawing boards of the theorists. Few of them focused their wrath and moral indignation upon the corrupting influence of privately owned utilities and the real estate interests on city councils. They were less bothered by the businessman who bribed the city council than by the machine politician who accepted the bribe. Yerkes and Whitney seldom warranted their attention in the way that Tweed did. They chose instead to focus responsibility upon the individuals who sat on councils and the political systems that elected them rather than upon the business interests that sought favorable franchises, tax favoritism, and city services, such as paving, sewers, and water, which enhanced the value of their enterprises.

The ideas of the theorists were not lost upon the practitioners and designers of good city government. The structural reformers began to design new forms of urban organization and to codify the ideas of the theorists into new city charters. Two decades of searching and theorizing produced the city commissioner and later the city manager systems.

The theorists provided the rationale for the most radical departure the American city took in all its history. The widespread adoption of the commissioner and manager systems late in the Progressive period brought about what one scholar called a "revolution in the theory and practice of city government." Although the commissioner system had its origins in an accident of nature, it and the manager plan soon became the favored devices for achieving what the old political system could not—namely, the large scale movement of businessmen and business-minded representatives into public office. Both systems were patterned after the modern business corporation and rapidly adopted its ideals. Henry Bruère, a director of the New York Bureau of Municipal Research, boasted that commission governments were often made a "part of the progressive programs of 'boosting' commercial organizations." "Money saving and efficiency" were pursued as key objectives under the manager plan. The "Godfather of City Managerism," Richard S. Childs, observed that the city managers at their fourth annual conference could "unblushingly point with pride" to an average savings of 10 per cent in tax levies in the cities under his brain child. The first city manager of the publicized "Dayton Plan," Henry M. Waite, admitted that the "main thing" the nation's fifty manager towns had accomplished up to 1917 was a "financial saving." "Economy, not service," James Weinstein correctly asserted, was the "basic principle" of both the commissioner and manager systems. As Harold A. Stone has suggested, and Weinstein has demonstrated, no important reform movement of the Progressive period was more peculiarly the captive of organized business than the commissioner and manager movements.[42]

Although the commissioner and manager systems achieved their greatest success in middle-sized and smaller cities, they represented the ultimate ideal of the earlier theorists (whose major concern had been large American cities). Commissioner and manager reorganization brought about in its finished form the structural arrangements that facilitated the movement into office of that class of people whom Bryce, Goodnow, Munro, and Shaw believed best fitted and qualified to rule the city. Chambers of commerce and the dominant business groups were the main force behind the movement, and, as James Weinstein and Samuel P. Hays have demonstrated, these new forms facilitated the inflow of the commercial and upper class elements into the centers of municipal power at the price of ethnic and lower class representation.[43] The business model of municipal government would eventually spread to nearly one-half of our cities, and the structural-reform persuasion would dominate the main stream of urban reform thought in the twentieth century.[44] This extension of the instruments and the ideology of the business world would help to return to power men with the temperaments of Havemeyer, Cleveland, and Low and considerably diminish the electoral prospects for men like Pingree, Jones, and Johnson—as well as like Tweed.

The conservative revolution in city government would also help to end the process whereby astute politicians and socially-conscious reformers used the political system to ease the shock of assimilation for newcomers into American life. The political machine may have been one of the most important institutions not only for acknowledging the immigrant's existence but for interpreting a new environment to him and helping him to adjust to a bewildering new society.

By concentrating on the mechanistic and bureaucratic aspects of city government and by throwing the weight of their influence behind the election of businessmen, the theorists grossly oversimplified the problems of the city. Wiping out lower class and foreign-born corruption unfortunately took precedence in their minds over the social needs of the city. The theorists confined themselves to dealing with the plumbing and hardware of city government and finally became narrow administrative reformers. In the process, they deceived themselves and helped to mislead a generation of reformers into thinking that they were dealing with the fundamental problems of the city, when in reality they were retooling the machinery of urban government to fit the needs of the business world.

Characteristically, the manager and commissioner movement, which represented the greatest achievement of the structural-reform tradition, experienced its greatest success during the twilight of the Progressive period and during the nineteen twenties,[45] when great expectations for social reform were withering and receding. This late triumph of good government reform was not an accident of historical timing. It was not a case of cultural lag, nor can it be attributed to a late blooming of the urban Progressive spirit. If anything, new concepts and systems of organization usually appeared sooner at the urban level than at the national. The victory of the manager-commissioner system during the age of Harding and Coolidge was an historical acknowledgement of the basically conservative nature of the structural-reform tradition. The nation had finally tailored the urban political organization and molded reform thought to respond to the most powerful economic forces in the city. In this instance it was not free silver but the chamber of commerce that became the cowbird of reform. This should not be surprising, for the chamber of commerce and its affiliates had also proved to be the greatest obstacle to social reform in Pingree's Detroit.

II

URBAN REFORMER IN THE STATE HOUSE

9

Urbanite Challenges
the State Legislature

Hazen S. Pingree's two terms as governor, from 1897 to 1901, were, in some respects, the most trying years of his life. His struggle against a reactionary legislature, elected by Michigan's 83 counties, put his political methods to a more difficult test than they had faced in Detroit. Although his role as Governor was not as freighted with victory for reform as was his urban career, he squeezed from a niggardly legislature far more in the way of reform measures than any of his predecessors had and cultivated popular support for future reforms. His victories helped to lay a solid foundation for the social reform side of the Progressive movement.

I

Pingree's decision to run for governor was made during 1895, when the popular repercussions of a smallpox epidemic propelled him into a major conflict with the Republican dominated state legislature. Because the legislature had voided reforms for which he was responsible, Pingree was faced with but one choice in order to save his Detroit program: to challenge Michigan's pre-eminent political leader, James McMillan, for control of the state political apparatus.

Detroit's smallpox epidemic of 1894–95 threw a pall of terror over the city. The fear of death, the crippling and disfiguring effects of the disease, and the city's inability to check its spread caused spasms of horror in the city. Despite the discovery of a preventive vaccine in the eighteenth century, few Detroiters had availed themselves of its protection. As the epidemic took hold in the city and continued into the winter, public fear grew to hysterical proportions. Physicians who had been associated in the public mind with the diagnosis of smallpox lost patients rapidly. A Dr. N. A. Goodwin who had been mistaken for a city contagion inspector complained bitterly to the press that he had been locked out of the homes of his patients, and he asked for the suppression of the names of all physicians attending smallpox cases. Morticians who handled victims of the epidemic suffered a similar fate, for Detroiters apparently were unwilling to entrust even their dead to potential carriers. The Geist Brothers, who claimed that the burial of an indigent person had ruined their business, instituted a suit against the city to recover damages. When a city hall employee was felled by the disease, a Police Court justice, acting under the popular miasma theory of contagion, passed out cigars to the jurors and ordered them to turn the room blue with smoke fumigations.

Detroiters were extremely tense and nervous from fear of smallpox. When a prankster walked into the detective office, dropped a coat on the sergeant's desk, and announced that it had belonged to a smallpox victim, pandemonium broke out as the officers wildly rushed for cover, shouting, "get rid of it, burn it, throw it out." It took the detective sergeant a full hour to restore order and to convince his men that the coat was untainted and the property of a macabre-minded individual.[1]

The burial of smallpox victims had a strange, medieval, black-death air about it. In order to avoid panic and minimize the danger of infection, deceased victims were normally removed from their homes during the night. Their bodies, sealed in sheets saturated by chloride of lime, were picked up by cemetery workers enshrouded in black, ground-length rubber slickers, wearing fishermen's helmets, and with their faces wrapped in gauze. After burial, the black-shrouded entourage returned to the home of the victim and ignited a pyre upon which were cast all the possessions of the deceased.[2] The impact of these almost pagan rites of death upon superstitious immigrant sectors of the city, where the epidemic appeared to have its deadliest effect, must have been terrifying.

Adding to the problem of disease control was the fact that many of the immigrants in the city were not aware of the modern techniques of dealing with an epidemic. Many Poles, according to one doctor, resisted large scale emergency vaccination programs because they feared that sore arms would prevent them from working for several days. Quarantining smallpox victims was equally difficult as shown by the case of Joseph Bilski, who, armed with a shotgun and supported by his wife, who held a kettle of boiling water, prevented the health inspectors from removing his infected daughter to the contagion hospital. Under these conditions the isolation of carriers became almost impossible. There was also a strong strain of peasant fatalism among the Poles, who accepted the epidemic as inevitable and resisted efforts to check it. The assumption was that the sooner the disease had run its course, the sooner the city would be rid of it.[3]

The internment of patients in the city's contagion hospital was viewed by many as a death sentence. Isolation was the sole function of the "pest house" or "death house," for there was little that medical science could do during the 1890's to cure the disease once contracted, except to comfort the patient. "Frightful" charges of willful incompetence and negligence were hurled at the city health commissioner, Dr. Duncan McLeod, who was accused of direct responsibility for the death of patients and charged with "murder" by an irresponsible city press. In one typical instance, it played up the story of a smallpox patient who expired unnoticed in the "pest house" and was left to lie there for two hours between two live patients, and implied that McLeod was responsible for these conditions. Reporters worked feverishly to pin the onus of guilt for the epidemic upon McLeod. When they lacked factual evidence of wrongdoing, they readily fabricated it. Stories of McLeod's alleged diagnosis of a case of smallpox as chickenpox or his failure to post a quarantine sign rapidly enough to suit the reporters were published under large headlines. The hysteria of the times clearly called for a scapegoat, and the city's press was not averse to finding one.[4]

On January 26, 1895, the Detroit *Evening News* added up the contagion lists and the death tolls which the press had been publishing for the previous six months and concluded that the city had experienced 200 cases of smallpox and 45 deaths from the disease. All Detroit's daily newspapers, the city's medical society, the silk stocking elements, and countless citizens from all walks of life, including many of Pingree's allies, demanded that the Mayor fire McLeod. Headlines which proclaimed: "Patients at the Pest House Crying For Want of Attention" and serpent-of-death cartoons which depicted the Mayor as shielding the evils of "McLeodism" behind the shabby pretense of home rule began to have their effect upon Pingree's popularity in Detroit.[5]

By January, 1895, the smallpox epidemic was no longer a municipal question but had moved to the state house, which the McMillan machine ruled and where many of Pingree's bitterest political opponents saw a superb opportunity to curb the power of Detroit's "Tartar," if not to kill him politically. In a fit of anger, state Senator William G. Thompson, who had miraculously survived the Pingree purge of 1894, warned, "Ping, we'll build a fence around you at Lansing so high that you won't know where you are."[6] With the co-operation of the McMillan machine, Thompson began a deft job of political alchemy which transformed the fear of smallpox into one of the most virulent "Ripper" and anti-Pingree sessions that the state experienced during the 1890's.

Pingree played into the hands of his enemies by committing two serious blunders. First, he failed to fire McLeod, who had become a liability to the city administration. During the early stages of the epidemic, Pingree had asked for McLeod's resignation, but the Mayor had not pressed the point, and the Health

Commissioner remained at his job. Later, when condemnation of McLeod was almost universal, Pingree refused to discharge him and staked the prestige of his administration on his retention. Pingree's decision baffled his friends, and the president of the Civic Federation, the Reverend D. D. MacLaurin, warned him that he would destroy much of his good work if he stuck perversely to his course. The Mayor offered little explanation for his obduracy other than the fact that McLeod was an underdog and that Pingree could not desert a friend in need.[7] What Pingree failed to recognize were the limits of personal power. Even he could not save the much-criticized McLeod. Disease and death are seldom amenable to political persuasion, as Pingree would discover.

Pingree's second serious blunder was his attempt to recast the smallpox question in terms of home rule and to call for public support on this basis. He adopted this tactic in an effort to stop Thompson, who, capitalizing upon the epidemic hysteria, was sponsoring a bill in the state senate which would deprive Detroit's Mayor of the power to appoint the health commissioner and the Board of Health and would abolish the city council's control over appropriations to the agency. Thompson saw his measure as the first installment of a "Ripper" movement aimed at the destruction of Pingree's political power. Failing to see Thompson's over-all design, Pingree was confident that he could convoke a massive rally in Detroit to support his home-rule proposals and to serve as a mandate for his policies. He had used such public gatherings in the past to crush his enemies and to coerce councilmen into supporting his reforms. Rejecting the advice of his closest aides that smallpox was not an issue he could control, Pingree rented an auditorium and waited for his mandate.[8]

The home rule rally turned into a bitter rout for Pingree. Many of his erstwhile allies in the council, reformist clergymen D. D. MacLaurin and L. Morgan Wood and Democratic state boss Don M. Dickinson, all of whom had stood with the Mayor during his fiercest battles, declared themselves unavailable to speak in his behalf. The same unwillingness to give or ask quarter which had always sustained Pingree during a time of crisis governed his actions now as he sought total victory but risked the possibility of total defeat. Brushing aside many of the portents of disaster which would have deterred a more reflective man, Pingree led his city hall contingent into the auditorium.[9]

The Mayor was unaware that the hall had been packed in advance by Detroit's "best" citizens of both parties, most of the city's physicians, and representatives of the various economic interests and their followers. The first rows were filled with medical students armed with horns instructed by Alderman Charles Wright to greet every remark by the Mayor with blaring. When Pingree attempted to present his resolution for home rule, he was booed, hooted at, and howled down for nearly two hours. One journalist noted that at times it seemed as if everyone of the 4,000 persons assembled was on his feet and shrieking at the top of his lungs. Pingree "went off the handle" and cursed his traducers in unrestrained fashion, while his enemies mounted chairs and led derisive chants. Shouts of "Ping, Ping, Small-pox Ping" and "Hang" McLeod drowned out every attempt of the Mayor to make himself heard over the uproar. During a pushing and shoving match to control the speaker's stand, William G. Thompson made a rush at Pingree but was stopped by the police. When the exhausted audience hesitated to catch its breath, state Representative John Atkinson correctly charged that many of those present "would like to have the number of smallpox cases doubled just in order to score against Pingree." Pingree was stunned by his first public repudiation.[10]

Pingree had discovered himself and his reform programs during a heated mass rally over the traction-franchise fracas of 1891, and now in 1895, ironically, the wheel of history had come to a full circle: a protest meeting had censured Pingree. Speculation was rife that Pingree's political career was approaching its end. For the first time in his public career, Pingree seemed to have lost his optimism and his confidence in himself. "I stand here today alone and friendless," he told the state legislature on February 14, and people tell me that "I have killed myself beyond redemption." Belatedly Pingree recognized the colossal proportions of his blunder. "The Doctor [McLeod]," the Mayor wrote, "was the whip with which I was to be lashed until I would cry for mercy, or the end gained of passing in Lansing a measure which I opposed." [11]

Thompson and the G.O.P. Wayne County delegation returned to Lansing with headline-making evidence that Detroit's master craftsman of politics had met defeat. Pingree seemed to be shorn of support after January 26, when Thompson and the state senate, with the public blessing of Senator McMillan, came within an ace of destroying Pingree's political power and severely damaging self-government in Detroit. Thompson's health bill passed with hardly a dissent. This was followed by a voter re-registration bill, which, it was estimated, would disfranchise at least 25 per cent of the foreign-born voters in Detroit. "I've driven the last nail into Mayor Pingree's coffin," announced its sponsor, Representative John A. Mathews. "It will take off the books just about enough Pingree votes to prevent his ever becoming mayor again." [12]

Continuing its course, the legislature then passed an act which required the Mayor to fill vacancies on the various city boards within fifteen days after the term of office of the incumbents had come to an end, thus putting an end to Pingree's practice of holding incumbents in office beyond their terms but without reappointing them in the expectation that this would ensure their loyalty to the administration. The actions Pingree had taken to introduce a "federal plan" or municipal "cabinet," thus to concentrate municipal authority and establish lines of responsibility, were overturned. Lastly, the legislature pushed through an anti-fusion law. This statute, which prohibited a candidate's name from appearing on two separate party tickets, was intended to stop Pingree from ever again accepting a Populist nomination or from using Populist support as a lever to force his renomination at G.O.P. conventions. [13]

The anti-Pingreeites also attempted to pass bills to prevent

Pingree from running for a fourth term, deprive him of the power to appoint members of Detroit's Fire Commission, Board of Public Works, Water Commission, create a bicameral school board one of whose branches would be appointed by the governor, and extend the term of the city's chief legal adviser for an additional year. This would have deprived Pingree of the power to dismiss an official whom he believed had compromised the city's best interests in his dealings with the street railway company. Every one of these measures was calculated to undercut the Mayor's authority and to weaken the Detroit voters' tenuous and indirect grip on municipal commissions. Self-government in Detroit was placed in serious peril. "The McMillan legislature," asserted the Detroit *Sun*, "has spent more time on measures to defeat Pingree . . . than has been devoted altogether to all the other measures which have been considered." Actually, however, although Senator McMillan permitted his stalwarts to pass the first four anti-Pingree bills, he withdrew his support from the other measures noted, and they failed to pass.[14]

The anti-Pingreeites also fought for a bill which would have hampered the expansion of the administration sponsored three-cent street railway in Detroit by requiring the consent of every abutting property holder before a single rail could be laid upon any street. The measure failed to be enacted not because of Pingree's political influence, which was at its nadir in the spring of 1895, but probably because Tom Johnson of the Citizens' Company planned to expand his line and did not wish to be hampered by a "spite" law passed to injure Pingree.[15]

The legislature systematically rejected some sixty bills (many of which Pingree had championed) to strengthen the regulation of the state's railroads and increase the taxes imposed upon them. Of the three innocuous bills passed, the railroads objected to one which provided for interchangeable passenger tickets, and that measure was pocket vetoed by Michigan's faithful business watchdog, G.O.P. Governor John T. Rich. Pingree sarcastically observed that "farmer" Rich had stirred but twice from his bucolic torpor, once to kill an appropriation bill which would have provided $25,000 for a publicly owned light plant on the University of Michigan campus and the second time to support a $116,000 appropriation for a home for the feeble-minded. Pingree quipped that Rich apparently loved darkness more than light and suggested that in his sponsorship of the bill to aid the feeble-minded, the Governor certainly recognized his own.[16]

When the legislature adjourned its biennial session in May, 1895, the Detroit *Evening News* called for a "genuine patriotic blowout" to celebrate the end of one of the worst legislative sessions the state had ever seen. Pingree's invocation to the city council asked that "God grant that we may never be cursed with another lot of so-called representatives like those who bartered the people's rights. . . ." Pingree referred to the body as the "skunk legislature" and called it a "heap of bribery compost." When Governor John Rich appeared before Detroit's Michigan Club to defend the achievements of his administration, the *Evening News* entitled his speech "The Explosion of a Bladder." [17]

What had begun with a smallpox epidemic in 1894 had ended as a bitter anti-Pingree and anti-home rule movement in 1895. It had revealed to Pingree how vulnerable his municipal machine and his urban reform programs were to attack from Lansing. Unleashed temporarily by Senator McMillan, the legislature had destroyed much of the home rule that Detroit had slowly achieved over the decades. Although McMillan had stopped the "Ripper" assault when he perceived that public opinion had changed from support to opposition, he had demonstrated that regular Republicans could use the state house to impose control upon the city and discipline political mavericks. Pingree had to face the real possibility that the next McMillan legislature might repeat or even improve upon the performance of its predecessor. The lesson of the "Ripper" session was clear: if Pingree hoped to protect his urban achievements and press his reform programs further, he would have to control the state house. By the fall of 1895, the Mayor's hat was in the gubernatorial ring.

Pingree's earlier efforts to secure the gubernatorial nomination in 1892 and 1894 had provided him with the necessary experience to wage a strong campaign for the office in 1896. He launched a vigorous pre-convention campaign aimed at winning support for his nomination. Especially attractive to labor in the state was Pingree's effort to force arbitration in the Pullman strike and his condemnation of President Cleveland's dispatch of federal troops to Chicago during the strike. Pingree offered the voters positive programs that demanded state regulation of the railroads and imposition of additional taxes upon the lines. He called for an equalization of the tax burden between individuals and corporations, supported an income tax, and demanded vigorous antitrust action. Closing each address with a plea for both Democrats and Republicans to pack the G.O.P. caucuses and elect Pingree delegates, the Mayor encouraged the widespread belief that if he were denied the Republican nomination, he would bolt to a third party or to the Democrats.[18]

The evidence indicates that Senator James McMillan capitulated to the widespread G.O.P. view that Pingree would be needed to carry Michigan for William McKinley's election, but McMillan found the thought of a Pingree nomination politically embarrassing. He resolved his problem by resigning the state chairmanship, which he had held for the past decade, and passing it on to the politically inexperienced Dexter M. Ferry. This left the party confused and without an effective leader. Some Detroit businessmen whose economic interest had suffered at Pingree's hands sought to rid the city of Pingree and worked for his nomination.[19] Nevertheless, Pingree's immense popularity with the masses was the key to his nomination.

At the state convention in early August, the Rich forces and the state central committee under Dexter Ferry made a futile effort to stop Pingree, but he was nominated on the fourth ballot. In accepting the nomination, Pingree refused to embrace either the national or the state G.O.P. money planks, both of which, in effect, endorsed the gold standard, and he left the convention to campaign for his soft money, railroad regulation, and equal tax heresies. Pingree campaigned with a greater sense of confidence and unrestrained exuberance than he had ever exhibited in his mayoral campaigns, and he made no effort to check his political lieutenants who were calling for a Pingree-Bryan vote. The party made a final effort to discipline Detroit's maverick by denying him financial support.[20]

When the vote began coming in on November 3, the early afternoon count in Detroit revealed that the silk stocking residents in the first, second, and fourth wards were cutting Pingree as badly as they had during the mayoralty elections, but later in the evening, when the working class vote began mounting, the trend reversed itself. The Detroit and Wayne County totals showed that Pingree had polled 41,068 votes to his Democratic opponent's 21,961, while Presidential nominee McKinley had garnered but 36,400 votes to Bryan's 26,231. The same pattern occurred at the state-wide level, where Pingree led the party and amassed 304,431 votes to his opponent's 221,022, in comparison to McKinley's 293,336 to 237,166 victory over Bryan. Only once before had a Michigan G.O.P. gubernatorial candidate outpolled his party's Presidential nominee. In addition to his dynamic campaign at the state level, Pingree had worked diligently for the election of a Republican council in Detroit; prominent among those Democrats whom the Pingree machine helped to defeat was the Mayor's old enemy, John Chris Jacob.[21]

Pingree's election as governor in 1896 signalled the end of farmer-oriented executives in Michigan. "Farmer" Winans and "farmer" Rich had sat in the governor's chair for the previous six years, partly as the result of the widespread agrarian distress of the late 1880's and 1890's, but they were the last of their breed. An urban reformer had moved to the state house to defend his achievements in Detroit and to extend his programs to a larger constituency. The politics of smallpox, ironically, had run an unpredictable course.

II

With Jeffersonian simplicity, Pingree avoided what he called "flapdoodle" and took the gubernatorial oath of office on January 12, 1897, in a modest, unceremonious fashion. When he was in-

augurated, he was the nation's only Governor-Mayor, since he
had refused to relinquish control of his Detroit office. "I was
elected on the street railway issue, and am going to stay mayor
until it is settled," he announced.[22]

Since Pingree's political and business opponents had no intention of putting up with him as Mayor while he also served as
Governor, they instituted legal proceedings to force him to resign his municipal office. After three months of litigation, the
Michigan Supreme Court, in March, 1897, ousted Pingree from
his Detroit position and declared the mayor's seat vacant. Senator McMillan, who had been unable to purge Pingree for six
years, told his son, William, "Well I see Pingree is down for
once," and added pessimistically, "but I presume this *blow* will
help him in some way." [23]

Even though he had been evicted from his seat of power in
Detroit, Pingree sought as Governor to advance the cause of
urban reform. He fought vigorously but unsuccessfully for legislation to permit the sale of public power to private consumers, to
install a "federal system" and "little cabinet" and thereby centralize municipal responsibility under the mayor, for a new charter
which would permit Detroit to regulate utility rates, and for an
improved primary election law. A liberal public works bill which
authorized the city to engage in city street paving was passed. So
was the Eikhoff home rule bill, which empowered the Detroit
electorate as well as the state legislature to initiate charter
changes. Pingree also pressed through the state legislature a
quasi-municipal ownership bill for Detroit's street railways, but
the Michigan Supreme Court ruled the measure unconstitu-
tional. Since Pingree had learned as mayor that state "ripper"
laws could destroy municipal reforms as rapidly as they were
implemented, he persuaded his legislative supporters to quash
such measures whenever they were brought forward.[24]

Resolving to make the problem of equalizing taxation "the
principal effort" of his administration, Pingree directed the legislature to tackle the worst of the "tax dodgers," the railroads.
These corporations, he pointed out in May, 1897, paid but one-

tenth of the rate of taxes paid by all other citizens, with the depot companies contributing even a smaller proportion, one-fifteenth. "Every change in the system of taxation from 1869 to the present time," Pingree told the legislature, "has resulted in decreasing the proportion of taxes paid by railroads," while the burden of taxation on others had "enormously increased." In lieu of the payment of a property tax and other state and local taxes, the lines had initially paid a ½ to 1 per cent tax upon capital stock; this was replaced in 1869 with a 1½ per cent tax on gross earnings for the "general law" roads. Despite a tremendous increase in the number of lines, the volume of business, and the size of profits, the proportion of taxes paid by the railroads to the state had dropped precipitously from 72 per cent of all state taxes paid in 1855 to 35 per cent in 1870 and then to a meager 22 per cent in 1895.[25]

Michigan's "specific tax," or gross earnings tax, had "worked disastrously" against the state and had opened the "door for fraud" against which there were no safeguards, Pingree informed the Senate. Not only did the state lack the power to inspect the books of the carriers, but it had to rely completely upon the roads for a report of expenses and profits before a specific tax could be levied. Loading expense accounts, the Governor pointed out, was easy to accomplish, and interstate roads, for tax purposes, could simply juggle their accounts to register higher costs and lower profits in Michigan. The specific tax had been grossly abused by lines, such as the Chicago and North Western, which had computed their gross income in such a fashion as to show a smaller percentage of profits originating in Michigan than was actually the case, thereby decreasing their tax payments to the state. In addition, the specific tax exemptions granted in 1891 had permitted six roads, worth $15,000,000, to escape taxation completely despite the fact that some of them were subsidiaries of profit-making systems. Clever bookkeeping alterations of the earnings statements by parent firms could easily wipe out the state tax liabilities of branch lines. Although Michigan had 1300 more miles of railroads than Indiana, the

state collected but $740,000 in taxation annually from the rail-
roads in comparison to Indiana's annual income of $2,250,000
from this source. Michigan's system of self-taxation for the railroads was "robbery under the name of legislation," Pingree told
the lawmakers.[26]

The Michigan Central, politically most influential of the state's
roads, had hoodwinked the legislature in 1893 by ostensibly sur-
rendering its charter-guaranteed capital stock tax provision to
come under the specific tax system. At that time, the public had
been led to believe that Michigan Central's voluntary change to
the gross earnings system was a genuine concession favorable to
the taxpayers. The public, however, had been deceived, asserted
Pingree. His study of the tax reports revealed that Michigan
Central had paid only $145,000 in taxes in 1895 as compared to
the $190,000 it would have had to pay under the capital stock tax
provision. By 1897 the Michigan Central had saved itself more
than $200,000 in taxes by converting to the specific tax.[27] The
Michigan Central was not content to live under the gross earn-
ing system, however; when self-interest dictated in 1899, the firm
refused to pay its taxes and announced that it would return to
the capital stock tax. The carrier apparently believed that it
could accept or reject state tax laws as it saw fit.[28] Perhaps more
than those of any other line, the irresponsible actions of the
Michigan Central provided Pingree with the kind of ammunition
he needed to fight against the inequalities of the tax system.

The Michigan legislature that Pingree faced in 1897 was over-
whelmingly Republican and was not favorably disposed to reform;
like its G.O.P. predecessors in 1893 and 1895, it was a bulwark of
conservatism. During the biennial session of 1897, Pingree worked
vigorously with his legislative allies to advance his equal taxation
and other reform programs. He attempted to secure the passage of
a railroad rate regulation bill to slash Upper Peninsula passenger
fares by 25 per cent since they were double those of the Lower
Peninsula. The measure failed to pass. The Governor also set into
motion a suit to compel the Michigan Central to surrender its
charter-granted three-cent rate and to force the line to sell tickets

priced at two cents per mile, the practice of most of the state's carriers. But the courts sided against the Governor.[29]

With great effort, the Pingree administration pushed bills through the lower house to provide for the payment of franchise fees by public service corporations, to promote stiffer factory inspection and regulation of child and female labor, to prevent adulteration and fraud in the manufacture and sale of food, to grant Detroit a modern charter and Wyandotte the right to operate its municipal power plant, to create commissions for the regulation of interest rates, banks, insurance companies, and savings and loan associations, and to repeal toll road charters and the special charter privileges of the Michigan Central Railroad. Every reform measure, however, was quashed by the Senate. Only Pingree's executive order forbidding state administrative officials from accepting free railroad passes went unchallenged in the Senate.[30]

The key measure in Pingree's reform program was the application of equal taxation to railroad, express, telephone, and telegraph companies. The fight for his bill was directed in the lower house by the deft parliamentarian Representative John Atkinson, whom the Governor called the "head and brains" of the floor fight. At Pingree's request, Atkinson had drafted a measure which abolished the entire specific tax system and subjected all corporations to an ad valorem tax that compelled them to share the tax load equally with all the state's taxpayers. The measure also provided for a careful assessment of all railroad property by a state commission that would presumably be immune to the pressures that often corrupted local assessors. After a heated debate, the Atkinson bill failed to clear the House. Meanwhile, Pingree began making speeches, collecting petitions, gathering public support, and using his patronage power to force some kind of reform bill out of the legislature.[31]

The Senate responded by passing the Merriman bill, which coupled the continuation of the gross earnings system with a trivial tax increase upon the roads. The bill, according to Senator George W. Merriman's former secretary, had been "created in the interest of the railroads, and at their dictation, and on their own terms." Under Pingree's direction, Atkinson led the House in doubling the rates in the Merriman bill, and a conference committee was then designated to work out a compromise. When the House Senate conference committee met, railroad lobbyists Schuyler Olds and Harrison Geer, in a brazen display of influence peddling, were able to secure the defeat of the House increases. The committee chairman flitted back and forth from the conference room like an errand boy to confer with Olds, presumably to incorporate railroad demands into the compromise. Geer boldly prowled the Senate floor in shoring up railroad alliances. All the tax increases were reduced to their original low levels, and the bill was emasculated of its meaningful reform features.[32]

Pingree called the Merriman bill a "sop" and threatened to hold over the legislature for an extra summer session in the hope that the weather would be as "hot as h—" and would help to force a better bill out of the Senate. He relented, however, after he realized that the Senate was determined to stop all reforms, and Colonel Atkinson reluctantly advised the House to "accept the contemptible installment offered us by the railroads." Pingree warned the obstructionists that he would point them out to the public as bad examples who should be defeated in 1898.[33]

Undeterred by his first setback, Pingree called a special session of the legislature for March, 1898, to extend equal taxation to the railroads through a resuscitated version of the Atkinson bill. In an effort to force his opponents into the open, he sent his stenographers into the legislative chamber to record all floor debates and to "put the cusses on record" for the election of 1898. The Governor also solicited and gathered petitions from 80,000 citizens and bombarded both houses with such citizen warrants as: "Go after them Gov. Pingree, with grape and cannister, submarine mines and torpedo boats and free at least our State from this worse than pestilence, these cloven footed, oily tongued, organized gang of tax-dodging millionaires, philanthropists." The master of the Michigan Grange, George B. Horton, sent the

Governor a cryptic: "Give 'em hell" message. Driven by Pingree's lash and Atkinson's masterful tactics, the House passed the equal tax bill by an overwhelming vote of 90 to 3.[34]

When the measure reached the Senate, it was given the treatment prescribed by Michigan's G.O.P. boss, United States Senator James McMillan, and Sky Olds. The former governor, a host of federal officeholders, and railroad lawyers descended upon the upper house and demanded that it delay all action on any equal taxation bill, and that it create instead a committee to investigate state taxation problems in general. The Senate complied by passing the Barnum bill. Not only had the Senate killed all hope for equal taxation in the special session, but it had also packed the investigating committee provided for in the Barnum bill with five "fossilized mugwumps" who would pervert the investigation into a meaningless charade. The representatives tabled the Barnum bill. The upper house also defeated a bill to repeal the tax privileges of the Michigan Central, thus creating a legislative stalemate.[35]

At this juncture the approach of the Spanish-American War interrupted legislative deliberations, and the conservatives took advantage of the public concern about this matter to jettison all reform bills. "[L]et us fight in Spain and not our home industries in Michigan," the Michigan Central's attorney, Henry Russel, told the lawmakers. The legislature was suddenly "filled with jingoes," Atkinson noticed, and as the international crisis grew, demands were made in the Senate that "war bills" take precedence over all other legislation. Recognizing that the war was a convenient excuse to avoid tax reform, Pingree was bitter about the state of affairs and complained publicly: "If the federal government is willing to allow its agents in this state to prevent the just taxation of railroads, then of course, the federal government does not expect the people of this state to make appropriations to establish the state militia on a war footing." The war hysteria, however, took hold of even the reformers, and the legislature passed a $500,000 bond issue to equip the Michigan National Guard for federal duty.[36]

Although Pingree opposed the war and believed that it would have been more sensible for the United States to have purchased Cuba, he accepted his full responsibility as state commander-in-chief and threw himself into the job of outfitting, arming, and training Michigan's untried militia. At the Island Lake staging area, Pingree was most solicitous for the well-being of his troops. He took a personal hand in recruiting, lectured the men on camp sanitation, and rendered assistance to those with special problems. Sparing no expense, the Governor purchased new summer-weight uniforms, improved the quality of food for the troops, and tried to buy modern rifles for them. When sickness broke out in the camps in the South to which Michigan's five regiments had been ordered, Pingree personally inspected conditions and loudly protested to Washington. At his request, a special hospital train was dispatched to return Michigan soldiers suffering from typhoid to their local hospitals. When the War Department established a convalescent camp in New York, Pingree sent his son Hazen Jr. and a corps of trained nurses to look after Michigan men who had caught the "Cuban fever." [37]

Pingree's antics at the Island Lake encampment and during the war revealed that nine years of rough-and-tumble political battling with the toughest of adversaries had taken their toll. His speech had become profane where once it had been correct, and his public behavior was not as decorous as it had once been. Pingree had begun to consume great quantities of food and drink, and often enjoyed out-drinking the "boys." After one drinking bout, according to A. M. Smith, the Governor led his cronies in a "gallant midnight charge" upon the object of his frustration, the detested Senate chamber, where they flung everything from one end to the other and ruined a portrait of General Lafayette. There were also reports that Pingree would wind up a long night's revel with an impromptu version of the can can on the streets of Lansing. At the militia encampment, according to one legislator, Pingree had appeared before a detachment of soldiers in a drunken condition, swinging his hat and shouting, "Hurrah! for the governor of Michigan, where is the regimental——? I want to see her." [38]

Although the war interrupted Pingree's reform program, it helped, ironically, to enhance his political power. A majority of Michiganders were pleased both with his tax program and with his solicitous care for the state's soldiers. "Politics has been knocked galley-west by the war," Chase Osborn was told by a Washington correspondent. Evidence of the Governor's political strength mounted as the 1898 state Republican convention approached. Senator McMillan reluctantly informed his stalwarts that "the work that Pingree is doing for the soldiers and their families has made him invincible and that is going to . . . hurt us." [39]

With what one reporter called the deliberation of "an exploding gas main," Pingree launched a major effort in the fall of 1898 to take control of the state party away from the McMillan regulars and to purge anti-reform legislators. The Governor set his sights on purging 17 obstructionists, and he was able, with some help, to prevent the nomination of 14 of them. The forced retirement at the hands of Pingree's old Detroit organization of Senator William G. Thompson, a railroad stalwart, was especially pleasing to the Governor. He dictated the entire Wayne County legislative slate and easily won renomination for himself. Pingree also worked hard for reform Democrats and was delighted to see two of them elected to the Senate in the place of two unreliable Republicans. When chided for his party irregularity in October, the Governor had said, "Hell! I don't care a damn for Republican majorities; it's Pingree men I want." The most stunning achievement of the campaign was Pingree's capture of the G.O.P. state central committee and the installation of his protégé Arthur F. Marsh as chairman. McMillan was understandably chagrined, for it was the first time in more than two decades that the regulars had lost control of the committee to maverick outsiders. [40]

The Republicans swept the elections for the legislature in

1898, and Pingree increased his 1896 percentage of 55.57 to 57.26. During the campaign, he had forced an equal tax plank into the G.O.P. platform, and he had secured public pledges of support for the plank from most of the successful legislative candidates. Pingree's victory was more apparent than real, however, for although he had secured the removal of many of the reactionaries in urban areas, his influence was considerably weaker in many remote districts, where federal postmasterships, collectorships, and judgeships gave power to the McMillan forces, and in the mining districts, where, as the Ironwood postmaster explained, "the managers of the mines control the conventions." He would also be handicapped in his fight against the railroads because his railroad commissioner, Chase Osborn, was secretly loyal to the railroads.[41] Finally, Pingree's equal tax cause was severely weakened by the death of his legislative floor leader, Colonel Atkinson, in August, 1898.

Nevertheless, Pingree continued to gain strength in his fight for equal taxation of the railroads. Early in 1898, the State Grange had offered its support for an equal tax bill, and the State Association of Farmers' Clubs, representing some 30,000 members, committed itself to support Pingree's measure in December. The Farmers' Alliance and Industrial Union endorsed the Atkinson bill at the beginning of 1899, and on February 10, the State Association of Supervisors demanded immediate passage as a "matter of justice." At a crucial point the bill was reintroduced when the "usually sleepless agents of the corporate interests had been caught napping," as Pingree explained, and it passed the lower house.[42]

The legislative hatchet men for the railroads and business interests in the Senate in 1899 were known as the "immortal nineteen." Led by Senator Theron W. Atwood, they were a formidable obstacle to reform, and they had the power to thwart the Governor's programs. The G.O.P. Senate caucuses were controlled by a small cadre of 7 "immortals," who, Pingree complained, were "more powerful than the other 125 members of the legislature." During the 1899 session the "immortals" defeated measures to increase the specific tax on railroad, express, telephone, telegraph, copper, and iron mining companies, quashed a proposal to repeal the special charter privileges of the Michigan Central, and crushed every other reform bill of any consequence.[43]

The real power in Michigan's upper house was James McMillan, who had fought against all tax reform. As public pressure for tax reform mounted, however, McMillan seemingly recanted and confidentially told the Michigan Central president, Henry B. Ledyard, that it "was absolutely necessary that some legislation should be passed" to appease popular demand. Ledyard was miffed by McMillan's assessment of the situation and spoke quite sharply to him. It was upsetting "after all I did for the railroads, when the legislature held its special session [1898]," protested McMillan, "that he should turn around and talk in that way." Apparently piqued by Ledyard's ingratitude and facing up to political reality, McMillan released the Senate. A large majority of the upper house, which hitherto had been implacably opposed to the Atkinson bill, "suddenly . . . changed front[s]," a puzzled Pingree noted, and approved the bill without a dissenting vote on March 9.[44]

On April 26 the Michigan Supreme Court voided the Atkinson act in ruling on a collateral case concerning a uniform method of determining assessments. It was widely rumored at the capital and confirmed by the "immortals" themselves that the "immortals" had allowed the Senate to pass the equal tax bill because they had foreknowledge that the court would invalidate it. Whether Atwood received advance notice of the court decision from McMillan cannot be determined from the available evidence, but it is a fact that no one in Michigan enjoyed the confidence of the state's judiciary to the extent that McMillan did. In any event, the Senate's behavior lent additional support, as Pingree saw it, to his earlier remarks to the Ingham County supervisors that there were "gentlemen, sitting about the house and senate of our legislature, who ought to be serving their sentences in Jackson [prison], and whose crimes are red with treason to the government of Michigan." [45]

Hoping to salvage something from the wreckage, Pingree pressed for the creation of a state tax commission to evaluate all corporate property, including that of the railroads, and to report inequities in tax rates to the legislature. The administration sponsored Oren bill, which provided for such a commission with broad powers to inspect, correct, and enforce local assessments at "cash value" and to examine corporation books and compare tax rates under both the specific and ad valorem systems, passed the House. The Senate, however, threatened to kill the Oren bill unless Pingree promised not to appoint three avowed friends of equal taxation as commissioners. "I'll appoint three men that they hate more than these three," muttered Pingree, "if I can find them in Michigan." Hoping to avert an impartial investigation, the Senate passed the Wagar temporary tax commission bill, which usurped the Governor's executive prerogative by appointing five "nondescripts," to use Pingree's word, to the commission. [46]

In the confusing closing hours of the fortieth session of the legislature, an imperfectly understood deal was arranged between the administration and the "immortals" whereby the Senate agreed to pass the Oren bill in return for Pingree's approval of the Wagar bill, which would have given the Atwood crowd control over the railroad investigation. When both measures reached his desk, Pingree signed the Oren bill but vetoed the Wagar bill, touching off an explosion among the "immortals." They fulminated and cursed Pingree for reneging on the deal, and the Speaker of the House threatened revenge with a tough inquiry into the Governor's handling of war funds. In the fast and slippery game of legislative politics, however, Pingree had learned how to use the Senate's ground rules. The Governor pointed out that he had agreed to sign the Wagar bill provided that the "19" would carry out their part of the agreement, which included both the passage of the Oren bill and the adoption of the joint resolution calling for the constitutional convention to solve the tax problem. "The senate, however, released me from that obligation," said Pingree, "when they threw the joint resolution in the air." The Oren bill would in time prove the validity of Pingree's assertion that it was the "most important law ever enacted by a Michigan Legislature" and that it was "more far-reaching in its consequences . . . than even its most enthusiastic friends and advocates anticipated." [47]

When the work of the tax commission was getting under way, Pingree devised a plan to forge an alliance with the United States Secretary of War Russell A. Alger in an effort to offset McMillan's power in the Michigan legislature. In the late spring of 1899, the Governor launched a campaign to rehabilitate the political fortunes of the nation's "embalmed beef secretary of war," who, as Pingree understood it, was yearning for the chance to succeed McMillan as Senator upon the expiration of his term in 1901. Pingree's goal was to stamp McMillan as a lameduck Senator, which would greatly diminish his power in the state, and, if possible, to replace him with Alger, who might agree to give the Governor a free hand with the legislature. Should his plan fail, Pingree was prepared to drop Alger in return for a McMillan commitment to abandon his resistance to Pingree's reforms.[48]

Pingree initiated his scheme by publicly exonerating Alger of the charges of corruption and incompetence directed against his management of the War Department during the Spanish-American War. The shortcomings of the Department, Pingree claimed, were the result of the war itself rather than of Alger's actions. The Governor attributed reform sentiments to the Secretary (which he probably did not subscribe to) and described him as "absolutely sound" and on the "right side of the two greatest questions of the day," the trusts and the popular election of senators. Alger was flattered by and grateful for the lavish praise heaped upon him by Pingree at a time when the rest of the nation was clamoring for his head. Alger naïvely accepted Pingree's offer of assistance to obtain the senatorship.[49]

After Alger agreed to work with the Governor, Pingree revealed the second phase of his plan, which was for Alger to return to Michigan to run for the senate seat. Pingree knew that political promises were only as good as the men who made them, and Alger's record as an opportunist seemed to call for an extra guarantee. Pingree therefore unleashed a series of abusive attacks on President McKinley, which received nationwide press coverage.[50] Alger tried desperately to counter the newspaper stories by claiming that Pingree was for McKinley "first, last and always." "The question whether I am for McKinley lies with the President, not with me," retorted Pingree in the *New York Times.*

> If General Alger knows that President McKinley is opposed to territorial expansion, and is not an advocate of the murders and destruction being visited upon the innocent Filipinos, he has the right to say that I am for McKinley. If General Alger is informed that McKinley is opposed to trusts and to legislation which fosters, creates and encourages them, and in favor of legislation to restrict and suppress them, then I am closer to the opinions of McKinley than has generally been believed. If General Alger is assured that President McKinley is not in touch and sympathy with the disreputable political methods of Mark Hanna and his friends, and deprecates such leadership, then I am for McKinley.

In short, Pingree added, "I am for McKinley in everything he does which I consider right and against everything he does which I consider wrong." [51]

Alger was horrified by the Governor's attack on the President, which, he told a friend, puts "us together in a combine which would seem to hold me accountable for or endorsing the Governor's views." He pleaded for a cessation of Pingree's charges. Otherwise, lamented Alger, they "will force me to withdraw my candidacy or retire from the cabinet." [52] Alger was caught up in a Pingree-made dilemma, and he tried desperately to extricate himself. It was too late, however; the Detroit *Journal's* Washington correspondent informed Chase Osborn on July 18 that

"Alger is fighting for his life down here. He is liable to be forced out any minute. . . . He is entirely discredited." [53]

Part one of the Pingree plan worked precisely as the Governor had hoped: Alger submitted his resignation to the President on July 19. Alger's dismissal revealed a rather ignoble side of Mc-Kinley. He had ignored for almost a year the valid criticism of his Secretary's bungling by military officers, congressmen, and public officials, but then forced his resignation after he had become associated for a single month with Pingreeism and the Governor's attacks on the President.[54]

Pingree arranged a hero's welcome in Detroit for the fallen warrior which would have embarrassed even the immodest Admiral George Dewey. Pingree took the planning for what had been intended as an unpretentious ceremony away from Alger's G.O.P. friends and expanded it into a circus that included bands, bunting, banners, fanfare, a military escort, and lavish speeches by state and city dignitaries. "This demonstration is going into history," promised Pingree; "We want to hit this thing as hard as we can hit it—no love taps." [55] Pingree offered to send twenty-five prominent Michigan citizens to the White House to greet General Alger after he had submitted his resignation to the President. Pingree issued a gubernatorial proclamation calling upon the citizens of Michigan to assemble in Detroit to greet Alger, and he sent his staff in full military uniform to meet the General in Toledo and escort his train to Detroit. At the ceremony in Detroit, Pingree depicted Alger as a faithful public servant who had been "grossly abused and misrepresented" by his chief and spoke harshly of both McKinley and McMillan. "Each jab," reported the Toledo *News*, "was greeted with cheers," "howls of delight," and calls of "give it to 'em Ping," "Soak 'em Gov." [56]

Belatedly recognizing that he was being used as an anti-McMillan pawn by the Pingree forces, Alger withdrew his candidacy for the United States Senate. Actually there had been little love lost between Alger and Pingree; the *New York Times* correctly reported before the alliance came to an end that Pingree had nothing but a "sneering contempt" for Alger. The Governor's only regret was that he had been unable to use Alger's manufactured candidacy for a few more months in order to force concessions from McMillan.[57] The damage had been done, however, for Pingree had created a split within the hitherto solid ranks of the McMillan organization, and this seemed to offer some hope for the cause of reform.

Thinking that he had weakened the opposition through the Alger affair and by his constant propagandizing for reform, Pingree called a special session of the legislature for December 18, 1899. The Governor hoped to secure the passage of a joint resolution providing for a constitutional amendment that would permit equal taxation and legislation to repeal the capital stock tax privileges of the "chartered" railroads, to increase the taxes of the iron and copper mines, and to permit Michigan cities to engage in municipal ownership. During the session, the Senate "immortals" gained their threatened revenge for Pingree's veto of the Wagar act by exposing a major administration scandal: they co-operated with the Ingham County prosecuting attorney, whose inquiry into the conduct of the state's Military Board revealed that three of the Governor's aides had been implicated in defrauding the state. The Senate used the scandal as a convenient excuse for refusing to enact any reform legislation and passed a resolution pledging state funds to pay for the Ingham County inquiry, and then adjourned.[58]

Pingree called two additional legislative sessions in 1900 to achieve his long-sought reforms. The first, which met on the eve of the election on October 18, 1900, was perfectly timed. The Governor planned to force the Senate to go along with his reforms or to practice its obstructionism in the glaring publicity of an election campaign and thus court defeat at the polls. The House passed Pingree's measures by overwhelming majorities, and the Governor then applied heavy pressure on the Senate. The railroad forces, under Sky Olds, tried desperately to rally the faltering "immortals" with cries of "Pingree won't down as long as he is dealing with cowards." Senator McMillan, who needed a G.O.P. legislature to assure his re-election, was caught in a dilemma which hopelessly nullified his influence. "For once," asserted the Traverse City *Eagle*,

Pingree "had the cusses where he wanted them, and they knew it." The Senate "acted as if the business end of a buzz saw were after it," to quote the Port Huron *Daily Herald,* and passed in three days what it had denied Pingree for three years. The Governor sat in the Senate chamber as the measures passed, his face wreathed in smiles. The special tax privileges of the Michigan Central, Lake Shore and Michigan Southern, and Detroit, Grand Haven and Milwaukee railroads were repealed by an almost unanimous vote, and the joint resolution to submit the equal tax amendment to the Michigan voters passed with only two diehard "immortals" in opposition.[59]

The equal tax amendment, which empowered the state to levy a tax on the property of all railroad, express, telephone, telegraph companies, banks, and all other corporate property at its "true cash value," was approved by the Michigan electorate by an overwhelming vote of 442,728 to 54,752. No amendment in Michigan's history from the ratification of the first state constitution in 1835 to the corporation tax amendment in 1908 attracted such a large majority as Pingree's equal tax amendment in November, 1900.[60] It was a stunning victory for the now ailing and aging Governor.

After the election, Pingree called a second special session for December 12 to enact the Atkinson bill, which the amended state constitution now permitted. The House passed the bill for a fourth time, but the Senate, which was angered over Pingree's use of the election whip against its members, refused even to consider the measure. To deny Pingree the final fruits of victory, the legislature refused to pass the bill until Pingree had left office and the conservative Aaron T. Bliss had succeeded him. Neither contemporary nor subsequent observers have doubted, however, that it was Pingree's equal tax bill. "It is one of the anomalies of public life," said Professor Henry Carter Adams, "that Governor Pingree, to whom belongs the credit . . . of taxing railway properties on the basis of valuation, should not have been permitted to sign this bill, but that it should have been signed by his successor, Governor Bliss, who, to say the least, seemed indifferent to the success of the measure." [61]

The equal tax amendment, the Atkinson act, and the Oren act

brought about some of the most fundamental reforms in Michigan during the early years of the Progressive period. The tax board, created after passage of the Oren act of 1899, provided supporting data for the Governor's arguments with regard to railroads and helped to lay the foundation for the passage of the equal tax amendment and the Atkinson bill. The board's findings demonstrated, as Pingree had always contended, that the railroads were grossly undertaxed and paid but a pittance in taxation as compared to the average taxpayer.[62]

At the Governor's request, the Michigan Board of Tax Commissioners undertook a massive reassessment of taxable property and, between 1899 and 1902, conducted a diligent search for property that had evaded taxes. During the first year of its operation, the board discovered $350,000,000 worth of property to be placed on the tax rolls—about one-third the worth of all the assessed property in Michigan in 1899. Of the increase, $80,000,000 was found in the mining ranges of the Upper Peninsula, $104,000,000 among 1,175 other corporations in the state, and $133,000,000 in 780 Michigan cities. Very little of the increased assessable value had come from the "property of farmers, clerks, working men and other small property owners," Pingree noted.[63]

By 1902 the tax commissioners had eliminated the worst cases of corporate favoritism and had inspected the work of 1700 local assessors. The centralizing of assessment procedures in a state Board of Tax Commissioners, which was relatively immune to the influence of local corporations, was one of Pingree's great contributions to reform in Michigan.[64]

The work of the Michigan state commissioners paid dividends to a vast majority of the state's taxpayers. The ratio of assessed property shifted drastically from 85 per cent real and 15 per cent personal in 1899 to 76 per cent real and 24 per cent personal in 1900, and the benefits went to those with limited personal possessions. The change was in large part due to the discovery of the untaxed property of businesses and wealthy citizens. No state in the union had so high a percentage of personal property in relation to real property on its tax rolls in 1900 as Michigan then did. The small taxpayer and the average citizen had ample reason to be thankful for the work of Pingree's Commissioners when the tax rates dropped by 26 per cent, from $21.17 per thousand in 1899 to $15.47 per thousand in 1900.[65]

To implement the Oren Act, Pingree called in Professor Mortimer E. Cooley, of the University of Michigan, in August, 1900, to appraise the property of all Michigan's railroads and specific tax-paying corporations. No state appraisal of such magnitude had been conducted in the nation prior to 1900. No recognized or standardized method or procedure existed for making such an evaluation, nor was there any literature or developed theory on the subject. "Cooley, I'll tell you why I chose you to take charge of this work," said Pingree. "I knew that you didn't know a goddam thing about railroads, but I knew that you could find men who did, and that you would get the work done on time and make up theories that would justify everything you did." Pingree gave Cooley six months to complete the survey.[66]

Cooley first attempted to use company records to find the original cost of physical property on which to base his evaluations, but he found the records in "utter chaos." He also discovered that the railroads were withholding information from him. When he called to inspect the books of one road, the president told him to "go to hell." It became apparent to Cooley that the kind of appraisal he had to make could not be done with bookkeeper's methods. Cooley thereupon sent 75 engineers into the field to inspect and evaluate every tie, turntable, track, bridge, locomotive, and depot. The franchise evaluations were completed by Professor Henry Carter Adams, of the University of Michigan.[67]

The Cooley appraisal provided the basis for the state tax board's new assessment in 1902, which nearly doubled railroad taxation, raising it from $1,668,435 under the old specific tax system to $3,288,162 under the new general tax system. Although Pingree did not live to see it, he was indeed vindicated in a grand fashion that he would have enjoyed. The railroads conducted harassing court

tests against the new system, but it was so well conceived and exe-
cuted that it withstood all assaults, including even the conservative
trend in Michigan politics after Pingree's death.[68]

The "Michigan appraisal" was the first statewide railroad valuation undertaken in the country, and it was the "forerunner and
precedent maker for all subsequent work in the nation in [the]
valuation of corporation properties," asserted University of Michigan Professor Henry E. Riggs.[69] Robert M. La Follette, who was
apprised of Pingree's campaign for equal taxation by an aide, set
the appraisal of railroad property in his state in motion under the
direction of University of Wisconsin Professor W. D. Taylor, who
used the Michigan method as a model. The Michigan appraisal
during the Pingree administration was a pioneering piece of work
which enabled Michigan, Wisconsin, and other states to move toward equal taxation[70] and eventually toward the regulation of railroad rates with a scientific basis for establishing what the courts
would accept as "reasonable."

Pingree's last year as Governor, 1900, was filled with the kind of
success, some of the disappointment, and much of the drama that
had made the "Pingree era." The mining companies had been
brought to heel by the State Tax Commission, a scientific basis was
being laid for evaluations, corporate tax evading had been checked,
and the railroads had finally been forced to assume their share of
the tax burden. Sky Olds had lost his job with the roads and had
departed for Florida while a grand jury was conducting an investigation that might incriminate him. The Speaker of the House,
Edgar J. Adams, was under indictment for bribery, as was another
McMillan stalwart, State Land Commissioner William A. French.
This came as no surprise to Pingree, who had come to expect the
worst from McMillan's political henchmen.[71]

The Governor's personal and political prospects had, however,
begun to dim. Pingree had spent much of his own fortune, and he
was physically exhausted. After twelve years of strenuous public
life, his health was giving way, and occasionally he was unable to
muster the strength to speak when called upon. Mrs. Pingree, who
had been shocked by the character of her husband's tempestuous

career, had withdrawn into seclusion in the Pingree home. Although the first lady of the state, she never accompanied the Governor on any of his official appearances.[72]

The Michigan Military Board scandal which was uncovered in December, 1899, cut deeply into Pingree's political prestige and shook his confidence more so than any other event of the gubernatorial years. Three of the Governor's closest aides, Inspector General Arthur F. Marsh, Quartermaster General William L. White, and Eli R. Sutton, a University of Michigan regent in whom Pingree placed the greatest trust, had been involved with the Henderson-Ames Company of Kalamazoo in the fraudulent sale of military surplus during the demobilization that followed the Spanish-American War. When Pingree learned that some of his advisers were implicated in defrauding the state of $40,000, he was severely shocked. "I never had anything do me up so completely as this affair," the Governor muttered in disbelief. "I couldn't sleep at all for a week." [73]

Pingree dismissed the indicted military board members, but he insisted upon equal justice and demanded that the private parties to the conspiracy, the Henderson-Ames people, also be indicted and brought to trial. The young prosecuting attorney of Ingham County, Arthur J. Tuttle, who discovered the fraud, concentrated his investigation on the officials surrounding Pingree. Ambitious to build a reputation for himself and to generate as much newspaper publicity as possible from the affair, Tuttle, with the acquiescence of Circuit Judge Rollin H. Person, conducted a highly irregular series of grand jury hearings in 1899 and 1900, during which information which was highly prejudicial to the accused parties was leaked daily to the press. Tuttle brought Marsh and White to trial and obtained their convictions, but Sutton was acquitted. The young prosecutor refused, however, to ask for the indictment of the Henderson-Ames people.[74]

The indictments growing out of the grand jury hearings of such G.O.P. regulars as Speaker of the House Edgar J. Adams, former Attorney General Fred Maynard, and Land Commissioner William A. French were so carelessly drawn by Tuttle that Circuit Judge

Howard Weist reprimanded the young prosecutor and threw the indictments out of court. The court did manage, however, to bring Sutton back more than a year later and convict him of perjury arising out of his first trial. Pingree was furious over what he considered a travesty of justice; he called the judges a bunch of "judicial hypocrites" and pardoned White and Marsh in 1900. The pardons caused an uproar and led many one-time Pingree supporters to attack the Governor. "Villain thrice villain you are," charged a Hillsdale correspondent. "You Have Raised Potatoes By The Patch, But You Have Raised *Hell* By The Acre." The press and the clergy joined in the heated attacks on the Governor. Although no one questioned Pingree's personal honesty, his political influence was considerably diminished by the grand jury hearings, the trials, and the subsequent pardons.[75]

In the wake of the Governor's misfortune, Pingree's old antagonist, Senator McMillan, regained control of the Republican State Central Committee, although his power in the state party was considerably less than it had been in the pre-Pingree era. Pingree had so battered McMillan and weakened his grip on the state machine that it fell apart at the Senator's death in 1902, with squabbling and bickering factions scrambling for pieces. The Senator was the last of the McMillans to be a dominant figure in either the political or economic life of the state.[76]

Pingree, for his part, had had more than his share of personal disappointments. The Governor's aides Marsh and White had been disgraced; their careers as politicians were at an end. DeWitt Moreland, one of Pingree's early urban followers, turned into a hack politician who contributed little to Detroit's future. J. W. Walsh, a one-time secretary and confidant, vanished from the city. Alex McLeod, Pingree's right-hand man in the battle for urban reform, became a respectable owner of a motor company and devoted his abilities to making money. Colonel John Atkinson had died prematurely in 1898. Ralph Stone, a speech writer during the Lansing years, went into banking and was apparently content to forget his earlier radical associations. Eli R. Sutton, upon whom the Governor had lavished affection and placed great hope, was compromised by his perjury trial; he left the state and became a science-fiction writer. Pingree's only son, Hazen, Jr., offered little promise, led a dissolute life, and died at a young age. Except for his Railroad Commissioner, Chase S. Osborn, who could later lay claim to being the state's only reform governor of the Progressive period, and James Couzens, a maverick Detroit mayor who placed the streetcar system under municipal ownership, Pingree did not leave behind him a strong cadre of political leaders who could carry on his work.[77]

Suffering from poor health and upset by the Military Board scandals and his loss of control over the G.O.P. State Central Committee, Pingree decided not to contend for the governorship again in 1900. Popular support for reform continued, however, and many of Pingree's basic ideas, such as municipal home rule, municipal ownership, and public regulation of railroad rates, were written into the state constitution in 1907–08.[78]

Pingree left the scene in fiery and fitting fashion. Late in 1899 he had cheered the Filipino guerrillas in what he regarded as "their contest for independence," and he had ridiculed President McKinley for having "bought a revolution for $20,000,000." "Teddy Roosevelt a year or so ago characterized McKinley as a chocolate man," Pingree told a reporter in August, 1900, but "I have always contended that McKinley's backbone didn't reach far enough toward his neck to support his brains or his will power." With the Presidential election of 1900 approaching, the Governor broke with the G.O.P. and advocated voting for the Democrats, but he then recanted: "I shall probably hold my nose, vote for McKinley and hope for the best," he declared.[79]

In his exaugural address, given before the legislature on January 9, 1901, Pingree characterized the political elite of Lansing as "parasites" who fed upon state institutions and who were unfit to be entrusted with the state's capitol. He apologized to the citizens of Ingham County for not having removed their prosecuting attorney, Arthur J. Tuttle, who, Pingree asserted, was a "thief and a deceiver and a briber." He called the grand jury system a "relic of the dark ages" and the conduct of the Ingham County grand jury a "disgrace to the State." Embittered by the class and business interests that had throttled reform in every legislative body with which he had been associated, Pingree warned that unless there was a change in the "present system of inequality . . . there will be a bloody revolution in this great country of ours." [80]

When he delivered the address, Pingree was under a contempt-of-court citation for having publicly insulted an Ingham County circuit court judge. "If this young man thinks he has a monopoly on my contempt and that I have contempt for just his court alone, he is mistaken," Pingree told the lawmakers, "for I have contempt for dozens of courts in this State, knowing their methods of procedure." Pingree's last year of unrestrained assault upon practically everybody who resisted change or reform provoked demands for retaliation from some of the discomfited. When Representative Lawton T. Hemans was asked why the Governor had not been impeached, he replied: "Impeach Pingree! What good would that do? What can you do with a man who, when he is cited to answer a charge of contempt says: 'To hell with your court and your contempt,' and sails off to Africa." [81]

With his last salvo fired in January, 1901, Pingree had gone off to hunt elephants in South Africa, where he hoped to have a look at the Boer War and to visit Cecil Rhodes. He ended his trans-Atlantic itinerary in June in London, where he died at the age of sixty. He had earlier told a friend that he hoped to return to Detroit as mayor to finish his vital work as an urban reformer. [82]

Epilogue

The Detroit to which Pingree hoped to return had served the cause of reform well both at the urban and state level. The leadership and impulse for the reform spirit in Michigan had emanated from Detroit. Although the city's foreign-born community had failed to produce leaders, it had provided the political base for Pingree's programs. With the aid of his tight coterie of Detroit followers Pingree had pushed some of the state's most important reforms through the legislature. The Age of Reform in Michigan was clearly not primarily dependent upon the native-born middle and upper classes. Behind a dynamic and compassionate leader, newcomers had responded to the important issues of the age.

Although Pingree's accomplishments at the state level were not as manifold as his municipal achievements, he had imposed public control upon some of the most powerful financial interests in Michigan. Corporation tax evasion was corrected, and Pingree's battle with the railroads for equal taxation was won. Pingree also forced through a conservative legislature the first significant state-wide appraisal of railroad and corporation property and helped to establish a rational basis for railroad rate regulation and taxation during the Progressive period. Robert M. La Follette's Wisconsin was the first state to follow the Pingree pattern in corporate property appraisals and to popularize the technique during the Progressive period.

Pingree's influence as Governor cannot be fully measured by his legislative successes and failures, however, for he also left the state with a more important legacy, popular support for reform that continued for years after his death.

Pingree's reforms in Detroit had challenged some of the major assumptions behind the good government movement of the late-nineteenth and early-twentieth centuries. Contrary to the opinion of municipal experts, the city could produce political leaders who were concerned with honesty and efficiency without sacrificing social responsibility. The Mayor had avoided the nostrums of the good government reformers and spared his programs from drying up in the narrow confines of administrative reform. Recognizing the sterility of the "framework" school, Pingree rejected a course which many of his contemporaries followed. Similarly he had dismissed the dogma of the 1890's which held that businessmen were the "natural and inevitable directors of local affairs." Although he was a self-made businessman, Pingree's experience at the center of municipal power had disabused him of the illusion that the civic renaissance must begin with the commercial classes. Battle with the traction, gas, and light interests had taught Pingree that the aristocracy of business and birth had no monopoly on civic virtue.

The Pingree administrations had demonstrated that urban democracy was not bankrupt: the Mayor's political partnership with the immigrant and the poor had not corrupted the city. Pingree had shown that it was not necessary to sterilize the municipal apparatus with a dose of civil service reform or to fashion political systems which purged ethnic and lower class representatives before moving to substantive social reforms. Detroit's public light plant was established and functioned efficiently long before the adoption of the merit system. Pingree's keen concern with utilities, taxes, and transit had demonstrated to Detroit's masses that they had a genuine stake in a better urban society.

Pingree had linked his administration to newcomers in the only meaningful way possible—through political action. It is doubtful if a democratic society can produce an adequate substitute for the political system. The municipal government of Pingree's period was probably one of the most successful institutions for channelizing ethnic hostilities, sounding out urban discontent, and redirecting human energies. It also provided a constructive instrument for effecting social change and for creating unity in a fragmented society. Pingree's Detroit had reflected and responded to the physical and psychological needs of the unfortunate in an urban society. This became less possible where the anti-democratic persuasion of the structural reform tradition gained momentum in the twentieth century.

Notes

PREFACE

1. James Bryce, *The American Commonwealth* (New York, 1888) I, 608–13.
2. *Ibid.*, p. 614.
3. Wallace S. Sayre and Nelson W. Polsby, "American Political Science and the Study of Urbanization," *The Study of Urbanization* ed. Philip M. Hauser and Leo F. Schnore (New York, 1966), pp. 115–16, 120.

CHAPTER 1

1. Cyril A. Player, "Hazen S. Pingree: The Biography of an American Commonplace" (MS, 1931), pp. 1–13, Burton Historical Collection (hereafter, B.H.C.); *Cyclopedia of Michigan* (Detroit, 1890), p. 74.
2. *Compendium of History and Biography,* (Chicago, 1909), pp. 344–45; "Pingree—The First Insurgent," *Detroit Saturday Night:* December 9, 1911.
3. F. Clever Bald, *Michigan in Four Centuries* (New York, 1954), pp. 161–62; C. M. Burton, *The City of Detroit Michigan 1701–1922* (Detroit, 1922), I, 533, 537; Silas Farmer, *History of Detroit* (New York, 1890), I, 972; Almon E. Parkins, *The Historical Geography of Detroit* (Lansing, 1918), pp. 291–92.
4. George B. Catlin, *The Story of Detroit* (Detroit, 1926), pp. 574–75, 652–56.

5. *Ibid.*, pp. 477, 495–99, 664.

6. Sidney Fine, *Laissez Faire and the General-Welfare State* (Ann Arbor, 1964), pp. 142–43; *Cyclopedia of Michigan*, pp. 260–61.

7. Fred C. Hamil, "Charles H. Smith, Junior Partner of Pingree and Smith," *Michigan History*, VL (March, 1961), 45–48; Charles R. Starring, "Hazen S. Pingree: Another Forgotten Eagle," *Michigan History* XXXII (June, 1948), 130–31.

8. *Compendium of History and Biography*, pp. 344–45; Hamil, "Charles H. Smith," pp. 45–48.

9. *Labor Leaf:* May 13, 27, 1885; June 3, 10, 24, 1885; July 1, 1885; March 24, 1886; *Unionist:* June 10, 1887.

10. *Cyclopedia of Michigan*, p. 75; *Detroit in History and Commerce* (Detroit, 1891), p. 64.

11. Frank H. Croul, undated, as cited in Pingree Papers; interview with Mrs. Wilson W. Mills (Hazel Pingree), October 14, 1963; Detroit *Evening News:* June 23, 1901.

12. *Cyclopedia of Michigan*, p. 75; *Detroit in History and Commerce*, p. 64; Henry A. Haigh, *The Michigan Club 1884: The Alger Movement 1888* (Detroit, 1923), pp. 2–7.

13. Silas Farmer, *The History of Detroit and Michigan* (Detroit, 1884), pp. 136–40; Edward Bemis, "Local Government in Michigan and the Northwest," Johns Hopkins University *Studies in Historical and Political Science,* v (March, 1883), 7.

14. *Detroit Journal Yearbook For 1890* (Detroit, 1890), pp. 81, 85.

15. *Official Directory and Legislative Manual of the State of Michigan 1889* (Lansing, 1889), p. 5 (hereafter *Michigan Manual 1889*).

16. Farmer, *The History of Detroit and Michigan*, pp. 145–46; councilmanic lists cited in Pingree Scrapbook, January-February, 1891, B.H.C.

17. *Report of Vital and Social Statistics in the United States at the Eleventh Census: 1890* (Washington, 1896), IV, Part II, 43, 46 (hereafter *Eleventh Census: 1890*); Mark O. Kistler, "The German Language Press in Michigan: A Survey and Bibliography," *Michigan History* VIL (September, 1960), 321; Sidney Glazer, "Labor and Agrarian Movements in Michigan 1876–1896" (Ph.D. thesis, University of Michigan, 1932), pp. 52, 54, 57.

18. "Pingree—The First Insurgent," *Detroit Saturday Night:* November 25, 1911; Detroit *Evening News:* November 9, 1887.

19. For the relative socio-economic position of various ethnic groups see *Eighth Annual Report of the Bureau of Labor and Industrial Statistics 1891* (Lansing, 1891), pp. 152, 430–31; *Ninth Annual Report of the Bureau of Labor and Industrial Statistics 1892* (Lansing, 1892), p. 409; John A. Russell, *The Germanic Influence in the Making of Michigan* (Detroit, 1927), p. 309; "Roman Catholics in Detroit," *Michigan Pioneer and Historical Society* (Lansing, 1889), VIII, 409; *Eleventh Census: 1890*, pp. 219–23.

20. *Patriotic American:* June 20, 1891; Detroit *Evening News:* March 11, 20, 1886; George Pare, *The Catholic Church in Detroit 1701–1888* (Detroit, 1951), pp. 557–58.
21. Felix A. Lemkie to Cyrus G. Luce, January 29, 1889, GII Elections Box, Michigan Historical Commission, Lansing.
22. *Eleventh Census: 1890,* p. 46; Henry M. Utley, Byron M. Cutcheon, and Clarence M. Burton, *Michigan as a Province, Territory and State* (New York, 1906), IV, 265–66. A study of Polish sources sets the population of Poles in Detroit at 22,000 in 1885. Mary R. Napolska, *The Polish Immigrant in Detroit to 1914* (Chicago, 1946), p. 30; Detroit *Free Press:* June 27, 1890; Detroit *Evening News:* June 28, 1890.
23. George N. Fuller, *Historic Michigan* (Washington, 1925), II, 819–20; Farmer, *The History of Detroit and Michigan,* pp. 844–45; Fred E. Farnsworth to Cyrus G. Luce on November 7, 1888, Fred E. Farnsworth Papers.
24. *Michigan Manual 1889,* pp. 167–68, 370–79, 425–34, 586–87, 590–95.
25. John C. Lodge, *I Remember Detroit* (Detroit, 1949), p. 128.
26. Detroit *Advertiser and Tribune:* November 4, 1863; November 8, 1865; Detroit *Evening News:* November 5, 1873; November 4, 1874; November 3, 1875; November 8, 1876; November 7, 1877; November 7, 1878; November 5, 1879; November 3, 1880; November 9, 1881; November 8, 1882; November 6, 1883; November 5, 1884; October 30, 1889; Detroit *Free Press:* November 4, 1885; November 4, 1886; November 7, 9, 1887; November 8, 1888.
27. *Eleventh Census: 1890,* pp. 219–21, 368–69; Detroit *Free Press:* November 9, 1887; November 8, 1888.
28. Detroit *Evening News:* October 8, 1889.
29. Arthur Pound, "Don M. Dickinson," *Michigan in the Cleveland Era,* ed. Earl D. Babst and Lewis G. Vander Velde (Ann Arbor, 1948), p. 117.
30. Detroit *Evening News:* October 2, 3, 7, 8, 1889; Detroit *Free Press:* October 31, 1889.
31. William Livingstone, *Livingstone's History of the Republican Party* (Detroit, 1900), II, 316.
32. William P. Lovett, *Detroit Rules Itself* (Boston, 1930), p. 189.
33. "Pingree—The First Insurgent," *Detroit Saturday Night:* November 11, 1911.
34. The Democratic city ticket included Patrick J. Sheahan (Police Justice), Charles W. Casgrain (City Attorney), John Lennane (City Treasurer), James Phelan (Justice of Peace), Patrick Dee, and James V. Moran (Board of Estimates). Detroit *Free Press:* October 29, 30, 1889; Detroit *Evening News:* October 30, 1889; November 5, 1889.
35. *Ibid.,* November 9, 1887; November 4, 1889.

36. *Ibid.*, November 2, 4, 8, 1889; Pingree quoted in Starring, "Hazen S. Pingree," p. 132; "Pingree—The First Insurgent," *Detroit Saturday Night:* November 25, 1911; December 30, 1911.
37. Detroit *Evening News:* November 7, 1889. The "Big Four" of the Michigan Club were James L. Edson, William H. Elliott, Clarence A. Black, and Hazen S. Pingree.
38. The election gave the G.O.P. control of sixteen of the council's thirty-two seats. Detroit *Free Press:* November 6, 1889.
39. Detroit *Free Press:* November 9, 1887; November 2, 6, 1889; Detroit *Evening News:* November 2, 5, 1889; *Detroit Journal Yearbook 1890*, p. 85. The ninth ward reportedly included more members of the Knights of Labor than any other ward in the city and had provided the Labor candidate for mayor with 25 per cent of his vote in 1887. Only the Polish third precinct of the ninth ward had failed to provide the Labor candidate with strong support. The table below graphically illustrates the movement of the labor vote to Pingree in 1889.

Ninth Ward Election Returns for Mayor

	Pridgeon (Dem.)	Yemans (Rep.)	Robinson (Labor)
1887	1,008	617	403
	Pridgeon	Pingree	
1889	1,119	1,015	(no Labor candidate)

40. The ethnic character of these precincts was adduced from the general description of nationality groups and their relative location in wards given in *Eleventh Census: 1890*, pp. 219–27; Napolska, *The Polish Immigrant in Detroit to 1914*, pp. 89, 93–94, 96–98; Lois Rankin, "Detroit Nationality Groups," *Michigan History Magazine*, XXII (Spring, 1939), 177; Phyllis K. Metzler, "The People of Detroit: 1889," *Detroit Historical Society Bulletin*, xx (January, 1964), 6, 7; Detroit *Tribune:* November 6, 1889; and Detroit *Evening News:* November 5, 1889. Election returns were obtained from Detroit *Free Press:* November 9, 1887; November 6, 1889; and Detroit *Evening News:* November 7, 1888.
41. Detroit *Free Press:* November 9, 1887; November 6, 1889; Detroit *Evening News:* November 7, 1888.
42. *Eleventh Census: 1890*, pp. 368–69; Detroit *Free Press:* November 6, 1889.
43. Detroit *Evening News:* November 5, 1889; Detroit *Tribune:* November 6, 1889; January 15, 22, 1890.

CHAPTER 2

1. *Journal of the Common Council*, 1890 (Detroit, 1891), pp. 1–2.
2. Detroit *Journal:* May 2, June 3, 1890, Pingree Scrapbook (hereafter, P.S.); *Journal of the Common Council*, 1891 (Detroit, 1892),

p. 5; Norman Beasley and George W. Stark, *Made in Detroit* (New York, 1957), p. 22; George B. Catlin, *The Story of Detroit* (Detroit, 1926), pp. 593, 598.

3. Detroit *Journal:* April 25, 1890; May 1, 2, 1890; Detroit *Evening News:* April 25, 29, 1890; January 11, 1897, P.S.; Catlin, *The Story of Detroit*, p. 593.

4. Detroit *Journal:* May 29, 1890; June 11, 1890; July 27, 1892; Detroit *Free Press:* June 4, 1890; June 8, 1892; Detroit *Evening News:* June 16, 1892; September 26, 1892; December 21, 1892; July 5, 1893, P.S.; *Journal of the Common Council*, 1890, pp. 131–36.

5. Detroit *Journal:* August 12, 1896, P.S.; *Twentieth Annual Report of the Board of Public Works, 1893–94* (Detroit, 1894), p. 8; Edward W. Bemis, "Detroit's Efforts to Own Her Street Railways," *Municipal Affairs*, III (September, 1899), 473.

6. Detroit *Tribune:* March 26, 1890; May 22, 1890; Detroit *Evening News:* May 22, 1890, P.S.; *Journal of the Common Council*, 1890, pp. 122–23.

7. Detroit *Free Press:* March 28, 1890; Detroit *Tribune:* April 24, 1890; May 23, 1890, P.S.

8. Detroit *Tribune:* March 29, 1890; February 4, 16, 1892; Detroit *Journal:* August 12, 1892, P.S.

9. Detroit *Journal:* March 25, 1892; Detroit *Tribune:* January 14, 1893; May 26, 1893, P.S.

10. Pingree quoted in Detroit *Tribune:* August 16, 1894; Detroit *Evening News:* August 16, 1894, P.S.; "Hazen S. Pingree, Mayor, Etc. v. The Board of Education of the City of Detroit," 94 *Michigan*, 404–8.

11. Hazen S. Pingree, *Facts and Opinions* (Detroit, 1895), pp. 201–2.

12. Detroit *Journal:* October 19, 1894; June 13, 1895; October 2, 1896, P.S.

13. *Journal of the Common Council*, 1890, pp. 395, 539, 667, 839, 860.

14. Unidentified newspaper clipping, P.S., March–April, 1892; Detroit *Tribune:* February 18, 1891; Detroit *Evening News:* December 8, 1892; Detroit *Free Press:* February 20, 24, 28, 1892; April 5, 1893, P.S.

15. Detroit *Tribune:* May 27, 1891; June 20, 1891, P.S.; *Journal of the Common Council*, 1891, pp. 6, 410, 522.

16. Lansing *State Affairs*, December 13, 1893; *Journal of the Common Council*, 1893, pp. 774–75; *ibid.*, 1895, p. 435; John C. Lodge, *I Remember Detroit* (Detroit, 1949), p. 65.

17. Pingree quoted in Detroit *Evening News:* April 10, 1895; July 31, 1896; *Journal of the Common Council*, 1893, p. 774; Detroit *Free Press:* June 22, 1894; September 1, 1895, P.S.; *Journal of the Common Council*, 1894, p. 4; *ibid.*, 1895, p. 1459; *ibid.*, 1897, p. 12.

CHAPTER 3

1. John A. Fairlie, *Municipal Administration* (New York, 1906), pp. 292–93, 296; Frederic W. Speirs, *The Street Railway System of Philadelphia: Its History and Present Condition,* Johns Hopkins University *Studies in Historical and Political Science,* iii-iv-v (March, April, May, 1897), 10, 28; James B. Walker, *Fifty Years of Rapid Transit* (New York, 1918), p. 5; Delos F. Wilcox, *Municipal Franchises* (New York, 1911), ii, 127.

2. Fairlie, *Municipal Administration,* p. 295; *Street Railway Journal,* v (March, 1889), 62; (July, 1889), 200, 202, 208; (October, 1889), 287, 316, 324; (November, 1889), 379; (December, 1889), 430–33, 427; vii (February, 1891), 82.

3. Edward W. Bemis Testimony, *Report of the United States Industrial Commission on Transportation* (Washington, 1901), ix, 88–89; Edward E. Higgins, "Municipal and Private Management of Street Railways," *Municipal Affairs,* i (September, 1897), 465–67. Edward W. Bemis "Columbus Attempts to Secure Three-Cent Fares," *Municipal Affairs,* v (December, 1901), 905. For Milwaukee, see John A. Butler "Street Railway Problem in Milwaukee," *Municipal Affairs,* iv (March, 1900), 212–17.

4. Delos F. Wilcox, *Analysis of the Electric Railway Problem* (New York, 1921), p. 75; Wilcox, *Municipal Franchises,* ii, 20–21, 350; Department of Commerce and Labor, Bureau of the Census, Special Reports, *Street and Electric Railways 1902* (Washington, 1905), pp. 11, 48–49; *Street Railway Journal,* xix (March, 1902), 372.

5. T. C. Martin, "The Social Side of the Electric Railway," *Street Railway Journal,* vi (April, 1890), 202–3; Wilcox, *Municipal Franchises,* ii, 9–10; Charles H. Cooley, "Social Significance of Street Railways," *Publications of the American Economic Association* (Baltimore, 1891), vi, 72; John R. Commons, *Social Reform and the Church* (New York, 1894), p. 143; Edward W. Bemis, *Municipal Monopolies* (New York, 1899), p. 508; A. H. Sinclair, "Municipal Monopolies and Their Management," *Street Railway Journal,* vii (October, 1891), 519.

6. Sam Bass Warner, Jr., *Streetcar Suburbs: The Process of Growth in Boston, 1870–1900* (Cambridge, 1962), pp. 62–64, 67; Eric Kocher, "Detroit's Substantial Families 1900," in "Economic and Physical Growth of Detroit 1701–1935" (MS, Michigan Historical Collections, 1935), Appendix [1]; *Report of Vital and Social Statistics of the United States at the Eleventh Census: 1890* (Washington, 1896), iv, Part ii, 219–27; Department of Commerce, *Street and Electric Railways 1902,* p. 27.

7. *Street and Electric Railways 1902,* p. 30; Cooley, "Social Signifi-

cance of Street Railways," p. 72; Warner, *Streetcar Suburbs*, pp. 15, 16, 21.

8. *Street Railway Journal*, VII (May, 1891), 529; *ibid.*, VIII (March, 1892), 136; (February, 1892), 89; *Report on Transportation Business of the United States at the Eleventh Census: 1890* (Washington, 1895), XIV, Part I, 688; *Street Railway Review*, V (August, 1895), 519; *Journal of the Common Council*, 1890 (Detroit, 1890), p. 2.

9. Graeme O'Geran, *A History of the Detroit Street Railways* (Detroit, 1931), pp. 29, 93–94; *Detroit Journal:* August 25, 1890; Pingree Scrapbook (hereafter P.S.).

10. *Detroit Journal:* March 28, 1891; April 17, 1891, P.S.; *Ninth Annual Report of the Bureau of Labor and Industrial Statistics* (Lansing, 1892), pp. 344–56.

11. Detroit *Tribune:* April 25, 1891, P.S.

12. Detroit *Evening News:* December 6, 1892; Detroit *Free Press:* April 23, 1891, P.S.; *Ninth Annual Report of the Bureau of Labor and Industrial Statistics*, p. 347.

13. Detroit *Evening News:* April 25, 26, 28, 1891; Detroit *Free Press:* April 23, 24, 25, 1891, P.S.; Harry Barnard, *Independent Man: The Life of Senator James Couzens* (New York, 1958), p. 26.

14. *Detroit Journal:* April 22, 1891; Detroit *Free Press:* April 23, 1891, P.S.

15. Hazen S. Pingree, *Facts and Opinions* (Detroit, 1895), pp. 37–40; Detroit *Free Press:* April 23, 24, 1891, P.S.; Hazen S. Pingree to Dwight Warren, July 18, 1894, Pingree Papers.

16. Detroit *Tribune:* May 19, 1891, P.S.; Pingree quoted in Pingree, *Facts and Opinions*, pp. 51–52.

17. Detroit *Tribune:* July 3, 1891, P.S.

18. Detroit *Evening News:* July 3, 1891, P.S.

19. Pingree, *Facts and Opinions*, pp. 52–54; Detroit *Tribune:* July 7, 1891, P.S.

20. *Journal of the Common Council*, 1891, pp. 553–54.

21. "Pingree—The First Insurgent," *Detroit Saturday Night:* January 13, 1912; Detroit *Tribune:* July 8, 1891; Detroit *Free Press:* July 8, 1891, P.S.

22. Malcolm W. Bingay, *Detroit Is My Own Home Town* (Indianapolis, 1946), pp. 230, 238.

23. Lodge cited in William P. Lovett, *Detroit Rules Itself* (Boston, 1930), p. 189.

24. Detroit *Free Press:* April 2, 1890, P.S.

25. Chase S. Osborn, *The Iron Hunter* (New York, 1919), p. 128; Detroit *Evening News:* July 15, 1801; June 23, 1901, P.S.

26. *Journal of the Common Council*, 1891, pp. 560–61, 627, 668, 702, 790–91; *Detroit Journal:* August 19, 1891.; Pingree quoted in

Hazen S. Pingree, "Detroit: A Municipal Study," *Outlook,* LV (February 6, 1897), 438.

27. *Journal of the Common Council,* 1891, pp. 993–94; *New York Times:* April 25, 1892; Cyril A. Player, "Hazen S. Pingree: The Biography of an American Commonplace," (MS, B.H.C., 1931), p. 123. For the McMillan family's financial interest in the Citizens' Street Railway Company see George M. Black to James McMillan, March 10, 1892, McMillan Papers; Detroit *Evening News:* November 29, 1890; Detroit *Journal:* October 10, 1891, P.S.

28. Detroit *Times:* October 20, 1891; Detroit *Free Press:* September 26, 1891; October 21, 27, 1891; November 4, 1891; Detroit *Critic:* October 25, 1891; November 1, 1891.

29. Detroit *Tribune:* September 13, 15, 1891; Detroit *Journal:* September 14, 1891; October 6, 1891; Catlin, *The Story of Detroit,* p. 622; Pingree quoted in Detroit *Free Press:* September 15, 1891. Temporarily out of view, the Hendries still retained ownership of the firm as bondholders. Detroit *Tribune:* March 31, 1892.

30. *Journal of the Common Council,* 1891, pp. 945–47; *ibid.,* 1892, pp. 3–4, 15, 22, 39; Detroit *Tribune:* March 5, 1892, P.S.

31. Detroit *Evening News:* March 15, 1892, P.S.; *Journal of the Common Council,* 1892, p. 139.

32. Detroit *Tribune:* March 16, 17, 31, 1892; Detroit *Free Press:* March 17, 18, 1892; Detroit *Journal:* March 17, 1892, P.S.; Elwood T. Hance to James McMillan, March 19, 1892, McMillan Papers.

33. Pingree quoted in *Journal of the Common Council,* 1892, p. 139; Pingree, *Facts and Opinions,* p. 56.

34. Detroit *Evening News:* December 6, 1892, P.S.

35. "City of Detroit *v.* Detroit City Ry. Co. *et al.,*" 56 *Federal Reporter,* 867–95.

36. "Detroit Citizens St. Ry. Co. *et al. v.* City of Detroit," 64 *Federal Reporter,* 628–47.

37. *Journal of the Common Council,* 1893, pp. 23–24; Pingree, *Facts and Opinions,* pp. 204–5, 207; Hutchins, *Jere C. Hutchins,* p. 132.

38. *Journal of the Common Council,* 1893, pp. 23–24, 37; Detroit *Evening News:* January 19, February 1, March 9, 1893; *Street Railway Employees Gazette:* September, 1892; Detroit *Tribune:* February 16, 1893, P.S.; "The City of Detroit *v.* The Fort Wayne & Belle Isle Railway Company," 95 *Michigan,* 456–62. Detroit was the only major city in the country to offer workingmen's fares; Toronto made them available in 1891 and Saginaw, Michigan, in 1895.

39. *Journal of the Common Council,* 1892, pp. 3, 200, 257, 406–7, 417; Detroit *Tribune:* May 9, 1892; October 19, 1892; Detroit *Free Press:* May 28, 1892, P.S.

40. Detroit *Tribune:* May 28, 1892, P.S.

41. Detroit *Journal:* August 9, 1892, P.S.

42. Detroit *Tribune:* December 9, 1892; July 12, 13, 1893, P.S.; *Journal of the Common Council,* 1893, pp. 599–600, 615–16.

43. Detroit *Evening News:* July 8, 1893; Detroit *Journal:* July 8, 1893; December 5, 1893, P.S. The city's rate structure in 1894 was five cents for a single fare, six tickets for twenty-five cents, and working-men's tickets at designated hours.

44. *Report on Transportation Business at the Eleventh Census: 1890,* XIV, Part I, 734; Catlin, *The Story of Detroit,* p. 623; 61 *Federal Reporter,* 3; Detroit *Journal:* November 23, 1893; December 20, 1893; *Detroit Journal Year-Book for 1890* (Detroit, 1890), p. 88; *Report of the U.S. Industrial Commission,* IX, 88–89.

45. *Journal of the Common Council,* 1894, pp. 7–13, 242–48; Detroit *Evening News:* March 16, 1894, P.S. Pingree's daughter, Gertrude, who had been ill for several weeks, died in March, 1894.

46. *Journal of the Common Council,* 1894, pp. 1083–84, 1130–33; Detroit *Tribune:* July 25, 1894; August 3, 10, 1894; Wright quoted Detroit *Evening News:* April 30, 1894; Detroit *Journal:* [August, 1894], P.S.; O'Geran, *A History of the Detroit Street Railways,* pp. 118–19.

47. Pingree, "Detroit: A Municipal Study," p. 438.

48. Pingree, *Facts and Opinions,* pp. 85–86, 122; *Journal of the Common Council,* 1893, p. 4.

49. J. N. Beckley, "Report of the Committee on Transfers on Street Railways," *Street Railway Journal,* x (November, 1894), 680; *Journal of the Common Council,* 1894, pp. 1130, 1416–17.

50. Charles Wright to James McMillan, January 14, 1892; M. E. Dee to James McMillan, July 23, 1894, McMillan Papers; Detroit *Journal:* January 11, 1893, P.S.; George Gates cited in "Municipal Progress," *Outlook,* LIII (March 21, 1896), 522; Detroit *Evening News:* January 11, 12, 1893, P.S.

51. *Ibid.:* March 8, 1893.

52. W. K. Anderson to James McMillan, October 28, 1893, McMillan Papers; Detroit *Free Press:* November 25, 1894; Catlin, *The Story of Detroit,* p. 622; Detroit *Evening News:* July 26, 1893, P.S.; *Journal of the Common Council,* 1893, p. 498. All of Pingree's opponents were listed in the social register. *Detroit Blue Book: A Society Directory for the City of Detroit* (Detroit, 1885), pp. 32, 49, 74, 79, 87, 96–97, 115–16, 118, 122, 138, 191, 195–97.

53. Pingree, "Detroit: A Municipal Study," p. 437.

54. Pingree quoted in Detroit *Tribune:* November 4, 1893; Detroit *Evening News:* January 12, 1893; Commons cited in Detroit *Free Press:* November 30, 1894, P.S.; Jane Addams to Henry D. Lloyd, December 22, 1895, Lloyd Papers, State Historical Society of Wisconsin; Webster quoted in Detroit *Journal:* January 19, 1894, P.S.; E. W. Bagley to Richard T. Ely, May 9, 1894, Ely Papers, State His-

torical Society of Wisconsin; *New Nation*, III (November 18, 1893),
407; Lloyd to Pingree, November 12, 1895, Pingree Papers.

CHAPTER 4

1. *Journal of the Common Council*, 1893 (Detroit, 1894), p. 1152
   and *ibid.*, 1894, p. 376.
2. Detroit *Times:* June 17, 1891, P.S.; *Journal of the Common Council*, 1891, p. 42; Pingree quoted in *ibid.*, 1892, p. 6.
3. Detroit *Evening News:* April 1, 15, 16, 1892, P.S.; Pingree quoted
   in *Journal of the Common Council*, 1893, p. 6; "The Detroit Transportation Company *v.* The Board of Assessors of the City Detroit,"
   91 *Michigan*, 382–90.
4. Detroit *Evening News:* February 16, 18, 1893, P.S. Pingree's figure
   of $5,000,000 was derived from the practice of assessing property
   at about 70 per cent of value.
5. Detroit *Tribune:* February 18, 21, 23, 1893; Detroit *Evening News:*
   February 21, 1893, P.S.
6. Detroit *Evening News:* February 24, 26, 27, 1893; January 12, 1894,
   P.S.
7. *Journal of the Common Council*, 1891, p. 6; George B. Catlin, *The
   Story of Detroit* (Detroit, 1926), p. 609.
8. Pingree quoted in Detroit *Journal:* December 23, 1892, P.S.; Catlin,
   The Story of Detroit, p. 610; *Journal of the Common Council*, 1892,
   p. 7; *ibid.*, 1895, pp. 7, 8; *ibid.*, 1897, p. 4.
9. Pingree quoted in *Journal of the Common Council*, 1893, p. 6 and
   ibid., 1895, p. 147.
10. Detroit *Journal:* December 7, 1895, P.S.
11. *Journal of the Common Council*, 1893, p. 756; Emory Wendell, ed.,
    Wendell's History of Banking and Banks and Bankers of Michigan
    (Detroit, n.d.) I, 256–57.
12. Pingree quoted in *Journal of the Common Council*, 1893, p. 756;
    ibid., 1895, p. 7.
13. *Eleventh Annual Report of the Bureau of Labor and Industrial Sta-
    tistics Michigan 1894* (Lansing, 1894), pp. 425, 438; Arthur B.
    Moehlman, *Public Education in Detroit* (Bloomington, 1925), p.
    146; *Fourteenth Annual Report of the Board of Poor Commissioners,
    1893–94*, p. 5; *Journal of the Common Council*, 1893, p. 1152.
14. Detroit *Evening News:* December 2, 1893, P.S.; Norman Beasley
    and George W. Stark, *Made in Detroit* (New York, 1957), p. 20;
    Catlin, *The Story of Detroit*, p. 613; *Journal of the Common Council*,
    1896, p. 978; *Census of the State of Michigan 1894* (Lansing, 1896)
    I, 216–27; *Fourteenth Annual Report of the Board of Poor Com-
    missioners, 1893–94*, pp. 5, 49.
15. *Fourteenth Annual Report of the Board of Poor Commissioners,*

1893–94, p. 49; *Twentieth Annual Report of the Board of Public Works, 1893–94* (Detroit, 1894), p. 42; Detroit *Free Press:* April 14, 1894; Detroit *Journal:* December 12, 1894; Detroit *Evening News:* August 25, 1893, P.S.

16. Detroit *Tribune:* September 8, 12, 1893; Detroit *Evening News:* December 9, 1893, P.S.

17. *Patriotic American:* October 31, 1893; July 14, 1894; August 4, 1894; *Michigan Catholic:* September 13, 1894; November 26, 1896; Detroit *Evening News:* February 14, 1893; August 28, 1893; Detroit *Journal:* December 23, 1893; March 31, 1894, P.S.; *Fifty-Second Annual Report of the Board of Education, 1894–95* (Detroit, 1895), pp. 14, 15, 38; *Fifty-Third Annual Report of the Board of Education, 1895–96* (Detroit, 1896), pp. 12–15, 121–24.

18. Detroit *Tribune:* September 7, 1893; April 20, 1894; Detroit *Evening News:* October 1, 1894; Detroit *Journal:* April 18, 1894, P.S.

19. *Twelfth Annual Report of the Bureau of Labor and Industrial Statistics, Michigan, 1895* (Lansing, 1895), p. 513; Detroit *Journal:* April 18, 19, 1894; Detroit *Evening News:* April 18, 1894, P.S.

20. *Twelfth Annual Report of the Bureau of Labor and Industrial Statistics Michigan, 1895,* p. 513; Detroit *Evening News:* April 19, 20, 1894; Detroit *Tribune:* April 19, 1894; Detroit *Free Press:* April 20, 1894, P.S.

21. *Michigan Catholic:* April 26, 1894; Detroit *Tribune:* April 20, 1894, P.S.

22. *Michigan Legislative Manual and Official Directory 1899–1900* (Lansing, 1899), p. 322; *Michigan Catholic:* April 19, 1894. For views of workers toward immigration, see *Eleventh Annual Report of the Bureau of Labor and Industrial Statistics, Michigan, 1894,* pp. 372–78.

23. *Ibid.,* p. 372; *Twelfth Annual Report of the Bureau of Labor and Industrial Statistics, Michigan, 1895,* p. 235; *Thirteenth Annual Report of the Bureau of Labor and Industrial Statistics, Michigan, 1896* (Lansing, 1896), pp. 52, 160.

24. *Journal of the Common Council,* 1893, p. 754; *ibid.,* 1895, pp. 16, 469, 489; *Tenth Annual Report of the Bureau of Labor and Industrial Statistics, Michigan, 1893* (Lansing, 1893), p. xxviii.

25. Pingree quoted in *Journal of the Common Council,* 1893, pp. 1152–53; *ibid.,* 1894, p. 376; *ibid.,* 1895, p. 16; Catlin, *The Story of Detroit,* p. 614.

26. *Journal of the Common Council,* 1893, pp. 1127, 1152.

27. Pingree quoted in *ibid.,* p. 1152; *ibid.,* 1895, pp. 4, 786–87, 1127; Catlin, *The Story of Detroit,* p. 613; *Forty-Third Annual Report of the Board of Water Commissioners, 1894* (Detroit, 1895), p. 8; *Fifth Annual Report of the Commissioners of Parks and Boulevards, 1893* (Detroit, 1894), pp. 5, 6; *Sixth Annual Report of the Commissioners of Parks and Boulevards, 1894* (Detroit, 1895), pp. 3, 4,

10, 21; *Twentieth Annual Report of the Board of Public Works,
1893–94* (Detroit, 1894), pp. 40, 73; *Forty-Fourth Annual Report
of the Board of Water Commissioners, 1894* (Detroit, 1895), pp. 5,
6; *Twenty-Second Annual Report of the Board of Public Works,
1895–96* (Detroit, 1896), p. 60: *Forty-Fifth Annual Report of the
Board of Water Commissioners, 1895* (Detroit, 1896), pp. 10, 11.

28. *Journal of the Common Council,* 1893, p. 1152; *ibid.,* 1894, pp. 1155–57.

29. Detroit *Journal:* December 22, 1893; May 3, 1894, P.S.; Pingree quoted in Detroit *Evening News:* May 3, 1894 and *Journal of the Common Council,* 1893, p. 1152.

30. Detroit *Tribune:* November 30, 1894; December 4, 1894; Pingree quoted in Detroit *Evening News:* December 2, 1894, P.S.

31. Leah Hannah Feder, *Unemployment Relief in Periods of Depression* (New York, 1936), p. 158; Detroit *Journal:* June 7, 11, 1894; Reverend James F. Dickie, "Reminiscences of Detroit," *Michigan History Magazine,* xiv (Autumn, 1930), 637; *Journal of the Common Council,* 1895, p. 147.

32. Detroit *Evening News:* June 11, 1894; Pingree quoted in Detroit *Free Press:* June 6, 1894, P.S.; Hazen S. Pingree, "Mayor Pingree's Potato Patch Plan," *Public Opinion,* xx (January 23, 1896), 109.

33. *Ibid.;* Detroit *Tribune:* July 21, 1894, P.S.; Hazen S. Pingree, "How Can a City Best Care for Its Poor?" *Our Day: The Altruistic Review,* xiv (May, 1895), 257.

34. Pingree quoted in *Journal of the Common Council,* 1895, p. 15; Cornelius Gardner, *Report of the Agricultural Committee, 1894* (Detroit, 1894), pp. 1–5; Catlin, *The Story of Detroit,* pp. 616–17.

35. *Fifteenth Annual Report of the Board of Poor Commissioners, 1894–95,* p. 20; *Sixteenth Annual Report of the Board of Poor Commissioners, 1895–96,* p. 19; Report of the Agricultural Committee, in *Journal of the Common Council,* 1897, pp. 5–9; *Journal of the Common Council,* 1895, pp. 15, 16, 493.

36. *New York Times:* November 20, 1896. Pingree quoted in the Detroit *Evening News:* December 15, 1896, P.S. A sampling of some of the literature generated by Pingree's potato patch plan includes Frederic W. Speirs, "Vacant-Lot Cultivation," *Charities Review,* viii (April, 1898), 74–6; Michael Mikkelson, "Cultivation of Vacant City Lots," *Forum,* xxi (May, 1896), 313–17; B. O. Flower, "A Successful Experiment for the Maintenance of Self-Respecting Manhood," *Arena,* xv (March, 1896), 545–51; "Detroit Plan for the Cultivation of Vacant Lots," *Annals of the American Academy of Political and Social Science,* vi (July, 1895), 191, 566–67; Allan Sutherland, "Farming Vacant Lots," *Review of Reviews,* xxxi (May, 1905), 567–68; *Outlook,* liii (April 4, 1896), 618–19; *ibid.,* lix (July 16, 1898), 660; and *American Magazine of Civics,* vi (May, 1895), 550–51.

CHAPTER 5

1. *Journal of the Common Council*, 1894 (Detroit, 1895), p. 2
2. Louis Stotz and Alexander Jamison, *History of the Gas Industry* (New York, 1938), p. 110; Harold C. Passer, *The Electrical Manufacturers 1875–1900* (Cambridge, 1953), pp. 19, 20, 41–42, 53–54, 56, 64; Arthur A. Bright, Jr., *The Electric-Lamp Industry* (New York, 1949), pp. 82–83, 94.
3. William H. Lane, *A History of Electric Service in Detroit* (Detroit, 1937), pp. 9, 18–19; George B. Catlin, *The Story of Detroit* (Detroit, 1926), pp. 601–2.
4. *Ibid.*, pp. 602–3; Lane, *A History of Electric Service in Detroit*, pp. 32–33; *Journal of the Common Council*, 1890 (Detroit, 1891), p. 2.
5. John A. Fairlie, *Municipal Administration* (New York, 1906), pp. 285–86; Luther R. Nash, *The Economics of Public Utilities* (New York, 1925), pp. 333–34; Delos F. Wilcox, *Municipal Franchises* (New York, 1910), I, 141; John R. Commons, "Municipal Electric Lighting," *Municipal Monopolies*, ed. Edward W. Bemis (New York, 1899), pp. 66–67.
6. Frank Parsons, *The City for the People* (Philadelphia, 1900), pp. 25–27.
7. James B. Cahoon, "Municipal Electric Lighting Opposed," *Municipal Affairs*, VI (Winter, 1902–03), 646; Raymond C. Miller, *Kilowatts at Work: A History of the Detroit Edison Company* (Detroit, 1957), pp. 34–35.
8. Detroit *Evening News:* October 19, 1892; Catlin, *The Story of Detroit*, p. 602; *Journal of the Common Council*, 1890, pp. 30–31; *ibid.*, 1891 (Detroit, 1892), p. 162; Detroit *Tribune:* November 17, 1892, P.S.
9. Pingree quoted in Parsons, *The City for the People*, p. 226 and Detroit *Free Press:* December 18, 1892, P.S.; *Journal of the Common Council*, 1892 (Detroit, 1893), pp. 5–6.
10. Detroit *Tribune:* December 17, 1892; Detroit *Free Press:* December 23, 1892, P.S.
11. *Journal of the Common Council*, 1893 (Detroit, 1894), pp. 4, 5.
12. Detroit *Free Press:* December 18, 1892, P.S.
13. Detroit *Tribune:* February 10, 17, 1893; March 18, 1893, P.S.; *Journal of the Common Council*, 1893, p. 5; Hazen S. Pingree to Richard T. Ely, March 10, 1893, Ely Papers, State Historical Society of Wisconsin. Assistant city attorney, David E. Heineman, quoted in *Municipal Affairs*, VI (Winter, 1902-3), 847.
14. "Pingree—The First Insurgent," *Detroit Saturday Night:* January 20, 1912; Detroit *Evening News:* February 23, 1893, P.S.; *Journal of the Common Council*, 1893, p. 216.

15. Detroit *Free Press:* April 8, 1893, P.S.
16. *Journal of the Common Council,* 1893, pp. 250–51; Pingree quoted in *ibid.,* p. 258.
17. Pingree quoted in Detroit *Tribune:* April 26, 1893, P.S.; *Journal of the Common Council,* 1893, pp. 270–71.
18. Detroit *Tribune:* April 26, 1893; Catlin, *The Story of Detroit,* pp. 603–4.
19. Detroit *Evening News:* May 23, 29, 1893; June 2, 1893, P.S.
20. Pingree quoted in *ibid.:* June 2, 1893; Catlin, *The Story of Detroit,* p. 604.
21. *Journal of the Common Council,* 1896 (Detroit, 1897), p. 10.
22. Edward W. Bemis, "Municipal Electric Lighting," *City Government,* v (September, 1898), 99.
23. Frederick F. Ingram, "Municipal Lighting in Detroit," 823–24; Joseph E. Lockwood, "Analysis of Municipal Electric Lighting in Detroit," 826–27, in *Municipal Affairs,* vi (Winter, 1902–3); Commons, "Municipal Electric Lighting," *Municipal Monopolies,* p. 171; Alex Dow quoted in Detroit *Free Press:* June 11, 1896, P.S.; Commons quoted in "Municipal Electric Lighting," *Municipal Affairs,* i (December, 1897), 643.
24. Frank Parsons, "The People's Lamps," *Arena,* xiii (June, 1895), 118–30; (August, 1895), 381–400; xiv (September, 1895), 86–109; (November, 1895), 439–63; "Municipal Ownership in the United States," *Social Review,* i (February, 1897), n.p.; "Municipal Control of Lighting," *American Gas Light Journal,* lxiii (December 30, 1895), 1050; M. Judson Francisco, "The Fallacy of Municipal Ownership," *American Gas Light Journal,* lix (September 11, 1893), 362–63; M. J. Francisco, *Municipal Ownership vs. Private Cooperation* (Rutland, 1898), pp. 3–146; "The Cost of Municipal Lighting in Detroit, Michigan," *The Electrical World,* xxxii (August 13, 1898), 162; Editorial, *Electrical World and Engineer,* xxxiii (April 15, 1899), 464; Edward W. Bemis and Alton D. Adams testimony on municipal ownership in *Report of the United States Industrial Commission on Transportation* (Washington, 1901), ix, 146, 277–81; John A. Fairlie, "Municipal Electric Lighting in Detroit," *Municipal Affairs,* iv (September, 1900), 606; John R. Commons, "Economic and Social Factors in Chicago Municipal Lighting," *Municipal Affairs,* vi (Spring, 1902), 109–15. Joseph F. Johnson, "The Recent History of Municipal Ownership in the United States," pp. 527, 531; Victor Rosewater, "The Case for Municipal Ownership of Electric Lighting," pp. 628–29; James Blake Cahoon, "Municipal Electric Lighting Opposed," pp. 640–43; Frederick F. Ingram, "Municipal Lighting in Detroit," pp. 823–25 in *Municipal Affairs,* vi (Winter, 1902–3). "Municipal Electric Plants," *City Government,* iv (February, 1898), 57; Bemis, "Municipal Electric Lighting," *City Government,* v (September,

1898), 99; George E. Warner, "Public Ownership of Lighting Plant," *City Government*, VI (March, 1899), 51; Parsons, *City for the People*, pp. 131, 242–48; Fairlie, *Municipal Administration*, pp. 285–86; Bemis, *Municipal Monopolies*, pp. 318–30, 271–78; Commons, "Municipal Electric Lighting," *Municipal Monopolies*, pp. 141–42, 171; Wilbur F. Crafts, *Practical Christian Sociology* (New York, 1906), p. 178; United States Bureau of Labor, *Fourteenth Annual Report of the Commissioner of Labor 1899 Water, Gas and Electric-Light Plants Under Private and Municipal Ownership* (Washington, 1905), pp. 511, 550–52, 554–55.

25. Cahoon, "Municipal Electric Lighting Opposed," pp. 638–40, 647; John A. Fairlie, *Essays in Municipal Administration* (New York, 1908), pp. 223–24; Commons, "Municipal Electric Lighting," *Municipal Monopolies*, p. 177.

26. R. R. Bowker, "Public Control, Ownership or Operation of Municipal Franchises?" *Municipal Affairs*, I (December, 1897), 629–30; John R. Commons, "Municipal Electric Lighting," *ibid.*, 668; Rosewater, "The Case for Municipal Ownership of Electric Lighting," *Municipal Affairs*, VI (Winter, 1902–3), 633–34; Cahoon, "Municipal Electric Lighting Opposed," pp. 640–43; Lane, *A History of Electric Service in Detroit*, p. 38; Ingram, "Municipal Lighting in Detroit," p. 824.

27. Cahoon, "Municipal Electric Lighting Opposed," p. 647.

28. Stotz, *History of the Gas Industry*, pp. 4–9, 16, 57; Silas Farmer, *The History of Detroit and Michigan* (Detroit, 1884), p. 468.

29. Bronson C. Keeler, "Municipal Control of Gas Works," *Forum*, VIII (November, 1889), 288; Edward W. Bemis, "Municipal Ownership of Gas in the United States," *Publications of the American Economic Association*, VI (July–September, 1891), 295–305, 307–8.

30. Bemis, *Municipal Monopolies*, pp. 592–93, 595–602; Parsons, *The City for the People*, pp. 42–45; John H. Gray, "The Relation of the Gas Supply to the Public," *Municipal Affairs*, II (June, 1898), 189–90.

31. Catlin, *The Story of Detroit*, pp. 434–36; Clarence M. Burton, *The City of Detroit Michigan 1901–1922* (Detroit, 1922), I, 386.

32. *Journal of the Common Council*, 1892, p. 3; Hazen S. Pingree, *Facts and Opinions* (Detroit, 1895), p. 143.

33. Hazen S. Pingree, "Detroit: A Municipal Study," *Outlook*, LV (February 7, 1897), 442.

34. *Journal of the Common Council*, 1893, p. 996.

35. Joy quoted in Detroit *Journal*: May 23, 1893; *ibid.*: December 24, 1892; Detroit *Evening News*: November 23, 1892; May 23, 26, 28, 1893, P.S.

36. *Ibid.*: May 24, 27, 28, 1893, P.S.

37. *Journal of the Common Council*, 1893, pp. 546, 996.

38. *Ibid.*, p. 996; Pingree, "Detroit: A Municipal Study," p. 440.

39. *Journal of the Common Council,* 1893, pp. 175, 539; Pingree quoted in Detroit *Free Press:* April 8, 1893; June 23, 1893 and Detroit *Evening News:* April 7, 1893, P.S.

40. *American Gas Light Journal,* LIX (October 2, 1893), 480; Detroit *Journal:* June 22, 1893; and Detroit *Free Press:* June 23, 1893, P.S.

41. *Ibid.:* June 23, 1893; Detroit *Evening News:* June 23, 1893, P.S.

42. Catlin, *The Story of Detroit,* pp. 436, 598–99; Detroit *Tribune:* February 3, 11, 1893; Detroit *Evening News:* September 14, 1893, P.S.; *Journal of the Common Council,* 1893, pp. 175, 545.

43. *Ibid.,* p. 539; Pingree quoted in Detroit *Journal:* June 14, 1893, P.S.

44. *Journal of the Common Council,* 1893, pp. 538–41; Detroit *Journal:* June 15, 17, 1893, P.S.

45. Detroit *Free Press:* April 12, 1893; Detroit *Tribune:* September 19, 1893, November 27, 1895; "Pingree *v.* Mutual Gas Company," 107 *Michigan,* 156–60.

46. *Journal of the Common Council,* 1893, p. 996.

47. Pingree quoted in *ibid.,* pp. 996, 1022–26 and "Pingree—The First Insurgent," *Detroit Saturday Night:* December 16, 1911; Detroit *Journal:* October 19, 20, 1893, P.S.

48. Catlin, *The Story of Detroit,* pp. 600–601.

49. Wilcox, *Municipal Franchises,* I, 217; Horace Coon, *American Tel & Tel: The Story of a Great Monopoly* (New York, 1939), p. 60.

50. Statement of Edward J. Hall, *Report of the United States Industrial Commission on Transportation,* IX, 822; James M. Thomas, "The Independent Telephone Movement," *Electrical World,* XXIX (June 26, 1897), 840.

51. U.S. Census, Bulletin 17, *Telephones and Telegraphs 1902* (Washington, 1905), pp. 20–23; Frank Parsons, "The Telephone," *Municipal Monopolies* ed. Edward W. Bemis, pp. 359–61.

52. Coon, *American Tel & Tel,* p. 76; *Social Review,* I (March, 1897), n.p.; Henry V. Johnson, "Municipal Ownership of Public Service Utilities," *City Government,* VII (September, 1899), 60; testimony of Frank Parsons, *Report of the United States Industrial Commission on Transportation,* IX, 177; Wilcox, *Municipal Franchises,* I, 238. During the period from 1880 to 1894 only 237,000 telephones had been installed in the nation under Bell domination, whereas under the spur of competition from 1895 to 1902 more than 1,500,000 telephones were installed.

53. Coon, *American Tel & Tel,* pp. 71–72, 80.

54. Wilcox, *Municipal Franchises,* I, 237–38, 265–66; Coon, *American Tel & Tel,* pp. 88, 91–92, 102; Ohio Independent Telephone Association, *A Discussion of Telephone Competition* (Columbus, 1908), pp. 6–9; Frank S. Dickson, *Telephone Investments and Others* (Cleveland, 1905), pp. 33, 35; U.S. Census, Bulletin 17, *Telephones and Telegraphs 1902,* p. 9.

55. Edward P. Burch, *Telephone Rates in Detroit* (Detroit, 1916), p. 226; *Journal of the Common Council*, 1896, p. 244.
56. Pingree quoted in *ibid.*, pp. 243–44; Detroit *Free Press:* July 24, 1895; March 11, 1896, P.S.
57. Pingree quoted in Detroit *Free Press:* November 25, 1894; *ibid.:* March 16, 1896; Detroit *Journal:* April 3, 1896, P.S.
58. *Journal of the Common Council*, 1896, pp. 239–41, 243–45; Detroit *Evening News:* June 3, 1896, P.S.
59. Burch, *Telephone Rates in Detroit*, p. 227; "The Detroit Telephone Company," *Electrical Engineer*, xxix (June 26, 1897), 838, 845.
60. Detroit *Journal:* February 22, 1897, P.S.; *City Government*, viii (February, 1899), 30.
61. Burch, *Telephone Rates in Detroit*, pp. 228–29; Stephen McCracken, ed., *Detroit in Nineteen Hundred* (Detroit, 1901), p. 17. The survey, which had been conducted by Professor Frank Parsons, showed that in its population class only Indianapolis had as low a residential telephone rate ($24 per annum) as Detroit had. *Report of the United States Industrial Commission on Transportation*, ix, 885.

CHAPTER 6

1. Hazen S. Pingree, *Facts and Opinions* (Detroit, 1895), pp. 59–61; Detroit *Tribune:* November 29, 1894, P.S.; *Journal of the Common Council*, 1894 (Detroit, 1895), pp. 1486–89.
2. Graeme O'Geran, *A History of the Detroit Street Railways* (Detroit, 1931), pp. 139–40; Detroit *Evening News:* July 8, 11, 1895, P.S.; Delos F. Wilcox, *Municipal Franchises* (New York, 1911), ii, 352.
3. Jere C. Hutchins, *Jere C. Hutchins: A Personal Story* (Detroit, 1938), p. 132; Carl Lorenz, *Tom L. Johnson Mayor of Cleveland* (New York, 1911), pp. 1–9; Eugene C. Murdock, "Life of Tom L. Johnson" (Ph.D. thesis, Columbia University, 1951), p. 15; Tom L. Johnson, *My Story*, ed. Elizabeth J. Hauser (New York, 1911), pp. 28, 48–50, 64, 68–70.
4. Johnson quoted in Detroit *Evening News:* June 3, 1896, P.S.; "Detroit Citizens Street Railway Co. v. City of Detroit," 110 *Michigan*, 384–96.
5. Johnson, *My Story*, pp. 21–24; Detroit *Free Press:* April 5, 1895, P.S.; Johnson quoted in *ibid.:* April 9, 1895.
6. Detroit *Evening News:* April 19, 1895, P.S.
7. Detroit *Free Press:* April 18, 19, 1895; Detroit *Tribune:* April 19, 1895, P.S.
8. Bemis, "Detroit's Efforts To Own Her Street Railways," *Municipal Affairs*, iii (September, 1899), 474–75; Hutchins, *Jere C. Hutchins*, p. 140; Wilbur F. Crafts, *Practical Christian Sociology* (New York, 1896), p. 424; Johnson, *My Story*, p. 92.

9. Pingree quoted in *Journal of the Common Council*, 1895 (Detroit, 1896), pp. 1006–9; *ibid.*, p. 1309; Detroit *Tribune:* September 4, 1895, P.S.

10. *Ibid.:* October 10, 1895; Detroit *Evening News:* July 1, 1895; September 10, 1895; November 19, 1895; Detroit *Free Press:* September 11, 1895, P.S. Pingree quoted in *ibid.:* September 19, 1895.

11. Johnson quoted in Detroit *Free Press:* September 23, 1895; Detroit *Evening News:* November 18, 1895, P.S.

12. Detroit *Free Press:* November 21, 25, 1895; Hutchins, *Jere C. Hutchins,* p. 141; O'Geran, *A History of the Detroit Street Railways,* p. 151; Detroit *Evening Press:* November 26, 1895; Detroit *Evening News:* November 21, 1895; December 6, 1895, P.S.

13. *Ibid.:* November 25, 27, 1895; December 12, 1895, P.S.

14. Hutchins, *Jere C. Hutchins,* p. 141; Detroit *Journal:* November 26, 27, 1895; Detroit *Tribune:* January 1, 1896, P.S.; James McMillan to James McMillan, January 6, 1896, McMillan Papers.

15. Detroit *Journal:* December 31, 1895; January 1, 1896; Detroit *Tribune:* January 1, 6, 1896; Pingree remarks cited in *ibid.:* January 7, 1896, P.S.; *Journal of the Common Council,* 1895, pp. 1667–69.

16. Albert Pack to Frank W. Fletcher, July 29, 1896, Fletcher Papers; Pingree quoted in George B. Catlin, *The Story of Detroit* (Detroit, 1926), p. 627 and Detroit *Evening News:* September 18, 1896, P.S.; Tom L. Johnson, "My Fight Against a Three-Cent Fare," *Hampton's Magazine,* xxvii (September, 1911), 368.

17. *Street Railway Review,* vi (September, 1896), 540; Detroit *Journal:* September 10, 1896; Detroit *Free Press:* December 14, 1896, P.S.

18. Pingree quoted in Detroit *Evening News:* August 28, 1896; September 18, 1896; January 7, 1897; Detroit *Free Press:* January 7, 1897, P.S.; Hazen S. Pingree, "The Problem of Municipal Reform. Contract By Referendum," *Arena,* xvii (April, 1897), 707–10.

19. Cleveland *Plain-Dealer:* February 14, 1896; Hartford *Weekly Examiner:* February 29, 1896; Baltimore *News:* March 9, 1896; Johnson quoted in Detroit *Free Press:* November 23, 1895, P.S.; *Street Railway Review,* vii (February, 1897), 75.

20. Buffalo *Express:* December 17, 1895; Providence *Journal:* January 25, 1896; Milwaukee *Daily Record:* February 21, 1896; New York *Sun:* August 10, 1895, P.S.

21. New York *Journal:* February 13, 1896; Boston *Post:* March 18, 1896; Hazen S. Pingree, "Public Control of Franchises" *Proceedings of the Second Annual Meeting of the National Municipal League* (Philadelphia, 1896), pp. 216–18. Detroit *Journal:* February 6, 1896; Pingree Speech Book, 1894–96, Pingree Papers.

22. Pittsburgh *Post:* January 4, 1896; Albany *Press:* January 12, 1896; Philadelphia *Item:* January 5, 1896; Philadelphia *Press:* January 30, 1896; New York *World:* February 11, 1896; St. Louis *Chronicle:*

February 12, 1896; Chicago *Times-Herald:* February 7, 1896; Chicago *Universalist:* February 22, 1896; Chicago *Journal:* December 12, 1896; Cincinnati *Post:* February 11, 1896; Boston *Evening Transcript:* February 15, 1896; Buffalo *Illustrated Express:* February 16, 1896; Washington *Evening Star:* February 15, 1896, P.S.

23. Unidentified clippings: November 30, [1897]; December 7, 18, [1897]; Detroit *Evening News:* March 9, 1897, P.S.; *Outlook,* LXI (April 13, 1899), 851–52; Henry D. Lloyd to William T. Stead and Albert Shaw, April 7, 1897, Lloyd Papers; Harvey S. Ford, "The Life and Times of Golden Rule Jones" (Ph.D. thesis, University of Michigan, 1953), pp. 95–97, 184, 307.

24. Philadelphia *Enquirer:* November 24, 1895; Detroit *Evening News:* December 17, 1896; New York *Journal:* February 12, 1896; *Report and Testimony of the Special Committee of the Assembly To Investigate the Desirability of Municipal Ownership of the Street and Elevated Railroads of the Various Cities of the State* (Albany, 1896), I, 20–22; *Street Railway Journal,* XIX (May, 1902), 597; Frank Mann Stewart, *A Half Century of Municipal Reform: The History of the National Municipal League* (Berkeley, 1950), pp. 57–58; Boston *Evening Transcript:* February 15, 1896, P.S.

25. Hazen S. Pingree, "Municipal Ownership of Street Railways," *Munsey's Magazine,* XXII (November, 1899), 222–24; Hazen S. Pingree, "3c. Fares—No. 3"; "3c. Fares—No. 6, [July, 1899], Ralph Stone Papers.

26. Detroit *Free Press:* May 24, 1899; June 15, 1899; Detroit *Evening News:* May 10, 1899; June 7, 25, 1899, Ralph Stone Scrapbooks, (hereafter S.S.); Johnson, *My Story,* p. 96.

27. *Report of Detroit Street Railway Commission* (Detroit, 1899), pp. 3–36; Detroit *Journal:* May 10, 1899, S.S.

28. *Ibid.:* May 10, 1899; June 9, 1899; Detroit *Evening News:* May 27, 1899; June 25, 1899, S.S.

29. *Ibid.:* June 16, 1899; Detroit *Free Press:* July 12, 1899, S.S.; *Outlook,* LXII (July 29, 1899), 692.

30. Detroit *Journal:* July 12, 14, 1899; Detroit *Evening News:* April 25, 1899; May 10, 1899; June 25, 1899; Detroit *Free Press:* April 29, 1899; July 14, 1899, S.S.; "Municipal Ownership of Street Railways in Detroit," *Quarterly Journal of Economics,* XIII (July, 1899), 455; for opposition see also Hazen S. Pingree to Richard T. Ely, July 20, 1899, Ely Papers.

31. Detroit *Tribune:* July 16, 1899, S.S.; "Attorney General, ex rel. Barbour *v.* Pingree" 120 *Michigan,* 550–72.

32. Bemis, "Detroit's Efforts To Own Her Street Railways," p. 273; O'Geran, *A History of the Detroit Street Railways,* pp. 173–74; Detroit *Journal:* July 15, 16, 1899, S.S.; Detroit *Evening News:* October 3, 1894, P.S.

33. Johnson, *My Story,* pp. 95–96, 107; Robert H. Bremner, "The

Civic Revival in Ohio: The Fight Against Privilege In Cleveland and Toledo, 1899–1912" (Ph.D. thesis, Ohio State University, 1943), p. 46; Johnson, "My Fight Against a Three-Cent Fare," p. 369.

34. Lorenz, *Tom L. Johnson*, pp. 2, 36–41, 49, 53–54, 61, 63, 64, 111, 153–54; Hoyt Landon Warner, *Progressivism in Ohio 1897–1917* (Columbus, 1964), pp. 55, 71–74; Tom Johnson quoted in *My Story*, pp. 91–92 and Detroit *Evening News*, November 25, 1896; O. Bingham, "Is Tom L. Johnson Sincere?" *Gateway*, VIII (January, 1906), 5–6; Hutchins, *Jere C. Hutchins*, p. 154; Eugene C, Murdock, "Cleveland's Johnson: First Term," *Ohio Historical Quarterly*, LXVII (January, 1958), 39–48; Murdock, "Cleveland's Johnson," Ohio *State Archaeological and Historical Quarterly*, LXII (October, 1953), 330; Murdock, "Life of Tom L. Johnson" (Ph.D. thesis, Columbia University, 1951), pp. 76, 174–75; Charles A. Barker, *Henry George* (New York, 1955), pp. 624–26. Although most of the scholars mentioned above have attributed Johnson's career as a reformer to a rather dramatic and Biblical conversion to the ideas of Henry George in 1883, there is little in Johnson's career as a traction magnate in Detroit or in his actions as a reform mayor of Cleveland that suggest the influence of Henry George. On the other hand, his Cleveland administrations do resemble those of Pingree in Detroit.

35. Wilcox, *Municipal Franchises*, II, 715–16; Lorenz, *Tom L. Johnson*, pp. 139, 170–75, 178–82, 193–94; Warner, *Progressivism In Ohio*, pp. 72–73; [W.B.] Gongwer to Brand Whitlock, December 29, 1909, Whitlock Papers; Bremner, "The Civic Revival in Ohio," pp. 197–99; Tom L. Johnson, "The Three-Cent Fare Fight in Cleveland," *Hampton Columbian Magazine*, XXVII (October, 1911), 502–4.

36. Catlin, *The Story of Detroit*, p. 631; William P. Lovett, *Detroit Rules Itself* (Boston, 1930), pp. 31, 185; Harry Barnard, *Independent Man: The Life of Senator James Couzens* (New York, 1958), pp. 114–15, 119, 123.

CHAPTER 7

1. Detroit *Tribune:* January 15, 1890; June 12, 1890; Detroit *Free Press:* June 11, 1890; Detroit *Evening News:* June 11, 1890, P.S.

2. Detroit *Free Press:* July 23, 28, 1890; Detroit *Tribune:* June 26, 1890; July 16, 23, 1890, P.S.

3. *Ibid.:* June 26, 1890; July 30, 1890; Detroit *Journal:* July 3, 1890; Detroit *Evening News:* July 23, 1890; September 24, 1890, P.S. English translation of *Prawda* [June, 1893] in Pingree Papers.

4. Detroit *Tribune:* October 22, 26, 1890; November 1, 1890; Detroit *Free Press:* October 22, 1890, P.S.

5. Henry M. Utley and Byron M. Cutcheon, *Michigan as a Province,*

Territory and State (New York, 1906), pp. 179–81; *Official Directory and Legislative Manual of the State of Michigan, 1891–1892* (Lansing, 1891), p. 373 (hereafter cited as *Michigan Manual.*)

6. Detroit *Journal:* November 5, 1890, P.S.
7. Detroit *Tribune:* November 11, 15, 1890, P.S.; "John Coll *v.* The City Board of Canvassers," 83 *Michigan,* 367–72.
8. Detroit *Tribune:* November 26, 1890; December 10, 11, 1890, P.S.
9. Detroit *Free Press:* December 17, 24, 1890, P.S.
10. Detroit *Evening News:* January 13, 1891; Detroit *Free Press:* June 4, 1891, P.S.; *Journal of the Common Council,* 1891 (Detroit, 1892), pp. 1–4.
11. For the details of Pingree's veto see Chapter III.
12. Detroit *Journal:* October 15, 1891; Detroit *Evening News:* October 15, 1891; Detroit *Tribune:* October 15, 1891, P.S.
13. Detroit *Free Press:* October 18, 23, 24, 1891.
14. *Ibid.:* September 17, 1891; October 18, 21, 1891; Detroit *Evening News:* October 26, 1891, P.S.; United States Census, *Report on Statistics of Churches in the United States at the Eleventh Census: 1890* (Washington, 1894), pp. 98–99.
15. Detroit *Free Press:* October 22, 1891, P.S.
16. Detroit *Tribune:* October 28, 1891; November 1, 1891; Detroit *Free Press:* October 21, 23, 1891; November 1, 4, 1891, P.S.
17. *Ibid.:* October 23, 1891, P.S.
18. Detroit *Evening Sun:* October 26, 1891; Detroit *Tribune:* November 1, 1891; Detroit *Evening News:* November 4, 1891, P.S.; *Journal of the Common Council,* 1891, p. 874.
19. *Ibid.,* 1891, p. 874; Detroit *Free Press:* November 6, 1891, P.S. For evidence of the working class composition of wards 9, 15 and 16, see *ibid.:* November 9, 1887; Detroit *Evening News:* November 5, 1889; November 3, 1891, P.S. For wards one, two, and four, see Eric Kocher, "Detroit's Substantial Families," Appendix [1] in "Economic and Physical Growth of Detroit 1901–1935" (Manuscript, 1935), Michigan Historical Collections.
20. Thompson quoted in Detroit *Tribune:* November 6, 1891, P.S.; *Journal of the Common Council,* 1891, p. 874. In a recent monograph, Donald L. Kinzer has concluded, with a lack of supporting evidence, that "In his successful re-election campaign in 1891, Pingree advocated the abolition of parochial schools, while Catholic priests had opposed the use of Freeman's *General Sketch of History* in the public schools for reasons similar to those advanced in Boston." Neither the abolition of parochial schools nor the use of Freeman's textbook was a question in Detroit's election of 1891. Kinzer has the wrong issues for the wrong candidate in the wrong city. The only issue in the mayoralty election of 1891 which might have been but was not remotely related to Kinzer's charge of anti-Catholicism was the question of free textbooks for the public schools, which Detroit's labor unions and 69 per cent of the voters

supported. There is no evidence of Catholic opposition to this measure, and even if there had been, it simply does not follow that free textbooks could be construed as an episode in anti-Catholicism. Donald L. Kinzer, *An Episode in Anti-Catholicism: The American Protective Association* (Seattle, 1964), p. 60; *Thirteenth Annual Report of the Bureau of Labor and Industrial Statistics,* 1896 (Lansing, 1896), p. 246; United States Census, 1890, *Churches,* pp. 98–99; *Patriotic American:* October 17, 31, 1891; November 7, 14, 1891; *Michigan Catholic:* September, October, November, 1891; Detroit *Free Press:* October 23, 1891, P.S.

21. *Journal of the Common Council,* 1891, p. 1002. Thompson quoted in Detroit *Tribune:* November 6, 1891, P.S.

22. For German settlements in Detroit, see Jack D. Elenbaas, "Democrats of Detroit 1880–1900," (M.A. thesis, Wayne State University, 1964), Appendix III, and Sidney Glazer, *Detroit A Study in Urban Development* (New York, 1965), p. 53. For foreign-born and native-born by wards, see United States Census *Report on Vital and Social Statistics in the United States at the Eleventh Census: 1890* (Washington, 1896), IV, part II, 220–21, 227, 368–69. In addition to infant and adult mortality rates, the value of homes is also an important gauge for determining the financial and social differences between the city's various wards. In the first and second wards the value of the average (mortgaged) home was in excess of $9,000 and in the fourth ward, it was $5,000, whereas in the third, it was $2,918 and in the sixteenth, $1,358. A decreasing scale in the value of homes could be observed as one left the inner and low-numbered wards at the heart of the city and progressed toward the outer and high-numbered wards. United States Census, *Report on Farms and Homes Proprietorship and Indebtedness in the United States at the Eleventh Census: 1890* (Washington, 1896), XIII, 471; *Patriotic American:* October 17, 1891.

23. *Journal of the Common Council,* 1891, pp. 957–59; *Michigan Manual 1892–93,* pp. 346–47; *ibid.,* 1893–94, pp. 283–89; James McMillan to J. S. Clarkson, January 5, 1892; John T. Rich to James McMillan, November 12, 1892, McMillan Papers.

24. Detroit *Evening News:* October 24, 1892; November 2, 1892, P.S.; Charles P. Collins to James McMillan, November 5, 1892, McMillan Papers.

25. Detroit *Evening News:* November 3, 1892; *Patriotic American:* November 5, 1892; *Michigan Catholic:* October 27, 1892; November 3, 1892.

26. Detroit *Evening News:* October 25, 1892; November 6, 10, 1892, P.S.; *Patriotic American:* November 5, 1892; *Journal of the Common Council,* 1892, p. 958; *Michigan Catholic:* November 3, 1892.

27. Detroit *Tribune:* January 23, 1893; Detroit *Free Press:* January 30, 1893; Detroit *Conflict:* August 29, 1893; Detroit *Evening News:* July 3, 1893, P.S.

28. *Ibid.:* September 29, 1893; October 18, 1893, P.S.
29. *Ibid.:* September 29, 1893, P.S.
30. *Ibid.:* September 26, 1893; Detroit *Journal:* September 29, 1893, P.S.
31. Detroit *Free Press:* October 8, 9, 14, 1893; Detroit *Conflict:* October 10, 31, 1893, P.S.; Louis P. Granger to Hazen S. Pingree, October 14, 1893, Pingree Papers; Richard Hofstadter, *The Age of Reform From Bryan to F.D.R.* (New York, 1960), pp. 22–130.
32. William C. McMillan to James McMillan, October 19, 23, 1893, McMillan Papers; Pingree quoted in the Detroit *Tribune:* October 18, 1893 and Detroit *Evening News:* October 17, 1893; November 1, 1893, P.S.
33. *Ibid.:* October 9, 11, 1893; Detroit *Tribune:* October 7, 9, 26, 1893, P.S.; Pamphlets, Broadsides and Letters, Pingree Papers.
34. Detroit *Free Press:* October 24, 25, 1893; November 6, 7, 1893; Detroit *Tribune:* November 7, 9, 1893, P.S.
35. Detroit *Evening News:* November 4, 1893; Detroit *Journal:* November 3, 1893. For English translations of *Prawda:* November 7, 1893; *Sonntags Herold:* November 5, 1893; and *Abend Post:* [September 16, 1893]—see Pingree Papers.
36. Pingree quoted in "Pingree—The First Insurgent," Detroit *Saturday Night:* December 16, 1911; Detroit *Evening News:* November 8, 1893; *Journal of the Common Council,* 1893, p. 1044.
37. *Ibid.,* 1893, pp. 1044–58; Pingree quoted in Detroit *Evening News:* November 8, 1893; C. W. Moore to James McMillan, October 31, 1893, McMillan Papers; *Census of the State of Michigan 1894* (Lansing, 1896), I, 279, 395.
38. *Journal of the Common Council,* 1891, p. 874; *ibid.,* 1893, p. 1044; Detroit *Journal:* November 8, 1893, P.S.
39. Detroit *Tribune:* November 9, 1893, P.S.
40. *Ibid.:* October 6, 25, 1894; Detroit *Free Press:* October 25, 1894, P.S.
41. Pingree quoted in Detroit *Tribune:* November 8, 1894, P.S.; *Journal of the Common Council,* 1894, pp. 1416–21.
42. Detroit *Tribune:* November 7, 1894, P.S.; *Michigan Manual, 1899–1900,* pp. 486–89.
43. Detroit *Journal:* August 9, 1895, P.S.; James McMillan to Frank J. Hecker, August 10, 1894, McMillan Papers.
44. M. Ryan to James McMillan, June 22, 1894, McMillan Papers; Pingree quoted in Malcolm W. Bingay, *Detroit Is My Own Home Town* (Indianapolis, 1949), pp. 234–35.
45. Detroit *Tribune:* September 11, 1895; New York *World:* January 5, 1896; Detroit *Free Press:* March 14, 1896; Pingree quoted in Howell (Michigan) *Herald:* March 27, 1896, P.S.
46. Detroit *Tribune:* October 1, 18, 1895; Sumner quoted in Detroit *Evening News:* October 18, 1895, P.S.
47. Detroit *Tribune:* October 26, 1895, P.S.

48. Detroit *Evening Press:* October 19, 1895; Detroit *Evening News:* October 10, 1895; Detroit *Journal:* October 21, 1895, P.S.
49. *Ibid.:* October 22, 25, 1895; Detroit *Evening Press:* October 22, 1895, P.S.
50. *Ibid.:* October 26, 1895; Detroit *Tribune:* October 21, 26, 1895; Detroit *Evening News:* October 21, 1895, P.S.
51. *Ibid.:* August 18, November 3, 1895, P.S.; Pingree address to Detroit Chamber of Commerce, November 2, 1895, Pingree Papers.
52. *Journal of the Common Council,* 1895, pp. 515, 525.
53. *Michigan Manual, 1899–1900,* p. 322; H. S. Pingree to J. T. Rich, March 1, 1895, Letters Concerning Legislative Matters, Michigan Historical Commission Archives.
54. John T. Rich to James McMillan, September 19, 1894, McMillan Papers.
55. Detroit *Evening News:* August 6, 7, 1895, P.S.
56. Detroit *Free Press:* September 6, 1893, P.S.
57. Pingree quoted in *ibid.:* October 19, 1895; Detroit *Free Press:* February 4, 1895, P.S.

CHAPTER 8

1. Henry Demarest Lloyd to Richard T. Ely, November 16, 1896, Lloyd Papers; Samuel M. Jones to Hazen S. Pingree, August 4, 1899, Jones Papers.
2. Pingree quoted in Detroit *Free Press:* November 27, 1896 and Detroit *Evening News:* March 17, 1897, P.S.
3. B. O. Flower to Hazen S. Pingree, February 1, 1896, Pingree Papers; Richard T. Ely to Henry Demarest Lloyd, November 12, 1896; Henry Demarest Lloyd to Samuel M. Jones, May 23, 1897, Lloyd Papers.
4. Richard Hofstadter, *The Age of Reform: From Bryan to F.D.R.* (New York, 1960), pp. 135–48.
5. Hazen S. Pingree address to Detroit Chamber of Commerce, November 2, 1895, Pingree Papers; Hazen S. Pingree, *Facts and Opinions* (Detroit, 1895), pp. 85–86; Pingree quoted in New York *Journal:* December 8, 1896, P.S.
6. Detroit *Tribune:* May 1, 1899, P.S.
7. Lincoln Steffens, *The Autobiography of Lincoln Steffens* (New York, 1931), pp. 374–75; Hewitt quoted in *Pilgrim,* III (December, 1901), 4.
8. Hazen S. Pingree, "Address to the Nineteenth Century Club of New York," November 11, 1897, p. 7; S. M. Jones to Josiah Strong, November 15, 1898, Jones Papers; Brand Whitlock, *Forty Years of It* (New York, 1914), pp. 172–74.
9. Frederic C. Howe, *The City: The Hope of Democracy* (New York, 1913), pp. 1, 2. For the elitist views of reformers who overthrew Boss Tweed, see Alexander B. Callow, Jr., *The Tweed Ring* (New

York, 1966), pp. 69–71, 265–67. Charles R. Adrian, "Some General Characteristics of Nonpartisan Elections," Robert C. Wood, "Nonpartisanship in Suburbia," both in *Democracy in Urban America*, ed. Oliver P. Williams and Charles Press (Chicago, 1964), pp. 251–66. For an exposition of the views regarding municipal government of one of the most prominent twentieth-century "structural" reformers, see Richard S. Childs, "The Faith of a Civic Reformer," *ibid.*, pp. 222–24. The "elitist commitments" of the city manager system (as prescribed in city government textbooks) can also be seen in Lawrence J. R. Herson, "The Lost World of Municipal Government," *American Political Science Review*, LI (June, 1957), 330–45.

10. Howard B. Furer, *William Frederick Havemeyer: A Political Biography* (New York, 1965), pp. 14, 144–54, 160; Seymour J. Mandelbaum, *Boss Tweed's New York* (New York, 1965), pp. 91, 97, 108, 111; Callow, *The Tweed Ring*, pp. 253–86.

11. Mandelbaum, *Boss Tweed's New York*, pp. 98–100, 111; Furer, *William F. Havemeyer*, pp. 156, 158, 160–61, 169.

12. *Ibid.*, p. 161; Mandelbaum, *Boss Tweed's New York*, pp. 112–13; William L. Riordin, *Plunkitt of Tammany Hall* (New York, 1963), p. 17.

13. Allan Nevins, *Grover Cleveland, A Study in Courage* (New York, 1941), pp. 61–62, 83–94.

14. Harold Coffin Syrett, *The City of Brooklyn 1865–1898, A Political History* (New York, 1944), p. 134; Steven C. Swett, "The Test of a Reformer A Study of Seth Low," *New York Historical Society Quarterly*, XLIV (January, 1960), pp. 8, 9; Lincoln Steffens, *The Shame of the Cities* (New York, 1966), p. 201.

15. Syrett, *Brooklyn*, pp. 104–6, 109–19, 134; Swett, "Test of a Reformer," pp. 7–9.

16. Albert Fein, "New York City Politics From 1897–1903; A Study in Political Party Leadership" (M.A. thesis, Columbia University, 1954), pp. 19–20; Swett, "Test of a Reformer," pp. 10–14, 16–18.

17. *Ibid.*, pp. 21–23, 26–31, 35–36; Roy Lubove, *The Progressives and the Slums, Tenement House Reform in New York City, 1890–1917* (Pittsburgh, 1962), pp. 153–54.

18. Swett, "Test of a Reformer," pp. 6, 32, 35–36, 38–41; Wallace S. Sayre and Herbert Kaufman, *Governing New York City Politics in the Metropolis* (New York, 1960), p. 695.

19. James D. Phelan, "Municipal Conditions and the New Charter," *Overland Monthly*, XXVIII (no. 163, 2nd series), pp. 104–11; Roy Swanstrom, "Reform Administration of James D. Phelan, Mayor of San Francisco, 1897–1902," (M.A. thesis, University of California-Berkeley, 1949), pp. 77–79, 80, 83, 85, 86; Walton Bean, *Boss Ruef's San Francisco: The Story of the Union Labor Party, Big Business, and the Graft Prosecution* (Berkeley, 1952), pp. 8, 9, 16, 17, 23; George E. Mowry, *The California Progressives* (Chicago,

1963), pp. 23–25; Fremont Older, *My Own Story* (San Francisco, 1919), pp. 27, 31, 65

20. William E. Leuchtenburg, Preface to Edwin R. Lewinson, *John Purroy Mitchel: The Boy Mayor of New York* (New York, 1965), pp. 11–13; Lewinson, *Boy Mayor*, pp. 93, 95, 100, 102, 117, 124.

21. Leuchtenburg, *ibid.*, p. 12; Lewinson, *ibid.*, pp. 18, 151–69, 175–88.

22. Leuchtenburg, *ibid.*, pp. 11–13; Samuel P. Hayes, "The Politics of Reform in Municipal Government," *Pacific Northwest Quarterly*, LV (October, 1964), pp. 157–69.

23. Lewinson, *Boy Mayor*, pp. 11–13, 18, 93, 95, 102; Riordin, *George Washington Plunkitt*, pp. 17–20; Swett, "Seth Low," pp. 8, 9; Allan Nevins, *Abram S. Hewitt: With Some Account of Peter Cooper* (New York, 1935), pp. 515–16, 529–30; Seth Low, "An American View of Municipal Government in the United States," in James Bryce, *The American Commonwealth* (New York, 1893), I, 651, 665.

24. Hoyt Landon Warner, *Progressivism in Ohio 1897–1917* (Columbus, 1964), pp. 32, 70–72; Whitlock, *Forty Years of It*, pp. 211, 252; Clarence H. Cramer, *Newton D. Baker: A Biography* (Cleveland, 1961), pp. 46–47; Steffens, *Autobiography of Lincoln Steffens*, pp. 477, 492–93; Frederic C. Howe, *The Confessions of a Reformer* (New York, 1925), pp. 98, 102–8; Pingree, *Facts and Opinions*, p. 196. For Mark Fagan, see Lincoln Steffens, *Upbuilders* (New York, 1909), pp. 28, 30, 33, 35, and Ransom E. Noble, Jr., *New Jersey Progressivism before Wilson* (Princeton, 1946), pp. 13–42. St. Louis Circuit Attorney Joseph W. Folk (1901–04), who began his career by investigating and prosecuting franchise "grabs," discovered that the real despoilers of municipal government were not minor city officials but promoters, bankers, and corporation directors who profited by misgovernment. After he became governor he dropped his crime-busting and supported progressive and urban reforms. Louis G. Geiger, *Joseph W. Folk of Missouri* (Columbia, 1953), pp. 32, 41, 81, 88, 93, 99–117. Robert Wiebe's assertion that the "typical business ally of the boss, moreover, was a rather marginal operator, anathema to the chamber of commerce" is at variance with what is known about the political influence wielded in Detroit by urban capitalists such as the Hendries, McMillans and Johnson or for that matter with the role played by Yerkes and Insull in Chicago, Mark Hanna in Cleveland and the Huntington interests in Los Angeles, just to cite a few examples. *The Search for Order, 1877–1920* (New York, 1967), p. 167.

25. Steffens, *Upbuilders*, pp. 3–45; Warner, *Progressivism in Ohio, 1897–1917*, pp. 71, 74; Cramer, *Newton D. Baker*, pp. 50–52; Howe, *Confessions of a Reformer*, pp. 90–93, 108–9; Carl Lorenz, *Tom L. Johnson, Mayor of Cleveland* (New York, 1911), p. 152; Steffens, *Autobiography of Lincoln Steffens*, p. 480; Detroit *Free Press*, March 14, 1896, P.S.; Samuel M. Jones to Henry D. Lloyd,

April 16, 1897, Lloyd Papers; Samuel M. Jones to James L. Cowes, April 27, 1897; Tom L. Johnson to S. M. Jones, May 3, 1902, Jones Papers; Harvey S. Ford, "The Life and Times of Golden Rule Jones" (Ph.D. thesis, University of Michigan, 1953), pp. 185, 284–85, 330; Whitlock, *Forty Years of It*, p. 212. William D. Miller has argued that "Boss" Edward H. Crump, who was Memphis mayor from 1910 to 1916, stands with "Golden Rule" Jones and Tom L. Johnson as a typical progressive of the period, but an examination of Miller's book raises serious doubts about that judgment. Although Crump occasionally employed reform rhetoric, established a few milk stations for the poor, and put screens on public school windows, he used most of the energy of his administration to enforce the laws and instill efficiency into the municipal government in the structural-reform tradition. Crump wiped out "policy" playing by Negroes, eliminated loafing by the garbage collectors and street pavers, forced the railroads to construct eleven underpasses, lowered city taxes, reduced waste in municipal government by extending audit procedures even to the purchase of postage stamps, and increased city income by selling empty bottles, feed sacks, and scrap. William D. Miller, *Mr. Crump of Memphis* (Baton Rouge, 1964), pp. 79–113. Brooklyn's Mayor Charles A. Schieren (1894–95), who gained some stature as a reformer by defeating a venal Democratic machine, also followed a well-trodden path of cleaning out "deceit and corruption" and installing "integrity, nonpartisanship, and routine efficiency." Like most of the reform mayors of his period, Schieren failed to advance or support social reform programs. Harold C. Syrett, *The City of Brooklyn, 1865–1898, A Political History* (New York, 1944), pp. 218–32. Geoffrey Blodgett has tried to show that Boston became for "a brief time the cutting edge of urban reform in America" under Mayor Josiah Quincy (1896–1900), who established a publicly owned printing plant and expanded the city's playgrounds. Although the Dover Street Bath House may have been a "monument to municipal socialism" as Blodgett contends, Mayor Quincy stopped his programs short of anything that would have threatened the vested interests in the traction and utility business. Geoffrey Blodgett, *The Gentle Reformers: Massachusetts Democrats in the Cleveland Era* (Cambridge, 1966), pp. 240–61. For Quincy's absurd notion that regular bathing would cause the "filthy tenement house" to disappear, crime and drunkenness to decrease and the death rate to drop, see Josiah Quincy, "Municipal Progress in Boston," *Independent*, LII (February 15, 1900), 424. Henry Demarest Lloyd was critical of Mayor Quincy's failure to resist the traction interests and referred to the Mayor's public baths as Quincy's "little sops." H. D. Lloyd to Samuel Bowles, December 13, 1898, Lloyd Papers.

26. Ford, "Golden Rule Jones," pp. 151, 166, 339; Samuel M. Jones to Dr. [Graham] Taylor, October 5, 1897; S. M. Jones to L. L. Dagett,

April 17, 1899, Jones Papers; Hazen S. Pingree address to Springfield, Massachusetts Board of Trade, March 3, 1894, Ralph Stone Scrapbook; Whitlock, *Forty Years of It*, pp. 252, 254.

27. Robert H. Bremner, "The Civic Revival in Ohio: The Fight Against Privilege in Cleveland and Toledo, 1890–1912," (Ph.D. thesis, Ohio State University, 1943), p. 25; Hazen S. Pingree, "The Problem of Municipal Reform. Contract by Referendum," *Arena*, XVII (April, 1897), 707–10; Cramer, *Newton D. Baker*, p. 46; Steffens, *Upbuilders*, pp. 28–30, 33, 35; Noble, *New Jersey Progressivism before Wilson*, pp. 25–26, 35, 38.

28. Tom L. Johnson, *My Story* (New York, 1911), p. 113; Ford, "Golden Rule Jones," pp. 136–37, 170, 339; Hazen S. Pingree, "Detroit: A Municipal Study," *Outlook*, LV (February 6, 1897), 437; Bemis quoted in Detroit *Evening News*: June 21, 1899, Stone Scrapbook; Whitlock, *Forty Years of It*, p. 221.

29. Whitlock, *Forty Years of It*, p. 221

30. Frank J. Goodnow, "The Tweed Ring in New York City," in James Bryce's *The American Commonwealth* (London, 1888), II, 335; Bryce, *ibid.*, p. 67; Bryce, *ibid.*, I, 613; Albert Shaw, *Political Problems of American Development* (New York, 1907), p. 66. According to Edwin L. Godkin, New York City's problems began with the establishment of universal suffrage in 1846 which coincided with the beginning of the great Irish migration. Edwin L. Godkin, *Problems of Modern Democracy*, ed. Morton Keller (New York, 1896, Cambridge, 1966), p. 133.

31. Bryce, *American Commonwealth*, II, 67; William B. Munro, *The Government of American Cities* (New York, 1913), pp. 308–9, 310, 312; Andrew D. White, "The Government of American Cities," *Forum*, x (December, 1890), 369; Alfred R. Conkling, *City Government in the United States* (New York, 1899), p. 49; Frank J. Goodnow, *Municipal Problems* (New York, 1897), pp. 150–53; Delos F. Wilcox, *The Study of City Government* (New York, 1897), p. 151; "Report of the Committee on Municipal Program," *Proceedings* of the Indianapolis Conference for Good City Government and Fourth Annual Meeting of the National Municipal League (Philadelphia, 1898), p. 11 (hereafter cited *Proceedings for Good City Government*).

32. Wilcox, *The Study of City Government*, pp. 237–38; Frank J. Goodnow, *Municipal Government* (New York, 1910), pp. 39, 149, 378–79; James T. Young, *Proceedings for Good City Government*, 1901, p. 230.

33. *Michigan Legislative Manual and Official Directory 1899–1900* (Lansing, 1899), p. 322; *Report of the Commission to Devise a Plan for the Government of Cities in the State of New York* (New York, 1877), pp. 35–36.

34. Goodnow, *Municipal Problems*, pp. 148–49.

35. Shaw, *Political Problems of American Development*, pp. 65–67, 82, 125; Munro, *Government of American Cities*, pp. 120–21; Bryce, *American Commonwealth*, II, 67.

36. Goodnow, *Municipal Problems*, p. 278; Conkling, *City Government in the United States*, p. 34; Richard T. Ely, *The Coming City* (New York, 1902), p. 29.

37. Walter T. Arndt, *The Emancipation of the American City* (New York, 1917), p. 12; Frank M. Sparks, *Government As a Business* (Chicago, 1916), pp. 1, 7; Goodnow, *Municipal Government*, pp. 150, 381–82; Munro, *Government of American Cities*, p. 306; William H. Tolman, *Municipal Reform Movements in the United States* (New York, 1895), p. 34.

38. Conkling, *City Government in the United States*, pp. 6, 32; Goodnow, *Municipal Problems*, pp. 262–65.

39. *Ibid.*, pp. 204–5, 265; Munro, *Government of American Cities*, pp. 241, 279–80; Albert Shaw, "Civil Service Reform and Municipal Government," in *Civil Service Reform and Municipal Government* (New York, 1897), pp. 3–7.

40. Goodnow, *Municipal Government*, pp. 142–46, 385–86, and *Municipal Problems*, pp. 66–67; Leo S. Rowe, "City Government As It Should Be And May Become," *Proceedings for Good City Government, 1894*, p. 115; White, "The Government of American Cities," p. 370; John Agar, "Shall American Cities Municipalize?" *Municipal Affairs*, IV (March, 1900), 14–20; C. E. Pickard, "Great Cities and Democratic Institutions," *American Journal of Politics*, IV (April, 1894), 385. The Boston mayor Nathan Mathews, Jr., asserted that the proposal to restrict municipal suffrage to the propertied classes was one of the most common remedies for the evils of city government of his age. Nathan Mathews, Jr., *The City Government of Boston* (Boston, 1895), p. 176.

41. Munro, *Government of American Cities*, pp. 294, 308–10; Goodnow, *Municipal Problems*, pp. 150–53; Leo S. Rowe, "American Political Ideas and Institutions in Their Relation to the Problem of the City," *Proceedings for Good City Government, 1897*, p. 77; William Dudley Foulke, *ibid.*, *1898*, p. 137; Frederic C. Howe, *The City, The Hope of Democracy* (New York, 1913), p. 1.

42. Henry Bruère, "Efficiency in City Government," *Annals* of the American Academy of Political and Social Science, XLI (May, 1912), 19; Richard S. Childs, "Now that We Have the City Manager Plan, What Are We Going to Do With It," *Fourth Yearbook of the City Managers' Association* (Auburn, 1918), pp. 82–83; Henry M. Waite, *ibid.*, pp. 88–89; Harold A. Stone, Don K. Price and Kathryn H. Stone, *City Manager Government in the United States* (Chicago, 1940), pp. 25–27; James Weinstein, "Organized Business and the City Commissioner and Manager Movements," *Journal of Southern History*, XXVIII (May, 1962), 166, 179.

43. *Ibid.*, p. 173; Samuel P. Hayes, "The Politics of Reform in Municipal Government in the Progressive Era," *Pacific Northwest Quarterly*, LV (October, 1964), 157–69.
44. Edward C. Banfield and James Q. Wilson, *City Politics* (New York, 1963), p. 148.
45. The peak period for the spread of the city commissioner and the city manager system was 1917–27. Leonard D. White, *The City Manager* (Chicago, 1927), p. 317; Harold Zink, *Government of Cities in the United States* (New York, 1939), p. 301.

CHAPTER 9

1. Detroit *Tribune:* January 25, 1895; Detroit *Evening News:* June 10, 1894; September 22, 1894; March 8, 1895, P.S.
2. *Ibid.:* June 8, 1894, P.S.
3. *Ibid.:* July 2, 1894; Detroit *Journal:* December 11, 1894; Detroit *Tribune:* January 14, 1893; December 26, 1894, P.S. For figures on resistance of Poles to vaccination, see *Annual Report of the Board of Health, 1895* (Detroit, 1896), pp. 3, 4.
4. Detroit *Journal:* January 25, 1895; Detroit *Evening News:* February 15, 1895; Detroit *Tribune:* June 19, 1894; February 15, 1895, P.S. Hazen S. Pingree to John T. Rich, February 26, 1895, Governor's File, Michigan Historical Commission Archives.
5. Detroit *Evening News:* November 3, 1894; January 8, 25, 26, 1895; and news clippings in P.S., 1895.
6. Detroit *Free Press:* November 7, 1894, P.S.
7. Detroit *Tribune:* February 16, 1895, P.S.
8. H. S. Pingree, "Proclamation," January 23, 1895, Pingree Papers.
9. Detroit *Journal:* January 25, 26, 1895, P.S.
10. Hazen S. Pingree, *Facts and Opinions* (Detroit, 1895), pp. 95–137; James H. McMillan to James McMillan, January 28, 1895, McMillan Papers.
11. H. S. Pingree, address to the state legislature, "On Home Rule for Detroit," February 14, 1895, Pingree Papers; Pingree, *Facts and Opinions*, p. 135.
12. Detroit *Tribune:* March 15, 1895; Detroit *Free Press:* March 6, 1895, P.S.; Charles Wright to John T. Rich, March 2, 1895; Hazen S. Pingree to John T. Rich, March 1, 1895, Letters Concerning Legislative Matters, Michigan Historical Commission Archives.
13. Detroit *Tribune:* March 15, 1895; Detroit *Journal:* June 15, 1895, P.S.
14. Detroit *Free Press:* March 9, 19, 27, 1895; Detroit *Sun:* May 26, 1895, P.S.
15. Detroit *Free Press:* May 16, 28, 1895, P.S.
16. *Ibid.:* June 6, 7, 1895; Detroit *Evening News:* May 29, 1895, P.S.
17. *Ibid.:* May 27, 1895; June 8, 1895; Pingree quoted in *ibid.:* June 6,

1895; February 22, 1896, and *Journal of the Common Council,* 1896, p. 13.

18. Pingree, *Facts and Opinions,* pp. 5–17; Detroit *Free Press:* April 4, 1896; June 7, 1896; Detroit *Evening News:* May 10, 1896, P.S.; James McMillan to W. R. Bates, March 11, 1896, McMillan Papers.

19. James McMillan to William C. McMillan, March 14, 1896, McMillan Papers. For the G.O.P. view that Pingree was needed on the ticket to carry Michigan, see James McMillan to William McKinley, August 13, 1896, McMillan Papers. For Mark Hanna's view that Pingree was needed to help McKinley, see Russell A. Alger to [William Shafter], November 26, 1900, Alger Papers.

20. Detroit *Evening News:* August 1, 3, 7, 1896; September 17, 1896; October 17, 27, 1896, P.S.; *New York Times:* August 18, 1896.

21. *Michigan Legislative Manual and Official Directory 1897–98* (Lansing, 1897), pp. 355, 446–555; Detroit *Tribune:* November 4, 5, 1896, P.S.

22. Pingree quoted in Detroit *Evening News:* December 11, 1896, P.S.

23. 112 *Michigan,* 146–74; James McMillan to William C. McMillan, March 23, 1897, McMillan Papers.

24. Detroit *Journal:* February 19, 20, 1897; July 15, 1899; Detroit *Tribune:* February 20, 1897; Detroit *Evening News:* May 31, 1899; June 1, 1899, P.S.

25. *Messages of the Governors of Michigan* (Lansing, 1927), IV, 63–65, 71, 234–35; Pingree quoted in *ibid.,* p. 65. Although the gross earnings system was graduated from 1½ to 3 per cent, most roads, because of loose drafting of applicable legislation, apparently had little difficulty in paying only the minimum rate. Wilbur O. Hedrick, *The History of Railroad Taxation in Michigan* (Lansing, 1912), pp. 22–24. The "general law" railroads were incorporated under the railroad act of 1855 and were subject to all general laws passed by the state legislature, whereas the "chartered" railroads were guaranteed certain privileges such as a capital-stock tax provision and the right to charge higher passenger fares, which could be altered only by a two-thirds vote of the legislature. *Ibid.,* pp. 9–11.

26. *Messages of the Governors of Michigan,* IV, 69–72; Hedrick, *History of Railroad Taxation in Michigan,* pp. 24, 33.

27. *Messages of the Governors of Michigan,* IV, 65–66.

28. Richard H. Barton, "Michigan Railroad Regulation" (M.A. thesis, Michigan State University, 1948), pp. 117, 121–22.

29. Detroit *Tribune:* May 13, 1897, P.S.; William P. Belden, "Governor Pingree and His Reforms," *American Law Review,* XXXIV (January–February, 1900), 39.

30. *Journal of the House of Representatives of the State of Michigan, 1897* (Lansing, 1897), III, 2708–17; Detroit *Journal:* February 17, 1897, P.S.

31. *Messages of the Governors of Michigan,* IV, 112, 117, 157–58, 235;

Detroit *Tribune:* May 20, 1897, P.S.; W. G. Thompson, speech in
*Report of the Conference Committee on the Merriman Railroad
Taxation Bill, 1897* (Lansing, 1897), p. 12.

32. J. L. Berkheimer, *A Peep Behind the Scenes: Michigan Railroad
Legislation Exposed* (Lansing, 1897), pp. 35, 37; Detroit *Free Press:*
May 20, 1897; Detroit *Journal:* May, 21, 1897, P.S.

33. Detroit *Evening News:* May 19, 21, 1897; Detroit *Free Press:*
May 26, 1897; Detroit *Tribune:* May 21, 1897, P.S.

34. *Journal of the House of Representatives of the State of Michigan
Extra Session, 1898* (Lansing, 1898), pp. 212, 238; citizen letter
quoted in *ibid.,* p. 116; Pingree quoted in George B. Catlin, *The
Story of Detroit* (Detroit, 1926), p. 637; Horton quoted in Detroit
Evening News: March 21, 1898.

35. *Journal of the Senate of the State of Michigan Extra Session, 1898*
(Lansing, 1898), pp. 209–10, 222; Senate Joint Committee on the
Atkinson Bill, Appendix, *ibid.,* pp. 35–43, 54–55; Joint Committee
of the House and Senate on Railroad Bills, Appendix, *House Journal
Extra Session, 1898,* pp. 49–58, 70–81, 90–100, 270, 272, 286, 368;
Atkinson quoted in *ibid.,* p. 296.

36. *Senate Journal Extra Session, 1898,* pp. 283–84, 303; *House
Journal Extra Session, 1898,* p. 295; Russel quoted in Joint Committee of the House and Senate on Railroad Bills, Appendix, *ibid.,*
p. 81; Pingree quoted in Detroit *Evening News:* April 7, 1898.

37. St. Ignace *News:* December 16, 1898, P.S.; Detroit *Evening News:*
April 24, 28, 30, 1898; July 4, 1898, P.S.; "Pingree—The First
Insurgent," *Detroit Saturday Night:* March 9, 1912.

38. A. M. Smith, quoted in Detroit *Advertiser:* October 28, 1898;
legislator George T. Mason, quoted in Owosso *Argus:* January 26,
1899, P.S.

39. W. J. Hunsaker to Chase S. Osborn, July 22, 1898, Osborn Papers;
James McMillan to W. R. Bates, September 9, 1898, McMillan
Papers.

40. Lansing *Journal:* October 29, 1898, P.S.; Detroit *Evening News:*
October 23, 26, 1898; November 9, 1898; Hazen S. Pingree (cir-
cular letter) to Chase S. Osborn, June 23, 1898, Osborn Papers;
James McMillan to W. R. Bates, September 26, 1898, McMillan
Papers; Pingree quoted in Allegan *Gazette:* October 29, 1898, P.S.

41. *Michigan Legislative Manual and Official Directory, 1899–1900*
(Lansing, 1899), pp. 323–26; Detroit *Evening News:* June 17,
1899, Ralph Stone Scrapbook; Calvin E. Houk (Ironwood Postmaster) to Chase S. Osborn, January 18, 1900; Chase S. Osborn
to E. Pennington (general manager of the Minneapolis, St. Paul
and Sault Ste. Marie Railroad), February 27, 1899, June 30, 1900;
to Marvin Hughitt (President, Chicago, and North Western Railroad), [1896], Osborn Papers.

42. Kalamazoo *Evening News:* January 30, 1899; Detroit *Tribune:*

December 17, 1898; *Journal of the House of Representatives of the State of Michigan, 1899* (Lansing, 1899), I, 352; Pingree quoted in address before the State Association of Farmers' Clubs, December 13, 1899, Stone Scrapbook (hereafter S.S.).

43. *Ibid.; House Journal, 1899,* III, 2628–29, 2674–76, 2679–80.

44. For report of the conversation with Ledyard, see James McMillan to William C. McMillan, March 3, April 12, 1899, McMillan Papers; Pingree quoted in address before State Farmers' Clubs, December 13, 1899.

45. 120 *Michigan,* 95–115; Pingree quoted in Grand Rapids *Democrat:* February 11, 1899, P.S.

46. *House Journal, 1899,* III, 2196–97, 2325, 2416–17; Pingree, quoted in Detroit *Free Press:* June 24, 1899, S.S.

47. Pingree quoted in Detroit *Tribune:* June 25, 1899, S.S. and *Messages of the Governors of Michigan,* IV, 236.

48. *New York Times:* June 24, 1899; James McMillan to C. W. Watkins, June 26, 1899, McMillan Papers; Ralph Stone (Pingree's secretary) to Chase S. Osborn, August 26, September 18, 1899, Osborn Papers.

49. Detroit *Evening News:* May 2, 1899; Detroit *Journal:* June 23, 1899, S.S.; *New York Times:* June 29, 30, 1899; Pingree, quoted in *ibid.:* June 24, 1899; Russell A. Alger to Chase S. Osborn, May 8, 1899, Osborn Papers.

50. Detroit *Tribune:* June 28, 1899, S.S.; *Outlook,* LXII (July 8, 1899), 514; James McMillan to William C. McMillan, June 29, 1899, McMillan Papers.

51. *New York Times:* June 27, 1899.

52. Russell A. Alger to Chase S. Osborn, June 27, 1899, Alger Papers.

53. Otto Caramichael to Chase S. Osborn, July 18, 1899, Osborn Papers.

54. Russell A. Alger to William McKinley, July 19, 1899, Alger Papers. The commonly accepted view that Alger was dismissed by the President because of his blundering as Secretary of War seems questionable. Alger's mistakes, which allegedly had cost hundreds of lives and numerous cases of sickness, had been publicized and criticized for almost a year by July, 1899, when McKinley finally dismissed him. A study of Pingree's reforms and the Alger and Osborn correspondence indicated that it was Alger's brief flirtation with political unorthodoxy that cost him the Secretaryship.

55. Detroit *Free Press:* July 24, 1899.

56. Detroit *Free Press:* July 24, 1899; Detroit *Tribune:* July 29, 1899; August 1, 1899, S.S.; Detroit *Journal:* August 2, 1899; New York *Tribune:* August 3, 1899; Toledo *News:* August 3, 1899; Alger Scrapbook.

57. Russell A. Alger to Chase S. Osborn, September 8, 1899, Osborn Papers; *New York Times:* June 24, 1899; Ralph Stone to Chase S. Osborn, September 18, 1899, Osborn Papers.

58. *Messages of the Governors of Michigan,* IV, 189–95, 200–208;

Lansing *Journal:* December 18, 1899; *Journal of the Senate of the State of Michigan Extra Session, 1899–1900* (Lansing, 1900), pp. 68–70.

59. *Messages of the Governors of Michigan*, IV, 217–26; *Journal of the Senate of the State of Michigan Extra Session, October, 1900* (Lansing, 1900), pp. 11, 18–31; Olds quoted in Detroit *Tribune:* October 12, 1900; Traverse City *Eagle* and Port Huron *Daily Herald* cited in Detroit *State Affairs*, October 19, 1900; Detroit *Evening News:* October 12, 1900.

60. *Senate Journal Extra Session, October, 1900*, p. 19.

61. Henry Carter Adams, "Recent Changes in the Taxing Laws of Michigan," *Quarterly Journal of Economics*, XVI (November, 1901), 118.

62. *Messages of the Governors of Michigan*, IV, 217–26, 228–33.

63. *First Annual Report of the Michigan Board of State Tax Commissioners, 1900* (Lansing, 1901), pp. 7, 121, 190; *Messages of the Governors of Michigan*, IV, 240–41.

64. *First Annual Report of the Michigan Tax Commissioners, 1900*, pp. 58–59, 121, 129–30; Harley L. Lutz, *The State Tax Commission: A Study of the Development and Results of State Control Over the Assessment of Property for Taxation* (Cambridge, 1918), pp. 288–90.

65. *First Annual Report of the Michigan Tax Commissioners 1900*, pp. 7, 152; *Messages of the Governors of Michigan*, IV, 240–42.

66. Henry E. Riggs, "Pioneers in Public Utility Regulation: Henry C. Adams and Mortimer E. Cooley," *Michigan Alumnus Quarterly Review*, LI (Summer, 1945), 299; Mortimer E. Cooley, *Scientific Blacksmith* (Ann Arbor, 1947), p. 150; Pingree, quoted in Henry E. Riggs, "The Cooley Railroad Appraisal of 1900," *Michigan Engineer*, LXI (Convention number, 1940), 11.

67. Riggs, "The Cooley Railroad Appraisal of 1900," p. 11; Cooley, *Scientific Blacksmith*, pp. 155–57.

68. Hedrick, *History of Railroad Taxation in Michigan*, pp. 38–40, 47–49, 52, 54; Barton, "Michigan Railroad Regulation," pp. 120–22; Catlin, *Story of Detroit*, pp. 638–39.

69. Riggs, "The Cooley Railroad Appraisal of 1900," p. 11.

70. Herbert Quick, "Governor Bob," *Saturday Evening Post*, CLXXXIV (September 23, 1911), 5; Lutz, *The State Tax Commission*, pp. 35, 258–60; Riggs, "Pioneers in Public Utility Regulation," p. 300. Professor W. D. Taylor, who studied "reproduction" and "depreciation" problems under Cooley followed the Michigan appraisal in every respect except for one deviation which Pingree and Cooley had learned by experience was dangerous. Instead of conducting an actual field engineering survey, Taylor, in order to "save money and time," used company records to establish his valuations. Taylor, however, cross checked his figures with those of the Michigan survey and was satisfied with the results. *Third Biennial Report of the Wis-*

consin Tax Commission, 1907 (Madison, 1907), pp. 81–87, 93–95, 269–70, 279, 283–93.

71. Lansing *Journal:* November 29, 1899, Arthur J. Tuttle Scrapbook; Detroit *State Affairs:* December 3, 1900.

72. *Ibid.:* October 19, 1900; Detroit *Evening News:* June 23, 1901.

73. Lansing *Journal:* December 18, 1899; Pingree quoted in Detroit *Journal:* January 1, 1900, Tuttle Scrapbook.

74. *Ibid.:* June 2, 1900; Lansing *Journal:* December 19, 1899; Lansing *State Republican:* March 4, 1901; Detroit *Tribune:* September 18, 1900, Tuttle Scrapbook; Arthur J. Tuttle to Frederic H. Britton (Detroit *Journal* reporter), November 24, 1899; Tuttle to Michigan Press Clipping Bureau, November 28, 1899; H. C. Sleeper (Michigan Press Clipping Bureau) to Tuttle, February 19, April 13, August 31, 1900, Arthur J. Tuttle Papers.

75. Lansing *State Republican:* March 4, 1901; Detroit *Evening News:* April 3, 1901; Lansing *Journal:* March 19, 1901; January 22, 1902; Pingree quoted in Detroit *Journal:* December 8, 1900, Tuttle Scrapbook; Catlin, *Story of Detroit,* p. 645; E. J. Marsh (Hillsdale) to H. S. Pingree [December, 1900], Pingree Papers.

76. Stephen B. and Vera H. Sarasohn, *Political Party Patterns in Michigan* (Detroit, 1957), pp. 15–18.

77. Detroit *Evening News:* May 11, 1901, Stone Scrapbook; Paul Leake, *History of Detroit* (Chicago, 1912), II, 617; Ralph Stone, "Hazen S. Pingree, The Man—Not a Statue," *Detroit Historical Society Bulletin,* IX (October, 1952), p. 5; Eli R. Sutton Scrapbook, Sutton Papers; Cyril Player, "Hazen S. Pingree: The Biography of an American Commonplace," (MS, 1931), pp. 80–82, Burton Historical Collection; Harry Barnard, *Independent Man: The Life of Senator Couzens,* (New York, 1958), pp. 84–85, 115, 119, 123, 283.

78. F. Clever Bald, *Michigan in Four Centuries* (New York, 1954), p. 338; Barton, "Michigan Railroad Regulation," pp. 124–26; Lutz, *The State Tax Commission,* pp. 291–92, 308.

79. Pingree address, October 17, 1899, Stone Scrapbook; Detroit *Journal:* February 24, 1899; Chicago *American:* August 28, 1900; H. S. Pingree telegram to editor of New York *Journal:* August 25, 1900, Pingree Papers.

80. *Messages of the Governors of Michigan,* IV, 288–89, 290–91, 310–311.

81. *Ibid.,* IV, 283; Hemans quoted in Lansing *State Republican:* April 6, 1901, Tuttle Scrapbook.

82. "Pingree—The First Insurgent," *Detroit Saturady Night:* June 1, 1912.

A Note on Sources

The following selected list of sources proved most helpful in a study of Reform in Detroit. No attempt has been made to cite every source which appears in the footnotes.

The most valuable collection for this study was the Hazen S. Pingree Papers, located in the Burton Historical Collection, Detroit. The Pingree Papers include 4 boxes of letters and 280 volumes of scrapbooks containing mostly newspaper clippings, some speech and article manuscripts, a few policy papers, and some correspondence on special topics. Also at the Burton Collection are the James McMillan Papers, which provided much detail about the opposition to Pingree and reform and shed light on the turbulent political climate of the 1890's, as did the Daniel J. Campau, Jr., Fred E. Farnsworth, Thomas W. Palmer, and the Arthur P. Loomis Papers. The University of Michigan Historical Collections contain several important sources, including the Chase S. Osborn Papers, which were very useful for the study of state politics and the influence of mining and railroad corporations. The papers of Charles R. Sligh, Frank W. Fletcher, Arthur J. Tuttle and the Ralph Stone, Fred Maynard, and David E. Heineman, and Eli R. Sutton Scrapbooks develop various aspects of politics and reform in Detroit and Michigan. The Russell A. Alger Papers at the Clements Library record the Secretary of War's ill-fated alliance with Pingree.

The Michigan Historical Commission Archives at Lansing yielded few references because most of the Governor's file (1896–1900) has been lost in a fire. The Richard T. Ely and the Henry Demarest Lloyd Papers at the State Historical Society of Wisconsin provided insights into urban and pre-Progressive reform in the 1890's, as did the Samuel M. Jones Papers in possession of Professor James H. Rodabaugh, Miami University. The Brand Whitlock Papers contain important materials about Tom L. Johnson and municipal affairs unlike the Louis F. Post Papers, both which are at the Library of Congress. Columbia University's Lincoln Steffens Collection has transcripts of interviews with Tom L. Johnson as well as some correspondence on the broader aspects of urban reform unlike the Seth Low Papers, which are at the same repository.

Helpful for the mayoralty years were Hazen S. Pingree, *Facts and Opinions or Dangers that Beset Us* (Detroit, 1895), the Detroit daily press, other metropolitan newspapers, and several short-run labor, religious, and reformist newspapers. Articles by and about Pingree and about urban problems appeared in the *Detroit Saturday Night, Outlook, Arena, Charities Review, Our Day The Altruistic Review, Municipal Affairs,* the *Proceedings of the Conference for Good City Government, Municipal Journal and Engineer, City Government, Social Review, Forum, Review of Reviews, Hampton's Magazine, Public Opinion, Gateway, Pilgrim, American Magazine of Civics, Munsey's Magazine, New Nation, Overland Monthly, Literary Digest, Publications of the American Economic Association, Quarterly Journal of Economics, National Municipal Review,* and state historical journals, such as *Michigan History,* XXXII (June, 1948), which contains Charles R. Starring's "Hazen S. Pingree: Another Forgotten Eagle." Public documents, such as the journals and proceedings of the Detroit common council, the city's administrative departments, and the state legislature, were crucial to following Pingree's struggles in Detroit and Michigan. The legislature's *Extra Session* journals for 1898, 1899, and 1900 were especially candid because Pingree sent in his stenographers to record floor debates and, in some cases, committee proceedings.

Background for Pingree's Detroit was gathered from biographical and business directories, and local and institutional histories, including George B. Catlin, *The Story of Detroit* (Detroit, 1926), Sidney Glazer, *Detroit A Study in Urban Development* (New York, 1965), Edward W. Bemis, "Local Government in Michigan and the Northwest," Johns Hopkins University *Studies in Historical and Political Science,* V (March, 1883), and Delos F. Wilcox, "Municipal Government in Michigan and Ohio," Columbia University *Studies In History Economics And Public Law* (New York, 1896) V. The Michigan political and social scene is covered by several older studies and more recently by F. Clever

Bald, *Michigan In Four Centuries* (New York, 1954) and Stephen B.
and Vera H. Sarasohn, *Political Party Patterns in Michigan* (Detroit,
1957).

Important for investigating social, economic, ethnic, and religious history in Detroit and Michigan are the state and national census reports
on vital and social statistics, farm and home proprietorship and indebtedness, religious affiliation, and state resources. The reports of the
Michigan Bureau of Labor and Industrial Statistics are valuable for employment, income level, and nationality data, and the views of foreign
and native-born labor toward immigration. Locating Detroit's "400" was
facilitated by Erich Kocher, "Economic and Physical Growth of Detroit
1901–1935" (MS, Michigan Historical Collections, 1935) and Detroit's
blue books and social directories.

My study of urban utilities was based upon a large number of sources,
including federal reports such as *Street and Electric Railways 1902*
(Washington, 1905), *Testimony* of the United States Industrial Com-
mission on Transportation (Washington, 1901), *Telephones and Tele-
graphs 1902* (Washington, 1905), the Fourteenth Annual Report of the
United States Commissioner of Labor, *Water Gas and Electric Light
Plants Under Private and Municipal Ownership* (Washington, 1905),
local studies including Graeme O'Geran, *A History of the Detroit Street
Railways* (Detroit, 1931), and William H. Lane's *A History of Electric
Service* in Detroit (Detroit, 1937), Raymond C. Miller, *Kilowatts at
Work A History of the Detroit Edison Company* (Detroit, 1957), the
analyses of traction problems by Delos F. Wilcox, Frederic W. Speirs,
James B. Walker, and Harry P. Weber, and technical journals such as
the *Street Railway Review,* the *Street Railway Journal,* the *Gas Light
Journal,* and the *Electrical World and Engineer,* which yielded informa-
tion not available elsewhere. A comprehensive bibliographical essay is
contained in my dissertation which is at the University of Michigan.

Index

Adams, Edgar J., 214, 215
Adams, Henry Carter, 211, 213
Addams, Jane, 54
Alger, Russell A., 8, 13, 16, 58, 132;
  alliance with Pingree, 207–10; dis-
  missed as Secretary of War, 209
Allegheny, Pennsylvania, 76
Altgeld, John Peter, 115, 160
American Bell Telephone Company,
  94–97, 99–100
American Protective Association, 65,
  135–37, 151, 243n20
American Telephone and Telegraph
  Company, 95
Ancient Order of the Hibernians, 136
Arndt, Walter, 175
Atkinson, John, 190, 199, 200, 201,
  204, 216
Atwood, Theron W., 204, 205, 206

Bagley, E.W., 54
Baker, Newton D., 169, 171
Baldwin, H.P., 6
Baugh Steam Forge Company, 58
Beals and Selkirk Trunk Company,
  39
Beamer, William, 119
Beck, George, 65, 102
Beck, Walter H., 65
Belle Isle Bridge, 29; Park, 30, 69

Bemis, Edward W., 36, 84, 87, 105,
  117–18, 120, 160, 171
Bilski, Joseph, 187
Black, Clarence A., 16, 53, 54, 62,
  78
Blades, F.A. "Elder," 17, 62
Bliss, Aaron T., 211
Boston, Massachusetts, 34, 36, 72,
  75; Mayor Josiah Quincy, 249n25;
  Mayor Nathan Mathews, Jr., cited,
  251n40
Boston Municipal Reform Party, 115
Bremner, Robert H., 121
Brooklyn, New York, 165
Brown, Charles F., 137
Bruère, Henry, 178
Brush Electric Company, 75–76, 77–
  78
Bryan, William Jennings, 114, 195
Bryce, James, 171, 172, 174, 179
Buffalo, New York, 164
Buhl, Christian, 58
Buhl, Theodore, 58
Burch, Edward, 100
Burghardt, Ernest, 17
Burt, Lou, 127

Cahoon, James B., 77, 84–86
Campau, Daniel J., Jr., 131, 138,
  148, 151

Canadians, population in Detroit, 12

Catholic Mutual Benefit Association, 136

Catholicism: and Poles, 12; and ethnic tensions, 65, 67; communicants in Detroit, 132; and 1891 election, 135; and 1892 election, 136–37

Catlin, George B., 24, 60, 83, 123

Chamber of Commerce: Detroit, 59, 110, 150; and nation, 179, 181

Chambers, Fitzwilliam H., 19

Chandler, Zachariah, 161

Chicago, Illinois, 29, 36, 37, 72, 76, 84, 85, 91, 194

Chicago Bar Association, 114

Chicago and North Western Railroad, 197

Childs, Richard S., 179

Christian Endeavor Society, 146, 151

Churches, 8, 20, 53, 71, 137, 138; religious census, 132

Cincinnati, Ohio, 34, 90

City commissioner and manager government, 163, 178–80

Civic Federation, 146, 151, 189

Cleveland, Grover, 52, 139, 164, 194

Cleveland, Ohio, 34, 37, 90, 91, 121–23

Coll, John, 129

Collins, Charles P., 66–67, 99, 136–37

Columbus, Ohio, 34, 35

Commons, John R., 36, 54, 84–85, 159

Conkling, Alfred, 173, 175

Cooley, Charles H., 36–37

Cooley, Mortimer E., 118, 213–14

Cooley, Thomas McIntyre, 6

Coon, Horace, 97

Corliss, John B., 145

Couzens, James, 39, 123, 217

Crafts, Wilbur F., 105

Crump, Edward H., 249n25

Currie, Cameron, 41, 46

Cutcheon, S.M., 53

Davis, George S., 5

Davis, William, 5

Dee, Michael, 52

Democratic party, 10; Irish domination, 11–12, 17, 18; and Poles, 11–12, 127, 142; controls Detroit, 14–15; ethnic division, 15, 130; collusion with contractors, 25–27; and Germans, 126; city party splits 1891, 131–35; loses Detroit, 150–53

Depression of 1893, 56–57, 61–73; influence on Pingree, 56–57, 72–73; and peoples' bonds, 63; and unemployment, 63–64; and poor relief and work relief, 64, 69–70; and class and ethnic tensions, 64–68; and Connor's Creek riot, 66–67; and xenophobia, 67–68; and cheap bread, 70; and potato patch plan, 70–72

Detroit: economic growth, 4–5; population, 8; form of city government, 9–10; foreign-born, 11–12; religious census, 132

Detroit Board of Trade, 8

Detroit Car Wheel Company, 58

Detroit Citizens' Street Railway Company, 44–53, 68, 101, 103–12, 116–18, 120–21, 192

Detroit City Railway Company, 5, 37–44, 48

Detroit Council of Trades and Labor, 19, 67, 133

Detroit Edison, 84

Detroit Electric Light and Power Company (DELPC), 76–82

Detroit Gas Company, 88–94

Detroit Gas Light Company, 87–90, 92

Detroit Pipe and Foundry Company, 58

Detroit Public Lighting Commission, 83, 85

Detroit Railway Company, 102–6, 108, 110–11

Detroit Telephone Construction Company, 99–100

Detroit Transportation Company, 58

Dickinson, Don M., 15, 40–42, 45, 57, 131, 138, 144, 148, 149, 152, 189

Dime Savings Bank, 53

Dingwall, George, 128

Dow, Alex, 83–85

Ducat, Francis J., 127–28

Duffield, Henry M., 16, 42

Duffield, Samuel P., 5
Dust, William T., 127, 150

Edson, James L., 132
Education: board scandal, 27–29; during depression, 63, 65; Pingree vetoes Bible readings, 158; under New York Mayor John P. Mitchel, 168
Elections, city: 1861–88, 14–15; 1889, 19–21; 1890, 129; 1891, 44, 131–35; 1892, 136–37; 1893, 138–44; 1894, 144–45; 1895, 147–51; 1896, 111, 195
Elections, national: 1856–88, 13; 1890, 128; 1892, 139; 1896, 195
Elections, state: 1856–88, 13; 1890, 128–29; 1896, 152, 195; 1898, 203–4
Elliott, W.H., 8, 53
Ely, Richard T., 43, 54, 84, 159, 175
Everett, Henry A., 101

Fagan, Mark, 169, 171
Fairlie, John A., 85
Farmers' Alliance and Industrial Union, 204
Farnsworth, Fred E., 62
Ferry, Dexter M., 5, 8, 16, 42, 44–45, 53, 132, 194
Ferry rates, 30
Fildew, Francis, 137
Fitzgerald, William H., 78, 80–83
Flicker, Ferdinand, 148
Flower, Benjamin O., 158, 159
Flowers, Charles, 99
Foley, Bishop John S., 65
Fort Wayne and Elmwood Railway Company, 37, 43, 47–49, 110, 111
Foster, Horatio A., 84
Franchise: alien, 10, 67, 151, 174, 191; "grandfather clause," 174; England, 177; Germany, 177
Francisco, M.J., 84
French, William A., 214
Fyfe, R.H., 40, 46

Gardner, Captain Cornelius, 62, 72
Gary, Elbert H., 114, 162
Gas: cost of, 87, 94; Pingree seeks price regulation of, 88–89; monopoly on production, 88; franchises

revoked, 92–93; Pingree wins case against, 93
Gates, George A., 53
Geer, Harrison, 200
General Electric Company, 75, 79–81
George, Henry, 59, 242n34
Gerecke, Bernard, 148
Germans: aldermen, 10; population in Detroit, 11–12; G.O.P. candidates, 17; and depression, 64; and 1889 election, 20; and 1891 election, 135; and 1893 election, 139; and 1895 election, 147–48; and city politics, 151
Gies, Paul, 148
Gladden, Washington, 159
Godfrey, Marshall H., 139, 141–43
Goebel, August, 5, 39–40, 148
Goldwater, Samuel, 42, 67, 109, 138, 149–51
Goodnow, Frank J., 171–77, 179
Goodwin, N.A., 186
Grand Haven and Milwaukee Railroad, 211
Grand Rapids, Michigan, 90, 99
Granger, Louis P., 62
Gray, John H., 86
Green, Andrew H., 163
Grenell, Judson, 62
Guthard, Jacob, 127
Guy, Hugh, 148

Hammond, D. Judson, 89
Hanchett, Benton, 46
Hanley, James, 25, 27
Hanna, Marcus A., 208
Harvey, W.H., "Coin," 114
Havemeyer, William F., 159, 163–64, 179–80
Hays, Samuel P., 179
Hearst, William Randolph, 113–14
Hecker, Frank J., 14, 53, 58, 60, 145
Hemans, Lawton T., 218
Henderson, Charles R., 40
Henderson-Ames Company, 215
Hendrie, George, 5, 37–38, 41, 47
Hendrie, Stratheam, 31, 37–39, 62
Herzog, Gustave, 138
Hewitt, Abram, 159
Higgins, Edward E., 35

Hopkinton, Massachusetts, 3
Horton, George B., 200–201
Howarth, John B., 7
Howe, Frederic C., 169, 178
Hudson, J.L., 39, 51, 54, 119
Hull House, 36
Huntington, Collis P., 93–94
Hutchins, Jere C., 48, 105, 107–8

Independent Telephone Association, 99
Indiana, 35; State Assembly, 116; railroad taxation, 197–98
Ingram, Frederick F., 85
Irish: and Democratic party, 10–11, 15, 17–19; and Church, 12; population in Detroit, 12; and 1895 election, 147–48
Italians, 66, 68

Jacob, John Chris, 15–16, 19, 20, 25, 41–42, 93, 102, 109, 125–26, 128–31, 135–36, 139, 148, 195
Jersey City, New Jersey, 169, 171
Johnson, Albert, 103, 121
Johnson, Tom Loftin, 102, 103–14, 116–21, 149, 192; as Cleveland mayor, 122–23; as social reformer, 160, 162–63, 169–71, 180
Jones, Samuel M., "Golden Rule," 115, 159–60; as social reformer, 162, 169–71, 180
Joy, James F., 8, 16, 53, 58, 88

Kansas City, Missouri, 34
Karrer, Charles P., 20
Kellogg, DeWitt C., 41
Kelly, James, 149
Kent, C.A., 46
Knights of St. John, 136
Kolasinski, Father Dominic, 12, 18, 21
Kronberg, Augustus G., 18
Kwiecinski, W.K., 64, 66–67

Labadie, Joseph A., 141
Labor party, vote in 1889, 226n39
Labor unions: strike Pingree and Smith, 7; strike street railways, 38–41; Polish Laborers' Alliance, 67

La Follette, Robert M., 214, 219
Lake Shore and Michigan Southern Railroad, 211
Law, William J., 133
Ledyard, Henry B., 45, 53, 205
Licht, Frank J., 109, 119
Lichtenberg, F. William, 132–33
Lighting, see Street lighting
Lloyd, Henry Demarest, 54–55, 159–60
Lodge, John, 43
Lorenz, Carl, 123
Lovett, William P., 123
Low, Seth, 160; as mayor of Brooklyn and New York City, 162–67, 180
Lowry, Joseph T., 41, 51, 81, 92, 138, 144
Luce, Cyrus G., 13

Mabley and Company, 39
MacLaurin, D.D., 189
Mandelbaum, Seymour, 164
Marsh, Arthur F., 203, 215–16
Marxhausen, August, 17
Mathews, John A., 191
Mathews, Nathan, Jr., 251n40
Maybury, William, 119–20
Maynard, Fred, 215
McClure, Samuel S., 162
McCracken, Stephen, 100
McGregor, James, 58
McKinley, William, 194–95, 208–9, 217
McLeod, Alex, 48, 62, 99, 145, 216
McLeod, Duncan, 187–91
McMillan, Hugh, 53, 58–59, 97
McMillan, James, 5, 13, 16, 45–46, 47, 52–53, 58, 62, 80, 88, 97–98, 104–5, 109, 132, 136–38, 143, 145, 152, 161, 185, 191–94, 196, 201, 203, 205, 207, 210, 216
McMillan, James H., 53
McMillan, William C., 53, 58, 88, 104
McVicar, John, 141
Meier, Jacob F., 129
Memphis, Mayor Edward H. Crump's reforms, 249n25
Meriwether, Lee, 115
Merriman, George W., 199; tax bill, 200

Michigan Bell Telephone Company, 97
Michigan Board of Tax Commissioners, 206–7, 212–14
Michigan Bureau of Labor, 63, 68
Michigan Car Company, 5, 57–60, 63
Michigan Central Railroad, 45, 198–99, 201, 205, 211
Michigan Club, 8, 10, 11, 16, 17, 54, 145, 193
Michigan Constitution: amended 1894, 67; amended 1900, 211
Michigan and Detroit Stove Works, 5, 39
Michigan Grange, 200–201, 204
Michigan legislature: and anti-home rule, 188–93; during Pingree's governorship, 198–218; and "immortal 19," 204–6, 210; House Speaker indicted, 214
Michigan Military Board, see Spanish American War
Michigan National Guard, 152, 201–3, 210, 215
Michigan (Natural) Gas Company, 87–88, 92–93
Michigan Telephone Company, 97–100
Milwaukee, Wisconsin, 34, 35, 90
Miner, John, 132–35
Minneapolis, Minnesota, 34, 37, 72
Mitchel, John Purroy, 162; as mayor of New York City, 167–68
Moore, C.W., 62
Moore, William A., 45, 53
Moreland, DeWitt, 62, 154, 216
Morgan, J. Pierpont, 165
Moses, Robert D., 168
Mulliken, John B., 45
Munro, William B., 172–74, 176–77, 179
Murphy, Robert H., 25, 130, 148
Murphy, Simon J., 44–45, 53
Mutual Gaslight Company, 87–88, 91–93

National Bureau of Reforms, 105
National Electric Light Association, 77, 84
National Municipal League, 116, 173
Negro, 141, 144, 174

Nevins, Allan, 164
Newberry, John S., 58, 62
New York City, 34, 72, 75, 163–68, 172, 174–76
New York state senate, 116

O'Geran, Graeme, 120
Older, Fremont, 167
Olds, Schuyler, "Sky," 89, 104, 200–201, 210, 214
O'Regan, William, 25
Osborn, Chase S., 43, 203–4, 217

Pack, Albert, 101, 110
Pack, Greene, 101
Palmer, Thomas W., 13, 42
Parke, Hervey C., 5
Parke-Davis Company, 5
Parsons, Frank, 77, 84, 114–15, 160
Paving, 24–26
Peninsular Car Company, 14, 53, 58–60, 63
People's party, 138, 140, 144, 191
Person, Rollin H., 215
Pettigrew, Richard F., 115–16
Phelan, James D., 160; mayor of San Francisco, 167
Philadelphia, Pennsylvania, 34, 75, 86, 115
Pickard, C.E., 177
Pingree, Frank C., 6–7
Pingree, Hazen S.: early years, 3; during Civil War, 3–4; shoe manufacturer, 6–7; family, 7, 202, 214–15, 217; social position, 7–8, 52–54, 160; as mayor, 22–196; as governor, 196–218; dies, 218
Pingree, Hazen S., Jr., 202, 217
Pingree, Mrs. Hazen S., 7, 214–15
Pingree and Smith Company, 6–7
Pittsburgh, Pennsylvania, 34, 77
Plunkitt, George Washington, 164, 168
Poles: social and economic position, 11–12; population in Detroit, 12–13; and politics, 18, 127–28; and depression, 64–67; and 1889 election, 20; and 1893 election, 142; and 1894 election, 145; and smallpox epidemic, 187
Police department, home rule restored, 40–41

Polish Laborers' Alliance, 67
Port Huron, Michigan, 99
Preston National Bank, 8, 52, 138
Pridgeon, John, Jr., 14, 16, 18–19
Prohibition party, 139–40
Prostitution: Pingree uses to silence opponent, 146; in Detroit, 158
Protiva, Charles P., 82

Quinby, William, 149
Quincy, Josiah, 249n25

Railroads: Pingree's program to tax, 196–214; specific tax, 197, 199; Barnum bill, 201; Atkinson bill, 199–200, 205, 211; state tax commission, 206–7, 212–14; tax privileges repealed, 211; "equal tax" amendment, 211; tax increases on, 213; M.E. Cooley tax appraisal, 213–14
Rasch, Frank A., 17
Reform: social and structural, 157–81, 220–21; and status revolution, 160
Reichenbach, George F., 129–30
Republican party, 8, 10; and temperance, 13; rural outlook, 13; business control, 14; appeal to foreign-born in 1889, 17–18; appeals to Poles, 127–28, 142; tries to deny Pingree nomination, 132–33; Pingree purges, 144, 147; appeals to Irish, 147–48; controls Detroit, 150–56; and anti-home rule, 188–93; struggle for control of state party, 203, 216
Rice, William E., 105
Rich, John T., 152, 192, 193, 195
Richert, William, 106
Riggs, Henry E., 214
Riots, see Depression of 1893; Street railways
Roosevelt, Theodore, 217
Root, Elihu, 165
Rowe, Leo S., 177
Russel, George H., 45, 46
Russel, Henry, 201
Russel Wheel and Foundry Company, 58
Russell, Alfred, 45, 46
Russell, Henry, 45

St. Louis, Missouri, 34, 77
St. Paul, Minnesota, 34, 37
Salvation Army, 158
San Francisco, California, 34, 75, 77, 167
Schehr, Henry, 129
Schmidt, Frank, 65
Schmidt, John A., 17
Schools, see Education
Scotten, Oren, 145
Seattle, Washington, 72
Sewers, 26–27
Shaw, Albert, 159, 172, 174, 176, 179
Simpson, "Sockless" Jerry, 103
Sinclair, A.H., 36
Sligh, Charles R., 152
Smallpox: epidemic, 146, 185–88; the politics of, 185–95
Smith, A.M., 202
Smith, Charles H., 6–7
Socialist Labor party, 138
Socialist party, 138, 140
South Africa, 218
Spanish American War, 201–3, 207; and Military Board scandal, 210, 215; and Philippines, 208, 217; see also Alger, Russell A.
Sprague, Frank J., 34
State Association of Farmers' Clubs, 204
State Savings Bank, 45
Stead, William T., 160
Steffens, Lincoln, 162, 169
Stinchfield, Charles, 45
Stone, Harold A., 179
Stone, Ralph, 216
Street lighting: United States: first station, 75; municipally owned, 76; cost of, 77; financing of, 77; municipal ownership debate, 84–85. Detroit: vendors of, 76ff; poor quality of, 77–78; Pingree sponsors municipal plant, 78–85; cost of, 78, 83–85; and bribery of council, 81–83
Street railways: United States: franchises, 34; financing, 34–36; social significance of, 36–37, 48; Pingree's influence upon, 112–16. Detroit: 5, 34, 36–37; strike and riot, 37–41, 131; litigation, 46–48;

workingmen's fares, 47–48; social significance of, 48; physical improvements of, 48–49, 51; Pingree asks municipal ownership of, 49; financing of, 50; three-cent fare, 50–52, 109–11, 116–17, 122, 192; vote for municipal ownership of, 52, 145; Pingree sponsors three-cent line, 101–13; Tom L. Johnson manages Citizens' Company, 102–13, 116–21; transfers abolished, 107; boycott of, 108; consolidated, 110–11; quasi-municipal ownership plan, 116–22; municipal ownership of, 123; alleged bribes of, 161

Streetcar Employees' Association, 38–41, 133

Strikes, see Labor unions

Strong, Josiah, 162

Sumner, William P., 147

Sutton, Eli R., 62, 215–16

Taft, William Howard, 47

Tammany Hall, 166, 168

Taxation, 57; shipping, 57–58; industry, 58–60; single tax, 59, 109; real estate, 60; personal property, 60–61, 212–13; Pingree advocates on churches, 71. See also Railroads; Telephone

Taylor, W.D., 214, 256n70

Telephone: United States: Bell monopoly, 95; independents, 95–97; rates, 96–97, 99. Detroit: tax exempt, 97; rates, 98, 239n61; usage, 98–100, 238n52; independent company, 99

Temperance, 13–16, 65, 139–40, 146, 151, 170

Thomas-Houston Electric Company, 75

Thompson, William B., 102, 119, 137, 143–44, 148, 152

Thompson, William G., 44, 131–35, 141, 188–91, 203

Tillman, Harry C., 12, 127

Toledo, Ohio, 37, 91. See also Jones, Samuel M.

Toll roads, 30–32

Tossy, Louis E., 41, 42

Travers, R.H., 39

Trevellick, Richard F., 133, 141

Tuite, Thomas P., 14, 18–19

Tuttle, Arthur J., 215, 217

Tweed, William M., 163, 178, 180

United States Department of Commerce and Labor, 35–37, 84

United State Industrial Commission, 35

University of Michigan, 193

Utley, Henry M., 12

Veiller, Lawrence, 166

Vernor, James, 8, 41, 51, 78, 81, 92, 102, 138, 144, 147

Waite, Henry M., 179

Waller, Thomas M., 44–46

Walsh, J.W., 62, 216

Ward, Eber Brock, 5

Warren, Homer, 109

Washington, D.C., 80, 104

Webster, Sheridan, 54

Weinstein, James, 179

Weist, Howard, 17, 216

Welton, Everard B., 144

Western Electric, 79

Westinghouse Electric Company, 75, 79

White, Andrew Dickinson, 173, 177

White, William L., 215–16

Whitlock, Brand, 169–71

Wilcox, Delos F., 35, 173

Wilson, R.T., 103, 105, 117

Winans, Edwin B., 195

Wisconsin, 35; and railroad appraisal, 214, 219, 256n70

Wood, L. Morgan, 138, 141, 155–56, 189

Wright, Carroll D., 84

Wright, Charles, 51–52, 92, 102, 109, 138, 147, 190

Yemans, Charles C., 14, 139

Yerkes, Charles T., 54, 178